The Riddle of Cantinflas

ALSO BY ILAN STAVANS

The RIDDLE of CANTINFLAS

REVISED AND EXPANDED EDITION

Essays on Hispanic Popular Culture

Ilan Stavans

UNIVERSITY OF NEW MEXICO PRESS   ALBUQUERQUE

Printed in the United States of America
17 16 15 14 13 12   1 2 3 4 5 6

The author would like to express his grateful appreciation for the support from
Amherst College.

Library of Congress Cataloging-in-Publication Data

Stavans, Ilan.
  The riddle of Cantinflas : essays on Hispanic popular culture / Illan Stavans. —
Rev. and expanded ed.
    p. cm.
  Includes bibliographical references and index.
  ISBN 978-0-8263-5256-9 (pbk. : alk. paper) — ISBN 978-0-8263-5257-6
(electronic)
  1. Popular culture—Latin America. 2. Kitsch—Latin America.
  3. Cantinflas, 1911–1993. I. Title. II. Title: Hispanic popular culture.
  F1408.3.S73 2012
  306.098—dc23
                          2012024672

Design and layout: Melissa Tandysh
Composed in 11.8/13.8 Fournier MT Std
Display type is ITC Mendoza Roman Std

CONTENTS

Conversations:

ILLUSTRATIONS

PREFACE

¡Viva el Kitsch!

*K*ITSCH IS KING IN THE HISPANIC WORLD. NOTHING
is original, and all things are their own parody. I say this not in a condescending tone: counterfeit is beautiful. The region is hypnotizing in its arti-
ficiality; everything in it is bogus; the Roman alphabet is, in and of itself,
an extraneous import, and so life must be lived in translation; likewise,
democracy, condoms, Aristotle, TV soaps, clocks, blackness, money, vio-
lins, Satan, and antibiotics are all foreign idols. No wonder its citizens aren't
skilled at producing, but at reproducing.

In fact, kitsch, as a concept, must be fully and painstakingly redefined
so as to capture its immense possibilities south of the Rio Grande. Clement
Greenberg believed it to be a counterpoint to bohemian art. "Where
there is an avant-garde," he would argue, "generally we also find a rear-
guard, . . . that thing to which Germans give the wonderful name of Kitsch:
popular, commercial art and literature with their chromotypes, magazine
covers, illustrations, ads, slick and pulp fiction, Hollywood movies, et cetera,
et cetera." Walter Benjamin saw it as the automatic attempt to turn a one into
a many, to make uniqueness into multiplicity. But these views apply solely
to Europe and the United States, where kitsch, "that gigantic apparition," is
a mass-made product. In the modern Latin American orbit, it encompasses
much more: high- and lowbrow culture and middle brow as well; the masses
and the elite; the unique and the duplicated—in short, the entire culture.
Everything in the region is slick, everything a postcard, everything a never-
ending et cetera, including, of course, those manifestations striving to be
pure and authentic at heart and designed to repel all foreign influences. What
is its population without these foreign influences?

All this leads one to conclude that the triumphant entrance of kitsch into history did not come about, as Greenberg falsely believed, with the rapid population growth that affected the industrialized nations in the first third of our century. Nor was it born, as Benjamin misstated in "The Work of Art in the Age of Mechanical Reproduction," as photography became a fashion in France and Germany. Instead, the origins of kitsch are to be found elsewhere; they are a product of the Spanish mediocrity, of its frivolity. Yes, honor to whom honor is due. If Spain can pride itself on any solid contribution to Western civilization, it is precisely that derivativeness, that hand-me-down-ness practiced from generation to generation light years before the Xerox machine was even invented. Only within its national borders is the art of copying, of imitating, a national sport, and it is apparent in all epochs, from the massively produced chivalry novels that accompanied the Iberian conquistadors in the colonization of the so-called New World to Pedro Almodóvar's fashionable *cursilería*. Kitsch, in Western eyes, carries along a sense of fraudulence, of sin, of imposture, of plagiarism, but not in Spain, where talent must be found in the lack of talent, where fantasy is congenital to the trite and repetitive. What is *Don Quixote* if not first-rate art born from exhaustion and duplication? How to explain the Spanish Golden Age if not by invoking Lope de Vega's 728 "original" *comedias?* What is baroque architecture if not a caricature of previous architectural modes? In fact, I am tempted to date with as much precision as is advisable the moment when kitsch became an inseparable stamp of the Hispanic idiosyncrasy: in 1614, when Fernández de Avellaneda, trying to beat a turtle-paced Cervantes, appropriated the characters of Don Quixote and Sancho and published the second part of *Don Quixote*. The age of illegitimacy was thus legitimated.

Analogously, the Americas, an outgrowth of Spain, are a sequel, an imitation of an imitation, a plagiarist plagiarizing another plagiarist, Velázquez's *Las Meninas* within Velázquez's *Las Meninas*. No wonder Simón Bolívar dreamt of becoming a South American Napoleon; no wonder the first modern novel in Spanish America, *The Itching Parrot* by José Joaquín Fernández de Lizardi, was modeled after *El Lazarillo de Tormes*; no wonder Cubans are called "the Jews of the Caribbean"; no wonder Benito Juárez is the Mexican Abraham Lincoln; no wonder Buenos Aires is London-on-the–River Plate; and no wonder Pierre Menard rewrites *Don Quixote*—that is, he doesn't set out to copy it verbatim, but simply to recompose it from memory, word by word and comma by comma. To recompose, to recreate, to revive.... If Spaniards are semimodels, Latin Americans are hypermodels, countermodels, and antimodels: Frida Kahlo's talent for turning pain into a fake emotion becomes a myth; Selena's virginal beauty is a hybrid, an in-between confused with the Virgen de Guadalupe; Subcomandante Marcos is not a freedom fighter but an actor; Cantinflas is Charlie Chaplin without conscience. Nothing is real but the surreal.

I have been infatuated by this duplicity, by this all-encompassing arti-ficiality, for quite some time. Its possibilities seem to me infinite. If asked to explain the reason behind my obsession, I am tempted to reply that I am myself a double entendre, a bit Jewish and a bit Hispanic and, lately, a bit American as well, neither here nor there—a faked self. The reply might not be convincing enough, but at least it insinuates what I've said elsewhere: that I live my life possessed by the feeling that others before me have already done the same things I do, that I am but a replica. So why do I matter? What are my role and purpose? To call attention to this deception, perhaps, to unveil this trickery only to find out, of course, that I am both the veil and the veiled, the searcher and the object of my search. In the present vol-ume I have collected explorations of the ins and outs of kitsch-as-life in the Hispanic world. Beware of looking for sequence, cohesiveness, and conclu-siveness in these pieces, though; they are but fragmentary sketches of my intellectual curiosity, germane to the culture they emerge from. Also, as a token of self-referentiality I have reprinted a couple of short reminiscences that show the fashion in which I myself became unadulterated kitsch—an image in the image.

[1998]

∽

Postscript of 2012: I have added several essays and three conversations to this expanded edition. Of the essays, "Immigration and Authenticity" began as a lecture at Congregation B'nai Israel, in Northampton, Massachusetts, and evolved into a disquisition on genuineness; "Mother of Exiles" is part of a dialogue I have with the Statue of Liberty, which started in "Immigration and Authenticity"; "A Dream Act Deferred" generated a vociferous response when first published in *The Chronicle of Higher Education* as the issue of immigration was contested in states like Arizona; "Arrival: Notes from an Interloper" recounts my origins as an social critic; "*¡Lotería!* or, The Ritual of Chance" celebrates a popular board game that is also a philosophical attitude toward life; "The Novelist and the Dictator" wonders if tyranny is good for literature; "Mario Vargas Llosa: Civilization versus Barbarism" is a statement about the role of intellectual discourse in our obscurantist present; and "The Art of the Ephemeral" ponders the value of posters and street art in general. Among the conversations, "Language and Empire" (with Verónica Albin) addresses the durability of the Spanish language; "Against Biography" (with Donald Yates) includes a series of feisty notes on becoming a biographer; and "Redrawing the *Historieta*" (with Neal Sokol) meditates on the subversive nature of comics.

IMMIGRATION
AND AUTHENTICITY

I HAVE NEVER OWNED A SOMBRERO IN MY LIFE. NOR
have my family, friends, or acquaintances. The reason is simple: I do not
often socialize with mariachis. Sound strange for a Mexican like me? In fact,
I do not know a single Mexican who ever had a sombrero.

Yet in the mid-eighties, upon my immigration to New York, one of the
first things people asked me was, where is your sombrero? Of course, they
were referring to the typical Mexican sombrero mariachis use in *ranchera*
bands. The most common sombreros are made of felt and are black with
golden or silver line decorations. But what makes them common is not their
accessibility. To buy one, one must go to a Mexican specialty store. On the
other hand, the touristy version of the sombrero is red, yellow, orange, and
blue and is available in souvenir stores. While I lived in Mexico, I only went
to one of those stores if a gringo relative needed to be traveled around.

Why did the first Americans I met insist on seeing my sombrero?
Because as far as stereotypes are concerned, a Mexican and a sombrero go
hand in hand. It satisfied no one when I answered that a sombrero for me
was as foreign an item as it was for them. Did they all wear short pants, have
a camera hanging from their necks, or use cowboy boots, as the archetype of
the gringo required? I could see how annoying my response was by people's
facial reactions.

⁓

I want to talk here about the crossroads where immigration and authenticity meet. To do so, I want to turn to the Bible. In Genesis 24, the patriarch
Abraham, wanting to find a wife for his son Isaac, asks an unnamed servant

1

to return to Ur Kaśdim, the land that belonged to the Chaldees—where Abraham originally came from before settling west, at God's request, in Canaan—and find a wife for Isaac. Abraham makes it clear to the servant: "Put your hand, pray, under my thigh, that I may make you swear by the LORD, God of the heavens and God of the earth, that you shall not take a wife for my son from the daughters of the Canaanite in whose midst I dwell. But of my land and to my birthplace you shall go, and you shall take a wife for my son, for Isaac."

I will leave for later my comments on Abraham's decision to find Isaac's bride in Ur Kaśdim and not in Canaan. What interests me now is the episode where the unnamed servant, after an initial reluctance, swears to Abraham that he will fulfill his pledge. Then the Bible says: "And the servant took ten camels from his master's camels, with all the bounty of his master in his hand, and he rose and went to Aram-Naharaim, to the city of Nahor." That is, a bride must be found without the groom at hand and through a surrogate. The rest of Genesis 24 is about the finding of Isaac's bride, who turns out to be Rebekah, "born to Bethuel, son of Milcah, the wife of Nahor, Abraham's brother." The chapter highlights the protocol of making the camels kneel outside the city, by the well of water at the eventide, as women show up in the area near the well. The camels drink water too and are eventually exchanged as part of the dowry in a ceremony with the brother of the future bride.

I am bewildered by the presence of the camels in this protocol. Robert Alter, in a footnote that in its own right is a masterpiece of literary historicism (*The Five Books of Moses* [New York: W. W. Norton, 2004], 118), writes:

> 10. *camels*. The camels here and elsewhere in Genesis are a problem. Archeological and extrabiblical literary evidence indicates that camels were not adopted as beasts of burden until several centuries after the Patriarchal period, and so their introduction in the story would have to be anachronistic. What is puzzling is that the narrative reflects careful attention to other details of historical authenticity: horses, which also were domesticated centuries later, are scrupulously excluded from the Patriarchal Tales, and when Abraham buys a gravesite, he deals in weights of silver, not in coins, as in the later Israelite period. The details of betrothal negotiation, with the brother acting as principal agent for the family, the bestowal of the dowry on the bride and betrothal gifts on the family, are equally accurate of

the middle of the second millennium BCE. Perhaps the camels are an inadvertent anachronism because they had become so deeply associated in the minds of later writers and audiences with desert travel. There remains the possibility that camels may have already had some restricted use in the earlier period for long desert journeys, even though they were not yet generally employed. In any case the camels here are more than a prop, for their needs and treatment are turned into a pivot of the plot.

This is the sentence that strikes my imagination: "Perhaps the camels are an inadvertent anachronism because they had become so deeply associated in the minds of later writers and audiences with desert travel." Alter implies that, given the way camels are used as a stereotype in the desert landscape, their presence in Isaac's betrothal story is perfectly appropriate. Yet historically camels are implausible here. Not because they are expected to appear in the tale should they actually be part of it. Unmistakably, there have been countless hands—authorial and editorial—refining the biblical narrative. If the archeological facts referred to by Alter are right, someone in the strenuous process of standardizing the Bible might have thought, why not have camels be used as the protocol and part of the dowry?

⌒

This anachronism is the reverse of what occurs in the Qur'ān. In my discussion of it, I take the lead from a lecture Jorge Luis Borges, the Argentine writer, delivered in Buenos Aires in 1951, at the Colegio Libre de Estudios Superiores, and included in his book *Discusión* (1957). Over the years, I have often returned to this lecture, reflecting on it in public, writing about it in, among other places, my memoir *On Borrowed Words*. The lecture, titled "The Argentine Writer and Tradition," deals with what is expected not only from an Argentine writer—What should that writer write about? What are his themes? Who is his audience?—but about the place of literature as a whole in society. Somewhere in the middle of the transcribed version of the lecture, Borges states (in Esther Allen's translation, included in *Jorge Luis Borges: Selected Non-Fictions*, ed. Eliot Weinberger [New York: Viking Penguin, 1999], 423–24):

A few days ago, I discovered a curious confirmation of the way in which what is truly native can and often does dispense with local color; I found this confirmation in Gibbon's *Decline and Fall of the Roman Empire*. Gibbon observes that in the Arab book *par excellence*, the Koran, there are no camels; I believe that if there were ever any doubt as to the authenticity of the Koran, this lack of camels would suffice to prove that it is Arab. It was written by Mohammed, and Mohammed, as an Arab, had no reason to know that camels were particularly Arab; they were, for him, a part of reality, and he had no reason to single them out, while the first thing a forger, a tourist, or an Arab nationalist would do is bring on the camels, whole caravans of camels on every page; but Mohammed, as an Arab, was unconcerned; he knew he could be Arab without the camels. I believe that we Argentines are like Mohammed; we can believe in the possibility of being Argentine without abounding in local color.

With the exception of the last remark on authenticity in Argentine literature (a literary mantra if there ever was one), the memorable clause here is "the first thing a forger, a tourist, or an Arab nationalist would do is bring on the camels, whole caravans of camels on every page." The problem with Borges's quote is that Edward Gibbon appears not to have read the sacred Muslim text, revealed to Mohammed by the Almighty through the angel Gabriel between the years 610 to 632 CE and recited to Mohammed's tens of thousands of followers.

That is, the Qur'ān, as a narrative, postdates Genesis, estimated to have been composed (although, needless to say, there is no consensus among biblical scholars about it), around the sixth and the fifth centuries BCE. Had Gibbon, whose many volumes of *Decline and Fall of the Roman Empire* appeared between 1776 and 1789, the years of the American and French revolutions, read the Qur'ān, he would have found camels. I have come across at least two examples. The first is Qur'ān 6:144, which refers thus to the beasts of burden created by the Almighty (in Ahmed Ali's translation, *Al-Qur'ān* [Princeton, NJ: Princeton University Press, 1993], 129):

And there are two of camels and two of oxen.
Ask them: "Which has He forbidden,
the two males or the two females,
or what the females carry in the wombs?"

The second example is 22:36:

We have made the camels signs of God for you.
There is good for you in this.
So promote the name of God over them
as they stand with their forefeet in a line.
When they have fallen slaughtered on their sides,
eat of their meat and feed those who are content with little,
and those who supplicate.
That is why we have brought them under your subjugation
so that you may be grateful.

There is also the emblematic section in 7:39:

Verily for those who deny Our signs
and turn away in haughtiness from them,
the gates of heaven shall not be opened,
nor will they enter Paradise,
not till the camel passes through the needle's eye.
That is how we require the transgressors.

This translation, by Muhammad Asad, an Austrian Jew who converted to Islam (*The Message of the Qur'ān* [Watsonville, CA: Book Foundation, 2003], 234), calls attention to the misunderstanding around the word *jamal*. Asad believes it is doubtful for it to mean camel. He notes several other spellings of the word, namely, *jumal, juml, jumul*, and, finally, *jamal*, which is the generally accepted one of the Qur'ān. All of them signify "a thick, twisted rope." Asad argues that God could not have coined so inappropriate a metaphor as "a camel passing through a needle's eye," since there's no relationship whatsoever between a camel and a needle's eye, whereas there is between the latter and a rope, which, after all, is but an extremely thick thread. Therefore, the rendering of *jamal* as "a twisted rope" is, in this context, preferable.

The fact that the latter rendering occurs in a somewhat similar phrase in the Greek version of the Synoptic Gospels (Matthew 19:24, Mark 10:25, and Luke 18:25) doesn't affect this contention, since one must remember that the Gospels were originally composed in Aramaic, the language of Palestine at the time of Jesus, and that those Aramaic texts are now lost. It is more than probable that, owing to the customary absence of vowel signs in Aramaic writing, the Greek translator misunderstood the consonant spelling *g-m-ı* (corresponding to the Arabic *j-m-ı*), taking it to mean "a camel." The mistake has been repeated since, by many Muslims and all non-Muslim orientalists.

In any case, Gibbon, and through him Borges as well, is right, if not fully at least tangentially. The references to camels in the Qur'ān are inconsequential, and the dromedary does not appear to play the role of protagonist. When it does show up, it is as an anecdotal artifact. Hence, the Bible features camels where it should not, and the Qur'ān does not include camels though it should. A bit like my nonexistent Mexican sombrero.

What does all this say about authenticity and immigration? Genesis is the quintessential story of the love-hate relationship between God and the chosen people, the Israelites. That story is delivered in a narrative set in the desert. Should not the depiction of the characters and their landscape be emphasized through stereotypes expected to show up in this scenario? But what if those stereotypes were not present at the time, meaning that their inclusion is anachronistic, as it happens in the Abraham saga? And, conversely, what if their absence in Mohammed's divine recitation, known to us as the Qur'ān, means he preferred to ignore such an obvious artifact, precisely because it was obvious?

An immigrant's life is experienced in the zone where the authentic is put to a test. Can a Turkish dweller who settles in Frankfurt become more Aryan than the Germans in her choice of attire, food, daily habits? Might a Mexican in Los Angeles who learns to speak English better than a native speaker turn out to be more obsessed with protecting the purity of Anglo culture than his native counterpart? Could a Palestinian Arab living in Jerusalem be more Israeli than her Jewish neighbors?

To put it another way, where are the camels in an immigrant's tale? Is not the immigrant by definition an anachronism, springing from one habitat, which is quickly turned to nostalgia as the years go by, and embracing another, where he will always be an outsider, a trespasser, an interloper, no matter how much effort he puts into fitting in? Does the immigrant need to place a flag of her adopted country out of her window as proof of belonging?

Finally, another literary reflection. I am struck by the first word of the first stanza of the first verse of Emma Lazarus's sonnet "The New Colossus," arguably the most famous poem on immigration, stamped on the plaque in the pedestal of the Statue of Liberty, about Lady Liberty as the Mother of Exiles: "Not like the brazen giant of Greek fame, / With conquering limbs astride from land to land; / Here are our sea-washed, sunset gates shall stand / A mighty woman with a torch . . ."

Not.

Lazarus did not accidentally place the word at the outset; instead, she meant it as an outright refutation: an immigrant's life starts with a rejection, an interruption of the narrative that is one's life. The Statue of Liberty is "not like the brazen giant of Greek fame," the Colossus of Rhodes, the statue of the deity Helios that stood on the Greek island of Rhodes, a trophy erected by Chares of Lindos to commemorate the victory by Rhodes, in 304 BCE, against the ruler of Cyprus, Antigonus I Monophthalmus. One of the lost Seven Wonders of the World, with an estimated height of more than 107 feet, it was among the tallest monuments of the ancient world. In other words, before Lazarus tells us what the Statue of Liberty is, she starts with a negative attribute: the Statue of Liberty is *not* the old Colossus, she is the *new* Colossus. Likewise, before an immigrant can find out who he is—and, needless to say, no two immigrants are alike—he must start by realizing who he is not.

Perhaps my owning a sombrero is irrelevant.

[2011]

MOTHER
OF EXILES

Try not to let anyone carry the burden of your own nostalgia.
—LI-YOUNG LEE, "Self-Help for Fellow Refugees" (2008)

𝒯HE STATUE OF LIBERTY IS, ARGUABLY, THE MOST
famous sculpture in the world as well as the most renowned immigrant to
New York. Copper clad, it is a massive 151 feet tall (with the pedestal and
foundation, it is even taller: 305 feet) and weighs 225 tons. For more than a
century, it has sat on the twelve-acre Liberty Island, once called Bedloe's
Island, in Upper New York Bay. But she wasn't always there.

Like many New Yorkers, she came from somewhere else: in her case,
France. And like millions of immigrants, she changed her name to become
an American. She was originally known as *La Liberté éclairant le monde*,
but her appellation is an English translation: *Liberty Enlightening the World*,
although people prefer to call her by her short name, Lady Liberty.

Although she made it to these shores before then, her documents date
her arrival—or, rather, her inauguration as a full-fledged patriotic icon—
on October 28, 1886. What is intriguing is the way that, perhaps as a result
of her assimilation, she came to represent something nobody at the time
could have predicted.

Lady Liberty was made by sculptor Frédéric-Auguste Bartholdi as a
celebration of the one of the three principles—the "liberté" in the motto
"Liberté, egalité, fraternité"—that linked France and the United States.
The French Revolution inspired the American War of Independence of
1776, and a century later the two republics were eager to emphasize their

connection through the ideals of republicanism. The sculptor and the French government donated Lady Liberty as a gesture of camaraderie.

It is generally acknowledged that the inception took place during an after dinner conversation in Versailles attended by Bartholdi, where Édouard René de Laboulaye, a politician and professor of jurisprudence, said: "If a monument should rise in the United States, as a memorial to their independence, I should think it only natural if it were built by united effort—a common work of both our nations."

Bartholdi took the suggestion as an incentive. Alexandre-Gustave Eiffel, who also designed the Eiffel Tower, ended up building the structure of the statue.

How was liberty replaced by immigration as the message Lady Liberty eventually projected to the world? Neither Bartholdi nor Eiffel ever contemplated the idea.

It was left to Emma Lazarus, a Jewish American poet, to do the job, quietly, maybe even inadvertently. Lazarus wrote her sonnet "The New Colossus" in 1883. She donated it for an auction of the Art Loan Fund Exhibition in Aid of the Bartholdi Pedestal Fund. The purpose of the fund was to raise money to build the platform for the statue on Bedloe's Island.

The poem is only tangentially about freedom. Its true theme is immigration. It was stamped on a plaque at the pedestal in 1903, thanks in large part to an effort by one of Lazarus's friends, Georgina Schuyler. Lazarus imagined Lady Liberty as a caring, protective female presence, a protector and caregiver embracing those left homeless by other countries, greeting them as they arrived, seeking a new start in the United States.

It's intriguing that the Mother of Exiles, as Lazarus calls Lady Liberty, was not, on her birth day, a mother of exiles! The absence of this specific meaning at the start of her life in America makes me think of a photograph I once saw of a house where my family lived in Copilco, the neighborhood in Mexico City where I was raised. I was brought to this house a few months after I was born and lived there for eighteen years, almost until I immigrated to New York. In my mind's eye, I see the house as the theater where I performed a generous portion of my life. Yet this specific photograph depicts my house the year before I was born, that is, before the house was mine.

What do I see in the photo? A strange past, a past without me. And a future that might be described as a reservoir of memories waiting to materialize.

Maybe that's what poetry is: an invitation to look at things without us attached to them or in ways that weren't part of the original intention.

My experiences and perception transformed that house into a symbol for me, just as the American experience and perception transformed a French statue from a symbol of the liberté that bridges France and the United States to a symbol of immigration. A lofty concept evolved to a reality of human beings who arrive with the goal of becoming Americans and whose languages, customs, religions, and presence continue to shape and define the United States. Speaking of poetry, Lazarus's sonnet, as engraved in the plaque, features a typo just above the lines I quote. "Keep, ancient lands, your storied pomp!" reads, "Keep ancient lands, your storied pomp!"

The difference is just a comma. The absence of it doesn't altogether affect the overall meaning, yet it displays the kind of carelessness toward English syntax that opponents of immigration often point to with hostility. Ironically, while American opponents to immigration may speak the English language clumsily, they demand that immigrants learn it well and fast, otherwise they shame them, accuse them of laziness, of lack of desire to assimilate, of anti-Americanism. As an anonymous attacker writes on the Internet: "I hate Mexican accents, they make my skin crawl and I feel like I loose IQ points when I hear it." *¡Ay, caramba!* Shouldn't the noun and pronoun agree in number? *Loose* or *lose?* Yet it is the typo that betrays what Lazarus aimed at: "Ancient lands, keep your storied pomp" and not "Keep your ancient lands and your storied pomp." The typo is a reminder that immigration is never a perfect endeavor.

In any case, although Lazarus remains a fairly obscure poet, "The New Colossus" is perhaps the country's most famous poem—and among the most hotly contested—distinctly in the last five lines in the concluding stanza, in which Lady Liberty speaks for herself. Children across the nation memorize them. Personally, I find the poem flat, mechanical, annoyingly predictable. It delivers its political message forcefully but doesn't leave room for the imagination.

By starting the first quarter with a rotund "Not" and concluding the last stanza by inviting those seeking shelter to go through "the golden door," the poem goes from rejection to acceptance, from denial to affirmation.

Lazarus herself wasn't an immigrant. She was the product of mixed Jewish heritage: one parent was Sephardic (a descendant of Jews from the Spanish expulsion in 1492), the other an Ashkenazi Jew with roots in Eastern Europe. Lazarus translated the poetry of Heinrich Heine from the German and, also from the German, some classic medieval Jewish poets such as Solomon ibn Gabirol, Yehuda Ha-Levi, and Moses ibn Ezra.

Interestingly, the same year Lazarus produced "The New Colossus" she wrote another sonnet called "1492." In her volume *Songs of a Semite*, it follows directly after the Statue of Liberty poem. It reads (from *Selected Poems and Other Writings*, ed. Gregory Eiselein [Peterborough, ON: Broadview Press, 2002], 233):

> Thou two-faced year, Mother of Change and Fate,
> Didst weep when Spain cast forth with flaming sword,
> The children of the prophets of the Lord,
> Prince, priest, and people, spurned by zealot hate.
> Hounded from sea to sea, from state to state,
> The West refused them, and the East abhorred.
> No anchorage the known world could afford,
> Close-locked was every port, barred every gate.
> Then smiling, thou unveil'dst, O two-faced year,
> A virgin world where doors of sunset part,
> Saying, "Ho, all who weary, enter here!
> There falls each ancient barrier that the art
> Of race or creed or rank devised, to rear
> Grim bulwarked hatred between heart and heart!"

The two sonnets have the exact same cadence—both are iambic pentameter—and, even more surprisingly, the same series of motifs: the "Mother of Exile" in "The New Colossus" becomes the "Mother of Change and Fate" in "1492"; and the "tired, poor, huddled masses" become the "children of the prophets of the Lord, / Prince, priest, and people." Lazarus portrays the Jews expulsed from Spain (according to historians, between fifty and two hundred thousand, although the exact number is impossible to grasp) as refuse: they are refused by the West and abhorred by the East; and they are rejected at every port and barred from every gate. Yet the Jews, in their globe-trotting, smile enduringly because the Mother of Change and Fate ultimately embraces them. Where do they arrive? The poet doesn't say, at least not in concrete terms. Still, the Mother of Change and Fate, just as the Mother of Exile, does say to them: "Ho, all who weary, enter here!" In this welcoming place the ancient barriers of race and creed and rank shall be debunked, and no hatred shall nurture the heart.

Is Lazarus talking in both poems about the United States? Does she have in mind, not the huddled masses in general, but Jewish immigrants in particular, in "1492" the Sephardic refuse from Spain and in "The New Colossus" the Ashkenazi forced out from the pogrom-ridden czarist lands? If so, the equation is clear: Jews and immigrants in general, for Lazarus, appear to be one and the same thing.

Be that as it may, by accompanying the statue and, thus, redefining its meaning, the Lazarus sonnet engraved in the pedestal of Lady Liberty bestowed upon the United States a quality—let us call it a responsibility— distinguishing it from other countries: its self-proclaimed exceptionalism.

What makes America different? Its biblical sense of mission: a beacon of freedom that is a model to other nations. There is no other country that dreamers desperately want to enter, seeking a better future for themselves and their offspring. But the dream is only as good as its dreamers.

Lady Liberty is my mother. She is the mother of millions of people, immigrants and otherwise. I've visited her at Liberty Island. I see her in dreams. And, naturally, I come across her image everywhere, since, as a good mother (and a *Jewish* mother to boot), she is ubiquitous. One really doesn't need to take the subway to Battery Park, in Lower Manhattan, and walk toward the bay to be acquainted with her. Her image, especially after World War II, has been a favorite selling point for the United States government and for entrepreneurial people of all backgrounds. Think about it: How long does it go without her watchful sight impending on us? Not long. She is on postage stamps, tourist postcards, school notebooks, license plates, Halloween masks. (At least she isn't on our dollar bills. Those are reserved for the presidential boys.)

Plus you will also see her in movies like *Planet of the Apes* as the sole surviving item after the apocalypse. And there is a crucial scene at the top of Lady Liberty in Alfred Hitchcock's *Saboteur*. (Did Andy Warhol make an artistic piece with it? Probably not, but she is as iconic as if he had.)

Yes, to Bartholdi and Eiffel, Lady Liberty represented liberté. For Emma Lazarus, the statue incarnated the very concept of immigration. And for the rest of us, she's the queen of consumerism. Indeed, such is her popularity that early in the twenty-first century the statue was one of some two dozen finalists in a competition to name the New Seven Wonders of the World. Sounds like a Disney movie: *Lady Liberty and the Seven Wonders*.

⁓

Is it at all surprising that from her moment of arrival to the present she's been marred with controversy?

Keeping the doors to a nation open isn't easy. Who might come in? How does the presence of newcomers affect those already inside? And after how long a stay do new arrivals stop being outsiders?

The Lazarus poem has garnished countless animated responses. One of the earliest and most famous came in 1905, just a couple of years after the sonnet engraved on the pedestal was unveiled to the public. Thomas Bailey Aldrich, a novelist, poet, and travel writer from Portsmouth, New Hampshire, and editor of the *Atlantic Monthly*, published an anti-immigration poem called "Unguarded Gates" that speaks against Lazarus's generosity of vision. Aldrich's poem (*An American Anthology, 1787–1900*, ed. Edmund Clarence Stedman [Boston: Houghton Mifflin, 1900], 68):

Wide open and unguarded stand our gates,
Named of the four winds, North, South, East, and West;
Portals that lead to an enchanted land
Of cities, forests, fields of living gold,
Vast prairies, lordly summits touched with snow,
Majestic rivers sweeping proudly past
The Arab's date-palm and the Norseman's pine
A realm wherein are fruits of every zone,
Airs of all climes, for lo! throughout the year
The red rose blossoms somewhere—a rich land,
A later Eden planted in the wilds,
With not an inch of earth within its bound
But if a slave's foot press it sets him free.
Here, it is written, Toil shall have its wage,
And Honor honor, and the humblest man
Stand level with the highest in the law.
Of such a land have men in dungeons dreamed,
And with the vision brightening in their eyes
Gone smiling to the fagot and the sword.

Wide open and unguarded stand our gates,
And through them presses a wild motley throng
Men from the Volga and the Tartar steppes,
Featureless figures of the Hoang-Ho,
Malayan, Scythian, Teuton, Kelt, and Slav,
Flying the Old World's poverty and scorn;
These bringing with them unknown gods and rites,
Those, tiger passions, here to stretch their claws.
In street and alley what strange tongues are loud,
Accents of menace alien to our air,
Voices that once the Tower of Babel knew!
O Liberty, white Goddess! is it well
To leave the gates unguarded? On thy breast
Fold Sorrow's children, soothe the hurts of fate,
Lift the down-trodden, but with hand of steel
Stay those who to thy sacred portals come
To waste the gifts of freedom. Have a care
Lest from thy brow the clustered stars be torn
And trampled in the dust. For so of old
The thronging Goth and Vandal trampled Rome,
And where the temples of the Caesars stood
The lean wolf unmolested made her lair.

At first, Aldrich chants to the unending beauty of the land and to its magnetic qualities. But as the poem develops, the tone becomes somber. Of Lady Liberty, whom he portrays as a "white Goddess," or maybe of liberty as a value, he asks: "Is it well to leave the gates unguarded?"

He fears that "a wild motley throng," the world's penniless and scorned, are entering unimpeded. They bring with them "unknown gods and rites." They pollute the air with strange tongues that sound menacing. Immigrants come "to waste the gifts of freedom."

Ominously, Aldrich concludes with a warning: just as the Goths and Vandals brought Rome down, will the United States be shaken from within by these unwieldy, undermining people? The poem is thus a conduit of mean-spirited nativism and outright xenophobia. *Close the gates quickly*, Aldrich stoically announces, *close them before heaven breaks loose!*

The most inflammatory statement in "Unguarded Gates" is "These bringing with them unknown gods and rites." Ah, how much I dislike this line! Of course immigrants bring their deities with them. Didn't the settlers arriving on the *Mayflower*, escaping religious persecution, bring with them an entirely new civilization, one foreign to these lands? Aren't settlers immigrants, too? Actually, with the exception of native Indians, who isn't an immigrant to the United States?

The tone and implication of Aldrich's line are in tune with an anonymous e-mail I received some time ago that contained the following untitled—and, granted, far less accomplished—poem. Its sender asked recipients to circulate it "to every American taxpayer you know." And so here it is. It ought to be read with a heavy Pakistani accent:

I cross ocean,
poor and broke,
take bus,
see employment folk.

Nice man, treat me
good in there,
say I need
to see welfare.

Welfare say,
"You come no more,
we send cash
right to your door."

Welfare check,
it make you wealthy,
Medicaid is good
to keep you healthy!

By and by,
I got plenty money,
thanks to you,
American dummy.

Write to friends
in motherland,
tell them "come
fast as you can."

They come in turbans
and Ford truck,
and buy big house
with welfare buck.

They come here,
we live together,
more welfare check,
it gets better!

Fourteen families,
we moving in,
but neighbor's patience
wearing thin.

Finally, white guy
move away,
Now I buy his house,
and then I say,

"I find more aliens
for house to rent.
And in the yard
I put a tent."

Send for family,
bring my honey,
and they, too,
get welfare money!

Everything is
very good,
and soon we
own neighborhood.

We have hobby
it's called breeding,
welfare pay
for baby feeding.

Kid need dentist?
Wife need pills?
We get free!
We got no bills!

American crazy!
He pay all year,
To keep welfare
running here.

We think America
darn good place!
Too darn good
for white-man race.

If they no like us,
they can scram,
got lots of room in
Pakistan.

As a taxpayer, I'm doing what the cowardly author, who keeps his name veiled, wants me to do: disseminate his trash, although not without contextualizing it. He is angry about the welfare system that rewards the underprivileged without exhorting them to embrace free enterprise. He is a racist, a chauvinist, maybe even an anti-Muslim bigot in our post–Bin Laden world. And he is upset because newcomers, in his view, don't conform to the norms of the welcoming land, instead becoming a passive threat.

Honestly, I've never met a passive immigrant. On the contrary, immigrants are engines of growth.

"If they no like us, / they can scram," the poet says, "they" being the immigrants, while we, proud old Americans, plot their undoing. This antagonism, clearly, goes against the nation's foundation: it betrays the principles of justice and equality on which the dream of the United States was established. Is this what Lady Liberty gets in response for embracing the tired, the poor, the huddled masses "yearning to breathe free"? Or one could read the lines differently, the narrator saying that if Americans don't like "us" (the immigrants), they (the Americans) can scram, can go to Pakistan because all the Pakistanis have taken over the United States. That is, if in the last stanza the narrator is still speaking, not the so-called poet interjecting his voice.

The view of America expressed by the immigrant voice in the poem, obviously penned by an anti-immigration American, does not reflect the response immigrants have upon coming to the country and seeing Lady Liberty. Millions of us thank her, although our gratitude is qualified. Our arrival in these lands might be, in hindsight, a happy event, but the art of departure from our homeland is never pretty. We left behind a home, our loved ones, and carry the memories along the way. These pains are deep, lasting, and conflicted.

Impromptu messages scrawled by people in transit, awaiting news of their fate, fill some walls on Ellis Island, nearby Liberty Island, and part of the Statue of Liberty National Monument, a site that functioned as gateway for millions of immigrants to the United States between 1892, a few years before the statue was officially inaugurated, and 1954. Those words expressed in the moment of transition are the collective statement of humans, a poem of poems expressing the journey from the *I have been* to the *I will become*.

৴৹

How I wish I had been present at the ceremony, on October 28, 1886, when the statue was officially given to the American people. The scene, in my eyes, is reminiscent of the moment in Mount Sinai when Moses descends from the top with the two tablets containing the Ten Commandments and offers them to the people of Israel.

I do know of someone who was present in New York at the time: another poet, the Cuban activist, journalist, and wandering soul José Martí.

Martí, to me, is a poet of homelessness. Just a year after the event, or maybe two, he wrote a poem I memorized the day I left Mexico: "Dos patrias," or "Two Homelands." He wrote it while living in the United States, when the island of his upbringing was a sheer thought. I love the Spanish original (*Obras Completas*, vol. 13 [Havana: Editorial Letras Cubanas, 1954], 172):

Dos patrias tengo yo: Cuba y la noche.
¿O son una las dos? No bien retira
su majestad el sol, con largos velos
y un clavel en la mano, silenciosa
Cuba cual viuda triste me aparece.
¡Yo sé cuál es ese clavel sangriento
que en la mano le tiembla! Está vacío

mi pecho, destrozado está y vacío
en donde estaba el corazón. Ya es hora
de empezar a morir. La noche es buena
para decir adiós. La luz estorba
y la palabra humana. El universo
habla mejor que el hombre.
Cual bandera
que invita a batallar, la llama roja
de la vela flamea. Las ventanas
abro, ya estrecho en mí. Muda, rompiendo
las hojas del clavel, como una nube
que enturbia el cielo, Cuba, viuda, pasa . . .

My English translation:

I have two homelands: Cuba and the night.
Or are they one and the same? No sooner
does his majesty the sun retire, with long veils
and a carnation in hand, silent,
than Cuba, like a sad widow, appears before me.
I know that bleeding carnation
trembling in her hand! It's empty,
my chest is destroyed and empty
where the heart once was. It's time
to begin dying. The night is right
to say goodbye. The light is bothersome
and the word is human. The universe
speaks better than man.
Like a flag
inviting us to battle, the candle's
red flame flickers. I open the windows,
overwhelmed inside. Mute, plucking
the carnation's leaves, like a cloud
darkening the sky, Cuba, a widow, passes by.

I too have two homelands . . .

Strictly speaking, Martí wasn't an immigrant, either to the United
States or to the other countries (Spain, Mexico, Venezuela, Uruguay, Costa
Rica, the Dominican Republic, Haiti, Jamaica, et cetera) where he lived,

sometimes for days, other times for much longer. Depending on how one sees those periods, he was an exile and refugee. The two terms might appear to be synonymous but in effect are distinguishable: a refugee is a person who flees from the native country to escape dangerous conditions and upon arriving seeks asylum, whereas an exile lives temporarily away from the native country for political reasons but waits to return soon.

Accumulatively, Martí lived outside Cuba longer than he lived on the island. That diaspora included stints in Florida and, especially, in New York, where he arrived for the first time in 1880, at the age of twenty-seven, and where he settled, on and off, until 1892, which was three years before his catastrophic death. After arriving clandestinely in Cuba, at La Playita, near the eastern tip of the island, to fight for his country's independence, he was killed in a battle against the Spanish.

Immigrants, for the most part, aren't poets, and, it goes without saying, not all poets are immigrants, at least not in the physical sense of the word. Poetry and immigration, metaphorically speaking, are siblings, and Martí's metaphors—Cuba represented by a widow with a bleeding carnation in her hand, who passed by slowly, at night, across a window—are emblematic of the pain that results from displacement.

From New York, Martí sent newspaper dispatches to various periodicals in Latin America. Those dispatches are an extraordinary record of life in the United States: a depiction of Coney Island, an assessment of the life of Indians and blacks, an account of an earthquake in Charleston, the inauguration of the Brooklyn Bridge, and so on. He also wrote about Whitman and Emerson. Martí's intention was "to explain the mind of the United States of the North to the minds of those who are in spirit, and will someday be in form, the United States of South America."

On October 29, 1886, a day after Lady Liberty became an American, Martí sent a lengthy, impassioned reportage to the Buenos Aires newspaper *La Nación*, which he titled "Fiestas de la Estatua de la Libertad." (It was published on January 1, 1887.) In the piece Martí talks about what liberty means for those who don't enjoy freedom, tangentially invoking dictatorial regimes that marred Latin American politics in the middle of the nineteenth century. He talks about the sculptor Bartholdi and the extent to which his gift to the United States wasn't innocent of ideology: the French, he suggests, perceived themselves as owning the idea behind a Panama Canal, and Lady Liberty was a strategy to keep the American government and private companies, to the degree possible, detached in the region. Nevertheless, his description in general is about the festivities on that rainy day, the popular enthusiasm, the speeches by national (President Grover Cleveland, among them) and foreign dignitaries, and, in general, the mechanism of the celebration.

All this to say that Martí was joyful. During his last years of life, he fought against the Spaniards, who had controlled his native home since colonial times and, in so doing, sought the help of the United States, a liaison that didn't blind him to its political ambitions in Latin America. In the chronicle on the festivities he mentions the expansionist drive behind the Mexican-American War of 1846–1848 and its effects not only in the bilateral diplomatic relations between the two nations but in the entire Western hemisphere. Still, the day Lady Liberty was exposed to the world—literally, as a curtain covering her was undone—Martí was full of enthusiasm. Expectedly, in his piece there is no mention of immigration policies, because Lady Liberty is an emblem of freedom, not of openness. Thus, that aspect, symptomatically, is absent. Martí, and most people enjoying the festivities, were unacquainted with Emma Lazarus—hers wasn't a familiar name—let alone "The New Colossus."

What if Martí had been given a glimpse of the future? How would he have written about Lady Liberty? Would he have thanked her for embracing "the homeless, tempest-tost"? Or would he, instead, have accused her of hypocrisy, since from before the time United States received the present from France the country's attitude toward the rest of the world had been marked by duality: on one hand, openness to those seeking shelter, and on the other, invasions, expansions, and capitalist voracity?

In any case, on that fateful day Martí didn't see the future. He only saw the present.

⁓

Still, I'm struck by the Mona Lisa–like gesture of Lady Liberty: she doesn't smile, nor does she appear upset. What kind of expression does she display? What is she gesticulating to us?

Some hate her because she's unexpressive. Others hate her because she's unfair to her children, allowing some to thrive and others to perish, and because she doesn't pay attention to the rest of the world.

Not surprisingly, the hospitality embodied by Lady Liberty has often been a target of threats, from expressions of passing anger to outright terrorist attacks. For instance, the FBI uncovered a 1965 plot against it by the Black Liberation Front, known for its acronym BLF. Yet that plot wasn't an objection to her hospitality but a statement about what the group perceived as American hypocrisy, as well as opposition to her as a symbol of America, whose values were being questioned by the BLF.

And in the aftermath of the terrorist attacks of September 11, 2001, which focused on other symbols of American-style capitalism (the Twin Towers and the Pentagon), the site is believed to have been contemplated as a target of Arab fundamentalists linked to Al Qaeda. The fact that Lady Liberty was not destroyed might be connected with the ulterior motive of the attacks: their quest was to cause the largest possible number of human casualties. As a result, the site has been closed to the public, who isn't allowed to climb through her interior, as people had—myself included—for decades.

Irony of ironies: the Mother of Exile is also the Mother of Security, an unapproachable relative, a caring but distant protector. She has assumed that identity as a result of her location as well as her stance: New York is the true capital of the United States, and Lady Liberty is the doorwoman.

And then again, she's a frequent target of jokes. And of acts of enchantment. These threats, this distance, the overexposure Lady Liberty has been through, and, more than anything else, the transformative power of history have left Lady Liberty partially naked. People clothe her for the role she plays for them. In turn, she is stripped down.

She isn't really, of course. Bartholdi dressed her up in a heavy toga. (On sunny days, she must be ready to let it go.) He crowned her, gave her sandals, placed a torch at the top of her raised right hand, and in the left hand he made her hold a *tabula ansata*, a tablet with dovetail handles where the date of the Declaration of Independence, JULY IV MDCCLXXVI, stands visibly frozen in time.

⁂

Let's face it: figuratively, Lady Liberty is no longer what she once was. Emma Lazarus made her motherly, but these days she's not even that. It is difficult to relate her to the immigrant experience today. She is a symbol of commerce: America as Disneyland, an amusement park with liberty as its central motif.

Yeah, three cheers for liberty! Yeah, all who seek America shall be redeemed, meaning they will be entertained with Hollywood stories about immigrant success. Not with tales of defeat. Not with tales where the immigrant doesn't find a raison d'être. Uplifting tales. Tales where the Statue of Liberty can be shown as an emblem of deliverance.

In any case, the statue is a symbol beyond poetry, far beyond the predictable words put into her mouth through an unimaginative verse.

Years ago on TV I saw one of those disappearing acts—masterful, really—that in the end brought the Mother of Exiles to her knees. It was a show by magician David Copperfield. There were spotlights, helicopters, cameras, and amused spectators in different places on Liberty Island. Copperfield pulled a series of large curtains around the statue, and *kaboom!* It was gone. The helicopters shone down lights to reveal that where the pedestal once stood, there was nothing.

Figure 1:
Daryl Cagle,
"Immigration and
Liberty." © Daryl
Cagle, 2010. Used by
permission of Political
Cartoons. www.
politicalcartoons.com

I've told the story countless times to my children and students. They are too young to have watched the Copperfield show. In my recounting I always stress the impossibility of it all. (The statue weighs the equivalent of an elephant calf.)

How did the magician do it? I have no idea, but I'm not attracted to the Houdini mechanics. Instead, I'm attracted to the magician's implications.

The disappearance of the statue is more important than how she disappeared.

That is because Lady Liberty, as an emblem of immigration, disappeared long ago. It is impossible to conceive of the arrival of the Italian, Polish, Hungarian, Norwegian, Danish, French, Czech, Portuguese, Jewish, and other boat-bounded immigrants from the second half of the nineteenth century to the first half of the twentieth without invoking her image, but since roughly 1950 newcomers do not come through New York Harbor. They might come to New York, but they make it by car, by bus, or, mostly, by plane.

To be sure, the majority cross the border, legally and otherwise, at diverse geographic points from the Florida reefs to the Tijuana streets.

Who greets us? Another symbolic family member: Big Brother. (The words ought to be pronounced with a thick Arizona accent.) During the hundred years in which Lady Liberty greeted them, the newly arrived were Caucasian. Perhaps that's why she herself has Caucasian features (other than the fact, obviously, that Bertholdi imagined her as having Greek descent, not a lineage that traces her ancestry to Korea, Ghana, or Mexico).

Needless to say, Big Brother will be nice to you if you're nice to Big Brother. And if you've been invited by someone: for instance, if you're an engineer from India with a lucrative salary from MIT and a house waiting for you in Brookline, the treatment you'll receive is a warm handshake, quite different from what you will encounter as a peasant from El Salvador hoping to earn the minimum wage cleaning houses in White Plains or picking strawberries in Oregon.

For does Lady Liberty and the people of the country she represents really want the tired and the poor? As far as she's concerned, they shouldn't bother: *mejor quedarse en casa*, better to stay home.

"Enough immigrants already!" cries she while scratching her teeth.

[2010]

A DREAM
ACT DEFERRED

*J*ORGE ARBUSTO ISN'T THE TYPE OF PERSON WHO seeks the limelight. In fact, for years he has thrived in the shadows. But ask him today what he wants, and his answer is unequivocal: to be recognized.

A sweet, passionate, steadfast student originally from Mexico, Arbusto (his name has been changed for this article) may be the only undocumented immigrant to successfully defend a doctoral dissertation in the United States. Certainly he is among a very small group. Yet his case poses questions that not only affect thousands of undergraduates today—some sources put it at around fifty thousand—but also challenge our ideas about hard work, the choices that colleges do or should make, the value of education (for students and society), and, yes, that thorn in our political side—immigration and the Dream Act, which is still stalled in Congress.

Having defended his dissertation on Spanish-language popular culture, Arbusto received his PhD in Hispanic studies this past spring. To reach this point, he has gone through astonishing hardships, which include beatings and imprisonment, not to mention the shame that comes with being illegal. He has endured all by focusing on achieving the highest academic degree. But now he may not be able to enjoy the fruits of his labor: no university I know of will offer him a full-time, permanent position.

Arbusto is a criminal with a PhD. Is that what America stands for, education without reward?

No one is certain how many undocumented immigrants there are in the United States. Estimates suggest that the number is between 10 million and 12 million—approximating the populations of countries like Greece, Portugal, and Tunisia. Last year alone, our government deported more than 300,000 of them. Dire economic conditions in Latin America constitute the principal reason people cross the border, but corruption in politics also plays an important role.

Some studies indicate that the recession may be decreasing the number of people entering America, as immigrants find it harder to get jobs, but it's difficult to know. Mexico, the source of the largest number of legal and illegal immigrants, is the world's eleventh most populous country, with in excess of 112 million people—more than 6 million of whom are thought to be in the United States illegally. Mexico is going through terrible times, and its people are ready to try anything to escape drug-related violence, poverty, and a bleak future.

By any measure, Arbusto is an overachiever. Within the United States, educational prospects for the Latino minority are bleak. The high-school dropout rate is astounding—more than 18 percent in 2008, and almost 20 percent for boys, compared with an overall U.S. rate of 8 percent. College-graduation figures are appalling; census data reveal that in 2009, only 13 percent of Latinos twenty-five and older had four-year degrees. The number receiving graduate degrees is minuscule.

Unfortunately, our immigration debate has succeeded in dehumanizing undocumented immigrants. Entering the United States without papers is against the law. That is all we see. Not who is entering illegally, why, or what their individual circumstances may be. In December what we call the Dream Act passed in the House of Representatives but failed in the Senate. It would have provided a path for students, like Arbusto, who were brought illegally to the United States as children to become citizens, helping them to attend college or enter the military. The *New York Times* estimates that some 1.2 million students would benefit from the act. President Obama has recently stepped up his support for liberalizing immigration laws and passing the Dream Act, and top Senate Democrats have urged suspending the deportation of students who would have been protected by the legislation. But until it becomes law, that suspension is not likely to happen in any systematic fashion.

At the same time, the situation in the states is contentious and confused. Many are tightening restrictions on immigrants: leaders in at least five states have said they will unite to seek legislation to deny U.S. citizenship to children born in this country to illegal immigrants. Indeed, Alabama's governor has just signed a bill forbidding undocumented students from enrolling in public postsecondary institutions in the state. But Maryland's governor recently signed legislation to grant in-state tuition to illegal immigrants, and the Illinois Senate has passed a bill to create a Dream Fund, with privately financed scholarships, to accomplish the same goals as the federal Dream Act for students brought to this country as children. In the meantime, the U.S. Supreme Court, in an eagerly awaited announcement, has declined to hear a challenge to California's law allowing some illegal immigrants to pay in-state tuition at public colleges. To say the least, the confusion and uncertainty leave students like Arbusto living in the shadows of their undocumented status.

I became acquainted with Arbusto's ordeal four years ago, when a colleague in the institution where he was enrolled contacted me, saying that the university had found out he was illegal. With strong support from the faculty and some members of the administration, he was allowed to stay. But all his funds (tuition, teaching assistantship) were immediately eliminated.

Arbusto and I met shortly after I received my colleague's e-mail. I asked around, at various institutions, to see whether anyone would let him teach a Spanish class. But no administrator was ready to bend the law. Learning that Arbusto's finances were tight, a restaurateur friend of mine arranged for him to have free meals.

Eventually his situation stabilized. He gave private Spanish lessons, and a high school allowed him to teach a couple of courses. Not much, but enough to finish his PhD and send his mother in Mexico $200 a month. (He says that she's old and can't keep on working and that her house is in need of repair.)

Arbusto and I remained in touch. I occasionally took him out for lunch. We talked about his dissertation, and when he asked me to be part of his doctoral committee, I accepted the honor, even though I taught at a different institution. As he began to describe the details of his ordeal, I became more and more impressed by his commitment to his work—and by his endurance.

Arbusto's current legal situation isn't exclusively the result of the poverty of his childhood. It is also related to his homosexuality. He left Mexico to escape a dangerously homophobic atmosphere. "I had an alcoholic, violent father and a devout Roman Catholic mother," he told me recently. "I was sexually abused by a local farmer when I was seven. I didn't tell anyone. You simply didn't talk about sex, because it was a sin. And because I was abused by a man, it was even more shameful."

He hated school—the education for which he would eventually sacrifice so much. "I told the priest that a man had touched me near the river. He replied that if I did well in my studies, I would be redeemed. 'Saca puro diez y te vas al cielo'—earn straight tens and you'll go to heaven." Discovering and understanding his homosexuality became the central puzzle of Arbusto's adolescence.

He was born in 1981 in the small town of Antúnez, near Apatzingán, in the Tierra Caliente valley of the state of Michoacán. Apatzingán is where the constitution of 1814 was signed, a highlight in Mexico's war of independence against Spain. But today it is notorious as the turf of La Familia Michoacana, the region's principal drug cartel. In a society ruled by machismo, Arbusto was a constant target of harassment. "Kids threw rocks at me. I only understood the seriousness of the problem when a gang member put a knife to my throat. He and his pals said, 'Swear you aren't a *joto* or we'll kill you.'" In Mexican Spanish, *joto* means "fag."

Arbusto said one of his uncles used to yell that effeminate guys belonged in the United States. An aunt had crossed the border, and Arbusto fantasized about following suit. At the age of fourteen, he began saving money from a variety of jobs, and then, with the help of a friend, he traveled north. He entered America three times. The first time, early in 1996, he crossed into California. He was caught, put in jail, and soon deported.

He waited. A week later, he tried a second time, without better luck. The third time, while he and the group with which he was traveling were already on the other side, their coyotes abandoned them, although not before stealing everything: watches, earrings, money. For two days Arbusto didn't know where he was, what to do. He passed out for several hours. He was lost in a forest. He hid in the bushes. When they were noticed, he and the others pretended to be part of a nearby factory's labor force.

Arbusto had five hundred dollars securely stored in his shoes. With the money, he paid another coyote, who led him to a house filled with other undocumented immigrants in the San Diego area, where he worked at a store. Unable to survive on his own, he moved in with his aunt near Fresno and finished high school in 1999, an outstanding student. That same year he enrolled in a local community college to get an associate degree, with which he could transfer to a four-year college. He did well enough to qualify for scholarships—private ones. He was afraid to apply for federal or state funds.

In a new country and a new culture, his attitude toward education had changed. "Only when spending time in school," he explained, "did I realize that through learning I would better understand my identity as Mexican and as a gay man."

To support himself, he worked at hard-labor jobs, but then he started mentoring Hispanic migrant children, working in elementary, junior, and high schools tutoring math, Spanish, and English. He wanted to give something back. And the classroom felt safe. "Nowhere did I feel happier than in the classroom. Less confused, more fulfilled. And I didn't feel persecuted.

"It was around then that I discovered that you don't need good grades to please God. Good grades don't get you to heaven—but do get you scholarships."

I wanted to find out why Arbusto hadn't crossed the border legally in the first place. He was unequivocal: "Given my situation, there was no way to do so. To get a visa, you must show documentation of a bank account, properties, family ties in Mexico. But *no tenía ni en qué caerme muerto*, I didn't even have a bed to sleep in. You need money to get an interview with an immigration officer, to buy a bus ticket to Mexico City."

In 2001, Arbusto transferred to a state university in California. He continued to excel academically, receiving his degree in Hispanic and French studies summa cum laude in 2004. His academic career landed him acceptance in an MA program in the Midwest. In the first year, he received a full scholarship; in the second, he was invited to serve as a TA. He graduated in 2006, at which point he applied to a doctoral program at an East Coast institution. Now, five years later, he has completed his PhD.

Arbusto's case raises a number of issues that lie beneath the debate on immigration. First there's the question of money and benefits. Arbusto has never filed a tax return in the United States, for fear of being caught. A couple of times, in California and again in the Midwest, his Social Security number was shown to be fake, and he was called into an administrator's office and asked to present proof of legal status. When he couldn't, he told the truth.

I asked him if any of the departmental assistants, advisers, or associate deans who had called him in had ever denounced him to authorities. "They knew my situation," he answered. "Depending on the occasion, they either allowed me to go on, or they told me I needed to resolve my status within a period of time. I knew these people were protecting me. That's one of the reasons I've moved from one school to another—not to put them in jeopardy. And to protect myself, too."

"Unfair," I can hear the critics yelling. "Illegal. Costing us money!" Yes, but that's our own fault. Arbusto would be glad to pay taxes, if he could without fear of being deported. "I want to pay back everything I owe," he told me unequivocally. The Dream Act would allow him to do just that.

Since 2001, eleven states have enacted legislation allowing illegal immigrants to pay in-state college tuition. In most of those states, legislators argued that doing so would give students who were here and willing to work hard the chance to become productive members of society.

According to the U.S. Department of Education, the average annual expenditure per K–12 public-school student is $10,792. The average yearly charge for tuition and fees at a four-year college is $9,000, according to the College Board. Leaving the emotional and intellectual facets aside, deporting someone like Arbusto represents a significant waste of investment. No doubt those were some of the issues confronted by educators who found out about Arbusto's status while he was enrolled at their institutions.

Then there *are* the emotional and intellectual issues. Arbusto has shown astonishing perseverance. He is grateful for his education. And he wants to pay back, not just the money it cost, but also what he learned—to communicate his knowledge, his love of learning, and the value of hard work to another generation. But how can he go openly on the job market?

And what about the human toll? One night in 2003, while he was walking down the street in Fresno, a bunch of drunken thugs surrounded Arbusto and the female friend who was with him. The story isn't pretty: The drunks broke his friend's jaw and punched him repeatedly in the head. When he and his friend were taken to the hospital, "they asked for all sorts of information I couldn't provide: a Social Security number, health insurance, a home address," he recalled. "I might have suffered a concussion, although I don't know, since I never received proper medical care. I didn't have money to pay, so I signed a form refusing treatment. There were policemen around the hospital, but I knew the law didn't protect undocumented people. I didn't want to get into more trouble. I was afraid of being deported again."

The memory of the incident plagues Arbusto. "The ambulance alone cost seven hundred dollars. I couldn't come close to paying that amount, even in my wildest dreams." As it turned out, the attackers knew him. "Shortly after the incident, while working in the computer lab at school, I went to the restroom, and when I came back, I found a message on top of my keyboard: 'Be careful! I know who you are.'" He realized that someone at the university had probably been involved, knew his legal situation, and was threatening to reveal it if he tried to pursue his attackers. The message was clear: Keep his mouth shut. "Of course, it has always been shut," Arbusto said.

It is time for America to recognize the human tragedy beneath the debate over immigration. That means following through with some kind of comprehensive reform plan that will recognize the complexities that Arbusto's story raises. But to do that, America needs a conscience, because behind every immigrant's ordeal is a story worth paying attention to.

Before us is a paradox. Some educators are allowing undocumented immigrants to be educated but are doing little to support the Dream Act.

The membership of the Modern Language Association has just ratified an amendment to the group's constitution in support of undocumented students' seeking legal status through higher education. It's time for more of us in education to do the same and do more to take a stand. We aren't only teachers; we are also leaders.

"My crossing the border was a matter of survival," Arbusto told me several times. "I might not be here, alive, had I not dreamed of being on the other side." Having defended his dissertation, he expresses a deep appreciation for those who helped him. "I've learned in American schools that talent is what this country is about—talent and merit. It is my turn now to help others realize what they're worth."

Arbusto's biggest challenge is still in front of him. His best hope of being able to find an academic job was the Dream Act. But if and when it is brought up again, it might not apply to him anymore: The provisions of the bill put the maximum age of those who could gain legal status at thirty. Arbusto defended his dissertation in the same month of his thirtieth birthday. "Unless a miracle happens, my chances of leading a normal, respectable life in the United States, a teaching life, are small," he said.

Arbusto may have to give up the benefits of his higher education and look for a job in construction. At least that way he can stay with his current partner and have a dignified life as a gay man. He has also applied to a PhD program in Canada, in the hope that with an acceptance in hand, he might have a legal status there as a student, even if that means he needs to get another doctoral degree. His partner, an American citizen and PhD, is willing to relocate. The university officials there are aware of Arbusto's situation and are looking for options to help.

Or Arbusto could return to Mexico, where he hasn't been for a decade and a half. That looks unlikely, though. "If Ciudad Juárez is hell," he told me, "Michoacán is purgatory."

Have we dismantled not only the Dream Act but also the American dream?

✍

Addendum: Democracy is a loud, messy affair in which citizens seek to persuade others through logical arguments. My essay on Jorge Arbusto's dilemma generated a huge number of responses—including those that came directly to me—close to a thousand. The responses might be divided in two groups: those from readers who saw Arbusto as a flesh-and-bones person, perhaps a symbol of perseverance, and those from readers for whom he was another excuse to denounce immigrants in general, Latinos in particular, and the quagmire the stalled Dream Act has become. I responded to every message sent directly to me that conveyed a genuine desire for dialogue, especially to those with a viewpoint different from mine. And I thanked (and do so again) all those offering direct ways to help Arbusto.

What truly fascinated me, though, were the e-mails I got from dozens of "dreamers" enrolled in institutions of higher education, whether Harvard University or community colleges, whose paths have been similar to Arbusto's. I quickly learned how sophisticated a support network there is out there. And, astonishingly, how undocumented immigrants have become a class unto themselves: clandestine, entrepreneurial, forward thinking.

Several e-mails were from twenty-something conversos: students born Christian who discovered, after years, their Jewish heritage dating back to the fifteenth century. That was when some of the Jews expelled from Spain—many of them living in public as Roman Catholics—fled to Latin America. My correspondents drew a connection between their parallel identities: hidden Jew and undocumented citizen.

No two periods in history are alike. And yet we must learn from history. The secretive, double identity of the early conversos of the Mediterranean basin—Christian in public, Jewish in private—had consequences. A number of scholars, like Yirmiyahu Yovel, a professor of philosophy at the New School, argue that they helped advance capitalism and liberal thought. It was precisely their dilemma that prompted a new mentality: secular, transnational, utterly individualistic. Baruch Spinoza, Uriel da Costa, Antonio de Nebrija, Luis de León, Teresa de Ávila, and Juan Luis Vives, maybe even Columbus and Cervantes, were conversos or had roots in this tradition. It fostered modernity in the midst of the stultifying hysteria and suspicion of the Spanish-speaking world.

Our own hysterics are obvious from many of the comments on my story and from the larger debate over immigration. Meanwhile, scores of undocumented immigrants are thriving, thanks to imaginative support networks that allow them to develop their talents. Dreamers are restless, ingenious, and creative. Indeed, a couple of colleagues corrected me: Arbusto isn't the first undocumented student to receive a PhD. And there are more than a handful with law degrees, not to mention those with journalism and medical credentials.

Some critics argued that a doctorate in Hispanic studies is useless. I suppose that means that the humanities are irrelevant now. Several readers (those with a PhD in Hispanic studies?) also noticed that "Jorge Arbusto" is a Spanish translation of "George Bush." My choice of pseudonym is a tribute to our former president and his father, both of whom were far more practical, and less dishonest, about solving our immigration challenge than our current president.

By the way, Jorge is employed and on his way to Canada.

[2011]

ARRIVAL

Notes from an Interloper

*℘*T WAS IN THE PAGES OF *TRANSITION*, I REALIZE AS I
look back now, where I calibrated my writer's voice. They became a platform for me to experiment on a variety of topics that, without knowing it
then, would become, one by one, the stepping stones that mapped my path
as a cultural critic.

I still think of myself at the time of my first encounter with the magazine staff as being fresh off the boat. This is silly because although I'm an
immigrant, I didn't leave home by boat. Nor did I cross the border by foot. I
landed in Kennedy Airport in 1985, so in the early nineties I had been in New
York City for over half a decade. Still, I felt as if my journey was long, very
long, and it wasn't over. Everything was strange to me, alien, impersonal.
In other words, I had departed, but I had not yet arrived.

I was married, had a two-year-old, and was teaching nonstop. To make
ends meet, I would also pick up sporadic translation jobs at an agency. My
dream leaving Mexico was to become a writer. Not just any writer: I wanted
to be an English-language writer. After the first few years, I was fluent. But I
wasn't interested in fluency per se. Coming in my midtwenties, I did not find
the process of acquiring the language easy. But a writer not only acquires
a language, he becomes comfortable in it. If he is to succeed, he must make
it his own. That hadn't happened to me, in spite of the countless sleepless
nights browsing dictionaries, the learning of jargon, the acquaintance with
different regional accents. I was still a foreigner.

✍

I heard of *Transition*'s new epoch, its American revival, when someone sent me a news clipping. I wasn't a reader of black periodicals. In fact, to that point I don't think I had ever read any. There was no connection whatsoever to blackness and its literary manifestations in Mexico. But while the short time I had spent north of the Rio Grande hadn't changed that, I had become exposed to certain figures, such as Henry Louis Gates Jr., one of the editors of *Transition*, and I recognized, in spite of the limited background I had on black culture, that he was trying to do what Irving Howe, one of my role models, had done to its Jewish counterpart: contextualize black culture. Howe had grown up speaking Yiddish, like I had. His essays were an exploration of literature, politics, and society. Even though he was a cosmopolitan who wrote about Stalinism, American literature (Edith Wharton, Sherwood Anderson, William Faulkner), radicalism, censorship, and the Cold War, Yiddish was the filter of his sensibility. Skip, as Gates was known (we eventually became friends), also used blackness as a filter, a platform for diverse, heterogeneous meditations on race and literature. Plus Skip could write with ease for different audiences, from scholars to the general public, becoming a bridge between what goes on inside the university setting and the outside world. I liked that in-and-out movement. Academia for me could be a solitary cell. It wasn't a place that fostered good writing, at least not among academics. Skip was an exception. Good writing is good when it is benignly appraised—indeed, enjoyed—by the many, who are its target, and not by a small, obtuse cadre of specialists.

I wanted to follow a similar path, with the Hispanic world as my base. As I saw it, there was a void in regard to Latinos, what they want, how they articulate their collective self, where they come from. This minority was already the nation's fastest growing. Soon it would surpass blacks in demographic numbers. But the country still lived in black-and-white, meaning that the old paradigms of ethnicity and culture needed to be tested. There was debate on the assets of multiculturalism, but these debates had yet to penetrate highbrow intellectual circles. If I could only break into these circles . . .

I decided to write Skip a letter. Would he be interested in an essay precisely on the complexity of understanding Latinos as a minority? In my letter I said they have elements that distinguish them from other minorities: many are immigrants, but others have been in this country since even before the country was founded; for those who are immigrants, the closeness of their original home makes the process of acculturation difficult because they can easily go back and, too, because the history of Latin America is intertwined with U.S. history in unique ways; Latinos aren't really one minority but many, thus incarnating the motto "E pluribus unum" in ways that make them a microcosm of the entire country; and their origins (geography, history, language) aren't quite unifiers, which results in a fractured, discordant, noncohesive group.

As I look back, I ask myself what prompted me to connect this topic to *Transition*. Why would a black intellectual magazine be interested in *Latinidad?* The answer isn't complex. Latinos in the nineties were facing the challenges of the road to assimilation that blacks had already faced decades before. Surely readers would be interested to see the similarities and differences. But there was more: although blacks and Latinos are perceived as different minorities, they overlap, since a large portion of Latinos are black. The concerns of one group, in my mind, were also those of the other. I could also see a larger issue, especially connected to academia, emerging from this coincidence: What do these cultures gain or lose by being juxtaposed? What was the status of Black Studies and Latino Studies? The former had made a strong incursion into the establishment, whereas the latter was in its incipient stages, beginning to find a space, to ask for recognition.

Being white and having been raised Jewish, I initially made the effort within the academic field to reach out, to imagine myself, and through myself the Hispanic identity I emerged from, as linked to Jewish culture. But my first steps in the intellectual world signaled me that there was another, equally attractive side I needed to explore: black life. *Transition* showcased blackness through a cosmopolitan lens, that is, as an open, nonexclusive place of encounter. For that reason, I saw it as a kind of Jewish journal of blackness.

At any rate, in those days I was frighteningly self-conscious about my nonnatural English-language style. Even to write an inquiry letter made me cringe. The effort could take me days, maybe a whole week. I had written for other publications, but my pieces were almost always short, and sometimes very short. If Skip said yes, how long would the essay take me? Would I be able to keep up a sustained argument? And what would I do to soften, to caress my linguistic awkwardness? My wife read my manuscripts, and so did a couple of friends. They were always generous in their comments. But no matter how much they praised my style, I knew I was an outsider. All of this to say that the moment I put the letter in the mail, I was already able to visualize the rejection: swift, categorical, flawless. Not that I deserved it: the idea I proposed to Skip was sound; my approach to it was original. But I secretly wanted Skip to say no so that I would feel I had been courageous to ask but would not be put painfully to the test.

I was therefore astounded when a week or so later, I got a short, reassuring note from Henry Finder, *Transition*'s managing editor. Skip had heard of me, and yes, he would be interested in the piece. Could I have it ready in four weeks? I was beside myself. A writer's beginnings are made of endless refusals. This feels all the more painful when the writer is an immigrant. I could have filled an entire wall, maybe two or three, with rejections. Many of those rejections were standard dismissals. The drop that tipped over the glass of water was when I got a negative response from the editor of a famous periodical. I had gone out of my way to make my letter pitch-perfect so that my immigrant's background wouldn't be apparent. Yet his answer was filled with typos: not one or two, but many, and clearly they were the product of carelessness. What gave the native writer the right to have typos? When would I be allowed the same right?

Henry Finder's letter was the beginning of a fruitful relationship between *Transition* and me that lasted for years and resulted in the publication of a dozen pieces. In that period, I visited the offices on maybe a couple of occasions. Aside from Finder, I met Skip and his coeditor, Anthony Appiah. I browsed through a stack of review copies of recently published books with the hope, as Henry put it, that something would ignite my imagination. But the majority of my work was done from far away (New York, Amherst, Mexico City, London, Lima, Madrid). Our editorial communication was by post, phone, fax, and e-mail. I would propose an idea and almost immediately get a response. Once the manuscript was submitted, I would receive a copyedited version with suggestions. Space was never an issue; in fact, I was always encouraged to expand rather than reduce. Since the magazine relied on provocative photographs, starting with that first piece I was encouraged to think of my writing, not in visual terms, but as aided by visuals. That is, the photos were not meant to tell the story; they were there to expand on it, maybe even to somehow upset it.

There was something foreboding about that first piece. I gained confidence while writing it, which made me proud. My outsiderness didn't hinder me; on the contrary, it gave me a sense of command. Moreover, I remember walking down Broadway one afternoon thinking to myself: this isn't just another exercise, it has gravitas; it might even be the seed of a lengthier meditation. Somehow, I found a calling in it, a mission. I had come to New York to be a writer, and now I was writing about something I had a stake in and was personally involved in. For although I was a Mexican immigrant, I was starting to feel like a Latino, a member of a broader community.

Finder took almost no time to read my manuscript. If memory serves me well, he called me by phone and said he liked it and wanted to run by me some small changes, mostly related to expressions. He faxed them to me. Finder had a soft, intelligent, nonintrusive, surgical touch as an editor. His comments made you see your work through clearer eyes. But what I most appreciated about him was his capacity to read the magazine's readership. He wanted *Transition* to be like the *New Yorker*—curious about global affairs, restlessly current—and, in addition, aesthetically demanding. Although *Transition* was released under the aegis of Oxford University Press, the audience, in his view, wasn't trapped inside campus walls. Or at least he wouldn't allow it to be. Since the magazine had a small circulation, the model was closer to *Partisan Review* in the forties, when it had become a gathering place for great writing and, as such, a mirror of its age, a tool to calibrate what the entire age was about. Finder, who was white, had a similar goal: he looked at the printed pages he produced as offering a viewpoint not available anywhere else, one in which blackness—and, in general, nonwhiteness—was equated with wholeness.

He made sure I trusted him from the outset. And indeed, I saw him as my target reader. I told myself that if I was able to get my point across to Finder, the rest of the readers would follow. For that reason, I didn't want to please him; I wanted to make him think, to approach things differently, to test him. I realize now that it was through my connection with him that I learned to appreciate what a fine editor can do: make you a better writer. A couple of years later, that first piece mutated into a book-long meditation, *The Hispanic Condition*. Published by HarperCollins, it has been reprinted numerous times, has gone through different editions, and, in general, was my breakthrough. It was publicly debated and served to introduce me into mainstream intellectual circles.

As it turned out, most of the essays I wrote for *Transition* were grasped by publishers and became books. My second piece was also controversial. It was on Octavio Paz, the most important Mexican man of letters of the second half of the twentieth century, the author of *The Labyrinth of Solitude*, and the recipient of the Nobel Prize for Literature in 1990. I titled the piece "Of Arms and the Essayist." I used Paz as a model of the Latin American intellectual whose literature is always ideologically engaged, even as he has gone from having an acknowledged left-wing stand (Paz was an early supporter of the Cuban Revolution) to embracing a centrist, perhaps even right-wing, and at that time Thatcherite, relationship with the state. I compared Paz to other writers from the region, notably Gabriel García Márquez, Carlos Fuentes, and Mario Vargas Llosa.

Paz was an editor of a monthly, *Vuelta*. It was thanks to it that I had first read Irving Howe and other "New York intellectuals," such as Daniel Bell, Irving Kristol, and Alfred Kazin. Paz had opened up Mexican literature to outside influences, mostly European, American, and Japanese. I didn't empathize with his poetry as much as I did with his lucid nonfiction. But having been born in the early sixties, I, like most in my generation, had an ambivalent feeling toward him (Paz's birth year is 1914). His erudition was superb, but his style was evasive. I put him to task for having been co-opted by the Mexican government, which regaled him with all sorts of prizes and anointed him with an official status of prodigal son. Plus Paz had become the trophy boy of Televisa, Mexico's biggest television conglomerate. There's nothing that annoys me more than writers falling prey to power. What I cherish most about the literary career is the capacity of saying what I want.

There were a number of attacks against me in the Mexican press. The managing editor of *Vuelta* was a historian, Enrique Krauze, who some years earlier had published a cruel review of Fuentes's work. Fuentes was on the *Transition* editorial board. Hence, I was guilty by association in some quarters: under Fuentes's umbrella, I had expressed myself against Paz. But Fuentes and I hadn't even met; my interest in his oeuvre was almost nonexistent by then, as it still is. In any case, I wasn't used to this type of critical exchange because there's little room for it in Mexican circles. *Vuelta* itself didn't publish letters to the editor. Ironically, voicing dissent was something Paz himself cultivated; he just didn't like to be the target of it. Anyway, it was through my pieces in *Transition* that I realized that such exchanges were an essential part of the job description because ideas need to clash, to be appraised, to be sharpened. When I talked to Finder next time around, he welcomed me to "the pugilist rink."

It was only the beginning. Strong reactions to subsequent essays of mine would ensue. In one of them, called "Two Peruvians," I analyzed the roots and impact of the recent arrest of Abimael Guzmán, the leader of the terrorist organization Shining Path. Metaphorically, I pinned Guzmán against another notable Peruvian, Vargas Llosa, the author of *Conversation in the Cathedral*, *The War of the End of the World*, and other novels, also a Nobel Prize for Literature recipient, and a one-time friend of Paz's, who had run for president of Peru. After an embarrassing loss, Vargas Llosa, a Europeanized intellectual, had left his country for Spain, where he had quickly been granted citizenship. Once again, I used literature to scrutinize politics and the other way around, since I was realizing already then that for me literature was about faith: faith in the self, faith in society, faith in ideas. For this piece, I was able to access recently released information by journalist Gustavo Gorriti on how Shining Path operated, a model that proved effective during a decade and a half, until Vargas Llosa's opponent in the presidential campaign, Alberto Fujimori, effectively dismantled the organization.

"Two Peruvians" was reprinted a number of times in different parts of the world; I found out it had even been translated into Spanish. The dichotomy between Guzmán and Vargas Llosa enabled me to delve into a long-standing tension between what the nineteenth-century thinker Domingo Faustino Sarmiento called "the battle between civilization and barbarism." That was the time when Samuel Huntington's theory of "the clash of civilizations" was gaining momentum. Huntington's views were based on his observations of Arab societies. Somehow, the dichotomy I returned to in Latin America between civilization and barbarism seem apropos to people in the media.

Another piece that defined my path was a close analysis of the serpentine flow of Gabriel García Márquez's novelistic talent. With the occasion of the publication of the English translation of a collection of his stories, *Strange Pilgrims*, I followed his path from Aracataca, the coastal town where he was born in Colombia, to his years as a reporter for various newspapers in Barranquilla, Cartagena, and Bogotá, his opposition to the dictatorship of Gustavo Rojas Pinilla mainly through the writing of a journalistic serial about a shipwreck, his years in exile, and the making of the classic *One Hundred Years of Solitude*, which came out in 1967, when García Márquez, another Nobel Prize winner (Latin America has had a total of six), was turning forty years old. My piece was snapped up by two publishers, who offered a generous advance for me to develop it into a full-fledged biography of the writer's early years.

Rereading *One Hundred Years of Solitude* for this piece was one of the greatest pleasures of my career. I had first discovered the novel as a young man in Mexico and had been impressed. But now I was critic and was writing in English. I read Gregory Rabassa's translation and was flabbergasted. García Márquez had once said that the English version is better than the original. I had found the comment disingenuous. But he might have been right: the English translation is careful, methodical, precise—in a word, superb. It made me want to go back to the original. Once I did that, I felt compelled to delve into *Don Quixote of La Mancha*, the other masterpiece of the Spanish language. This back and forth has occupied me ever since. I've written on translation. I've contrasted Cervantes to García Márquez. I've discussed the friendship of García Márquez and Vargas Llosa, who wrote his doctoral dissertation in Madrid about *One Hundred Years of Solitude* but then fought with his Colombian friend and has not spoken to him since then. I've also reflected on the role of classics in culture, on the way a classic makes a language solidify while pushing it to its edge.

⁓

A discovery connected with *Transition* emerged in a public conversation between Anita Desai, Caryl Phillips, and me, which took place in Amherst, Massachusetts, and dealt with questions of authenticity in literature. What makes a writer's voice authentic? To what extent is American literature defined by outsiders? Looking back, in that conversation I realized the potential of dialogue—spontaneous, improvisational—in awakening ideas that a writer on his own might not be able to reach. I'm not talking about an interview, which is something we contemporary writers are used to, but about candid tête-à-tête that involves "people of the word." I realized then that my function was to use the spoken word as well, to do live interactions, to enjoy the role of being a *causeur*, a conversationalist, which I found rewarding in private but now I understood as part of my public persona. One doesn't need to concentrate on particular topics; the art of talking is the act of wandering. Wandering and wondering. After the conversation was transcribed and edited, after each of the participants added or took away things, after I read the final draft, I remember thinking: there's a delicious genre here. Since then, I've been involved in numerous other such dialogues, in auditoriums, on TV, on the radio. The majority have been compiled in volumes. A handful have given place to book-long reflections on specific topics, such as love, censorship, and the Bible.

Then I wrote a piece about Jorge Luis Borges. My interest in the Argentine is long-standing: his literature is for me a Rorschach test through which I came of age as a writer. In my private library, I have a large collection of Borgeana. Some of these books are in different languages. I looked at his oeuvre as oscillating between two extremes: emphasizing the local, e.g., the Argentinean, aspects of his surroundings (*milongas*, *compadritos*, the classic nineteenth-century poem *The Gaucho Martín Fierro* by José Hernández) and to the extent possible avoiding those localisms by stressing his cosmo-politanism. Borges, I have no doubt, is the most durable of Latin American writers. *One Hundred Years of Solitude* might be the greatest of all modern Spanish-language novels, but Borges is an unparalleled genius. That is, he has a unique weltanschauung. Centuries from now, when most of us are forgotten, when nothing that defines us will be of relevance, Borges will still be read. He will be read along with Homer, Dante, Shakespeare, and Emily Dickinson. Through him, I'm convinced, readers will access what Latin America was all about today—and what it was not. Over the years there have been other writers I've fallen in love with, and I have turned that love into a written commitment: Pablo Neruda and Isaac Bashevis Singer, among them. Borges ignites in me more than commitment: he generates awe. Several publishers wanted me to transform my essay in *Transition* into a book. I haven't done it because what I have to say about Borges is still a work-in-progress.

After Finder departed to take a job at the *New Yorker*, I worked closely with his successor, Mike Vazquez. It was with Vazquez as editor that I wrote pieces less about specific authors than about themes, like humor and sexu-ality. One of them was "The Riddle of Cantinflas," investigating Mexican humor through the lens of a number of comic figures (Tin Tan, Chespirito, Los Polivoces), but concentrating on the career of the most successful Hispanic comedian of all time, Mario Moreno, known as Cantinflas, who did dozens of B-movies of enormous popular appeal. I had been fascinated by the dichotomy between the foreign-looking elite in Latin America, obsessed with being chic, and the working class, whose interests, it seems to me, are more authentic. I love Mexican popular culture: sugar *calaveras*, *lucha libre*, *telenovelas*, the children's game of *lotería*. My essay contrasted the types of humor that typified these classes, then attempted to explain why Cantinflas made the masses laugh out loud for years.

This essay enabled me to ponder a concept that I've come to see as cru-cial: *rascuachismo*. It is used among the Mexican working class to refer to the aesthetic of the downtrodden. But an artifact that is *rascuache* also empowers its user, since it stands as a refutation of bourgeois, American-type consum-erism. Rascuachismo was an essential idea for Chicano artists in the sev-enties. It offered them a justification to connect elements from pop culture with their ideological struggle. That connection was for me a revelation. It opened up a well of possibilities, which led me to a reassessment of *la raza cósmica*, the cosmic race, a term coined by José Vasconcelos in a founda-tional book of the same title released in 1925. In it Vasconcelos talked about *mestizaje* as the essential feature of Hispanic civilization. He even prophesied that mestizos would conquer the world. If that moment ever happens, the aesthetic that will reign globally will be rascuachismo.

Arguably the most contested piece I ever wrote for *Transition* is "The Latin Phallus," a study of machismo through crucial intellectual figures, such as Oscar "Zeta" Acosta, the self-destructive Chicano lawyer and friend of Hunter S. Thomson who is portrayed as the three-hundred-pound Samoan in *Fear and Loathing in Las Vegas*. Acosta, in my mind, is one of the most fascinating figures of the civil rights era. He disappeared in 1973 in the Mexican port of Mazatlán, having run for sheriff of Los Angeles County. Acosta left two significant books, *The Autobiography of a Brown Buffalo* and *The Revolt of the Cockroach People*. In the former, he talks about the size of his penis. I used that episode, among several others, to explore the duality at the heart of the archetypal macho, who is always in search of showcasing his power, even if in essence he's vulnerable, overwhelmed by feelings of impotence, maybe even nurturing an attraction to other men.

But this wasn't a piece only about machos. It was, overall, about Hispanic maleness. How are we different from men in other cultures? The responses were loud. The widow of Julio Cortázar, the Argentine author of *Blow-Up and Other Stories*, lambasted me for having discussed Cortázar's sexual interests, and Borges's own widow, María Kodama, didn't like the fact that I talked about Borges living with his mother throughout his life, with the exception of two stints: a brief first marriage to Elsa Astete Millán, in part because some people in Buenos Aires appeared to have been puzzled by his nonmarital status, and the second to Kodama, at the end of his life, to avoid leaving his estate to his family, from whom he was partially estranged. Even before writing "The Latin Phallus," I had been warned that the topic might generate discord because talking about male sexuality in the Hispanic world is anathema. The premonition was proven right. Years later, when a publisher asked me to write a new introduction to Cortázar's short stories, his estate complained, stopping the project without delay.

I also wrote an essay on Cesar Chavez, the civil rights activist behind the United Farm Workers union. The piece, an adaptation of the introduction I wrote for the reissuing of Peter Matthiessen's book *Sal Si Puedes* (1969), was something of a departure. I reflected on Chavez's humble beginnings, his formation as a public speaker without having attended college, his political career, and—the driving point of the essay—his shortcomings as a leader, the nepotism he was involved with in the latter years of his life, his corruption. With the exception of the first piece I published in *Transition*, my contributions dealt with Latin America. But the focus now was Hispanic civilization in the United States, that is, how Latin America exists *inside* its northern neighbor. In Chavez I see a parallel figure to the Reverend Martin Luther King Jr.: a dreamer, a path opener. But Chavez—and my writing again proved controversial in this area—wasn't a martyr. He hadn't died young, his work interrupted, unfinished. Instead, he had survived his own legend to the point of almost spoiling it.

My interest in Chavez was sparked only after I was done with the piece. I wanted to do more, to delve deeper, to explore him through the kaleidoscope of his time. That interest eventually led me to find a piece by him—actually, signed by Chavez but ghostwritten by someone else, one of the many anonymous pens behind his written legacy—called "An Organizer's Tale" and, soon after, to visit the archives at Wayne State University, where his papers are stored. Reading them was a revelation: Chavez, I realized, is an American hero whose complexities, his tortured self, are far from known. I ended up editing a collection of his speeches, a handful of them previously unknown. A full-fledged, brave, uncompromising biography is desperately needed.

Transition had allowed me to explore, to meditate, to wonder while I wandered. I had learned to be thorough, adventurous. My approach was always to look at a topic from both a wide and a wild perspective, to have as target a reader who was inquisitive, restless, interested in global affairs. Was I writing for a black audience? For a Hispanic audience? Neither of them. My target was an unidentified reader: everyone and no one. What I learned from not pinpointing my reader was to seek a general approach: informative, current, stylized. If my essays could be read in Kampala, Lima, or Los Angeles, why make a choice?

My last piece for *Transition* was "Packing My Library," and it became the first chapter of my memoir *On Borrowed Words*. In it the focus was on me: how I had become an immigrant, what Mexico meant to me from a distance, and how I fancied a view of things filtered through literature, which is for me a religion. Why did I stop writing? A superficial answer is that I was writing for other periodicals now, such as the *Nation*, the *Washington Post*, and *El País*; also that books, not essays, were occupying my time.

But the truth is I saw the magazine as a different kind of inspiration. When *Transition* moved from Oxford to Duke University Press, Mike Vazquez, in one of our Cambridge conversations, suggested that I conceive of a journal for Duke along the same lines, with Latinos as the center of gravity. The idea had been with me for a while. Vazquez simply teased it out. Within a few months, I was in conversation with various funders, contributors, et cetera. It took shape as a quarterly and came to be known as *Hopscotch*.

The periodical lasted a couple of years, before Duke closed shop and a vast number of its journals were canceled, including *Transition*. Those two years were astonishingly rewarding. I had switched roles: I had assumed Skip's role and, when at first we were short staffed, even Henry Finder and Mike Vazquez's. I commissioned pieces, I edited them, I laid them out along with black-and-white photographs. The magazine (actually, the Duke people described it as a "journalzine") sought to tackle the Hispanic world through a broad, cosmopolitan perspective. In it I published pieces (essays, interviews, stories, reviews) by scores of writers. At no point during the period did I think that the English language wasn't my home. But the effort was immense. I came to understand the amount of time and energy editing required. My role, my original dream, had been to write. And I wanted to return to it. When the opportunity came to sell *Hopscotch* to another publisher, I didn't embrace it wholeheartedly.

At that time, the invitation came to be the general editor of *The Norton Anthology of Latino Literature*, a project that I initially foresaw as taking two to three years to complete. (It ended up taking thirteen.) I was deeply honored by it, but my concentration would need to be full. I see today that even that honor was also a stepchild of *Transition*, since I came to the magazine through my admiration for Skip, and it was through Skip's groundbreaking work on an anthology of African American literature that the idea of embarking on wide-scoped, ambitious exploration of Latino literature first started. The writing I had done for his magazine, the editing of *Hopscotch*, were indeed my education for the Norton endeavor.

Furthermore, looking back I realize that the education I got was crucial in my understanding of how Latino Studies ought to be nonsectarian, border crossing, a place of encounter, an area of study that begets its gravitas by feeding from a number of different disciplines: literature, sociology, anthropology, political science, religion, American and Hispanic studies . . . It is precisely by means of a cosmopolitan approach that one might be able to fully appreciate the complexity of the Latino experience, which cannot be reduced to a single dimension. Latinidad is a springboard.

That is how I had always understood my Jewishness: as a facilitator, a catalyst. American Jews signify a break with the past: their degree of assimilation to American culture is unprecedented in Jewish history. That might be seen as a good and a bad thing. Anti-Semitism and bigotry are always being targeted in the United States, which allows for a welcoming level of comfort. Yet for centuries Jews have been pariahs. That position, while painful, enabled them to keep a double conscience: they were simultaneously insiders and outsiders, no doubt a wonderful dilemma to find oneself in. In my opinion, the fertile artistic and intellectual zest of Jews in Western civilization is a consequence of that position. Only minorities who understand the pros of a minority status can benefit from it. Latinidad, Jewishness—I saw these as qualities to be cherished in the life of the nonnative, the interloper.

It seems to me that *Transition* was prophetic in its mission. The world has caught up with its sophisticated perspective. It was then, as it is now, a black magazine about the entire world. No small aspiration, but why should an intellectual forum reach for anything else? The publishing world is quite segregated, and that segregation mirrors our own general cultural fragmentation today. The rise of the blogosphere has, on the surface, attempted to close the gaps that exist. But the Internet is too nervous a medium, too ethereal and unstable, democratic, yes, but noncentralized. Everything fits in it, but the abundance of information and the infinitude of viewpoints minimize its impact. I say all this with a certain degree of sadness. *Transition* continues to do the job of featuring thoughtful pieces that are well written. Good writing should come from within academia but not be restricted to it. In contrast, the amount of bad academic writing (specialized pieces for a minuscule readership) seems only to grow by the minute.

As I look at it now, I'm a stepping stone, a bridge, a link between worlds: north and south, the academic milieu and a general readership, the Hispanic, Jewish, and American realms. Hopefully my writing will not be trapped in its own time. Perhaps it will have opened new vistas. We're all more than the sum of our parts. Yes, we're individuals, but we're also characters in a larger narrative whose meaning is beyond us. No matter how in control of our actions we believe ourselves to be, what we do, who we are, is ultimately defined by forces outside us.

Anyhow, maybe what I've been discussing here is my actual arrival, making me the person I am today. *Transition* was my home. It made me feel comfortable in my own skin, it provided me a space to explore, it grounded me in a language. Arrival is synonymous with becoming.

[2012]

UNMASKING
MARCOS

Tout révolutionnaire finit en oppresseur ou en hérétique.

—ALBERT CAMUS

*T*HE SUBCOMANDANTE INSURGENTE MARCOS, OR EL SUP, as he is known in Mexico. His skin is bleached, whiter than that of his *compañeros*. He speaks with palpable erudition. The sword and the pen: he is a rebel, yes, but also an intellectual, a mind perpetually alert. And like some ranting dissenter, he is always prepared to say no: No to five centuries of abuse of the indigenous people of Chiapas and nearby Quintana Roo in the Yucatan Peninsula. No to the sclerotic one-party state that has mortgaged Mexico and her people for generations, and for generations to come.

No, no, and no.

El Sup is also like Sisyphus, or possibly like Jesus Christ: he bears on his shoulders an impossible burden, the aspirations and demands of an embattled people. He must know, in his heart, that the rock is too heavy, the hill too steep; his efforts will change very little in the way people go about their lives south of the Tortilla Curtain. His real task, the best he can do, is to call attention to the misery of miserable men and women. He isn't a terrorist but a freedom fighter, and a peaceable one at that.

He took up arms because debate is unfruitful in his milieu. He is a *guerrillero* for the nineties who understands, better than most people, the power of word and image. He uses allegories and anecdotes, old saws and folktales, to convey his message. Not a politician but a storyteller—an icon knowledgeable in iconography, the new art of war, a pupil of Marshall McLuhan. As he himself once wrote, "My job is to make wars by writing letters."

El Sup is a tragic hero, a Moses without a Promised Land. He stands in a long line of Latin American guerrilla heroes, at once real and mythical, an insurrectionary tradition stretching back nearly half a millennium. Figures like the legendary Enriquillo, who orchestrated an uprising among aborigines in La Española around 1518, about whom Fray Bartolomé de las Casas writes eloquently in his *Brief Account of the Destruction of the Indies*. And like Enriquillo's children: Emiliano Zapata; Augusto César Sandino, the inspiration for Daniel Ortega and the Sandinistas; Simón Bolívar, the revolutionary strategist who liberated much of South America from Spanish rule and who dreamed in the 1820s of La Gran Colombia, a republic of republics that would serve as a Hispanic mirror to the United States of America; Túpac Amaru, the Peruvian Indian leader of an unsuccessful revolt against the Iberians in 1780, whose example still inspires the Maoists in Peru; Edén Pastora, Comandante Cero, an early Sandinista guerrillero turned dissenter; and, of course, Fidel Castro and Ernesto "Che" Guevara. A robust tradition of revolutionaries, overpopulated by runaway slaves, *indios*, *subversivos*, muralists, and disenfranchised middle-class intellectuals.

El Sup: newspaper columnists and union organizers credit him with the wake-up call that changed Mexico forever. He had gone to Chiapas in 1983 to politicize people. "We started talking to the communities, who taught us a very important lesson," he told an interviewer. "The democratic organization or social structure of the indigenous communities is very honest, very clear." He fought hard to be accepted, and he was, although his pale skin marked him as an outsider. (Though the preeminent spokesman of the Zapatista movement, he could never aspire to a position greater than subcomandante, as the highest leadership positions are customarily reserved for Indians.) The next ten years were spent mobilizing peasants, reeducating them and being reeducated in turn. The rest, as they say, is history.

And rightly so: after all, on the night of January 1, 1994, just as the so-called North American Free Trade Agreement (NAFTA) among Canada, the United States, and Mexico was about to go into effect, he stormed onto the stage.

Lightning and thunder followed.

It was a night to remember. As José Juárez, a Chiapas local, described it, "It was on New Year's Eve when President Carlos Salinas de Gortari retired to his chambers thinking he would wake up a North American. Instead he woke up a Guatemalan."

No, said the subcomandante. Mexico isn't ready for the First World. Not yet.

Everywhere people rejoiced. *¡Un milagro!* A miracle! A wonder of wonders! So spoke Bishop Samuel Raúl Ruiz Garda, the bishop of San Cristóbal de las Casas, whose role in the Zapatista revolution angered conservatives, but who was endorsed by millions worldwide, turning him into a favorite for the Nobel Peace Prize.

With his trademark black skintight mask, El Sup was constantly on television. *Un enmascarado*: Mexicans turned him into a god. Since pre-Columbian times Mexico has been enamored of the mask. A wall between the self and the universe, it serves as a shield and a hiding place. The mask is omnipresent in Mexico: in theaters, on the Day of the Dead, in lucha libre, the popular Latin American equivalent of wrestling. And among pop heroes like El Zorro, El Santo the wrestler, and Superbarrio, all defenders of *los miserables*, masked champions whose silent faces embody the faces of millions.

Suddenly, the guerrilla was back in fashion. The "news" that the Hispanic world had entered a new era of democratic transition had been proven

Figure 2:
Dan Carman, *Subcomandante Marcos Pop Art*. © Dan Carman. Used by permission of the artist. www. canvas-icons.webs. com

wrong. Once again weapons, not ballots, were the order of the day. Within the year, the lost "motorcycle diary" of Che Guevara was published in Europe and the United States—a record of a twenty-four-year-old Che's travels on a Norton 500 from Argentina to Chile, Peru, Colombia, and Venezuela. A free-spirited, first-person account unlike any of his "mature" works, it recalled Sal Paradise's hitchhiking in Jack Kerouac's *On the Road*. El Sup had discovered new territory: the revolutionary as Easy Rider.

El Sup had a rifle, yes, but he hardly used it. His bullets took the form of faxes and e-mails, cluster bombs in the shape of communiqués and non-stop e-mail midrashim through the Internet. He wrote in a torrent, producing hundreds of texts, quickly disproving Hannah Arendt's claim that "under conditions of tyranny it is far easier to act than to think." In less than twelve months, during sleepless sessions on the word processor in the midst of fighting a war, El Sup generated enough text for a three-hundred-page volume. And he sent it out without concern for copyright. His goal was to subvert our conception of intellectual ownership, to make the private public and vice versa.

He was a master at marketing. By presenting himself as a down-to-earth dissenter, a nonconformist, a hipster dressed up as soldier, he made it easy to feel close to him. To fall in love with him, even. In one communiqué, for instance, he addresses the Mexican people:

> Brothers and sisters, we are the product of five hundred years of struggle: first against slavery; then in the insurgent-led war of independence against Spain; later in the fight to avoid being absorbed by North American expansion; next to proclaim our Constitution and expel the French from our soil; and finally, after the dictatorship of Porfirio Díaz refused to fairly apply the reform laws, in the rebellion where the people created their own leaders. In that rebellion Villa and Zapata emerged—poor men, like us.

In another, he writes to his fellow Zapatistas:

> Our struggle is righteous and true; it is not a response to personal interests, but to the will for freedom of all the Mexican people and the indigenous people in particular. We want justice, and we will carry on because hope also lives in our hearts.

And in a letter to President Bill Clinton, El Sup ponders:

We wonder if the United States Congress and the people of the United States of North America approved this military and economic aid to fight the drug traffic or to murder indigenous people in the Mexican Southeast. Troops, planes, helicopters, radar, communications technology, weapons, and military supplies are currently being used, not to pursue drug traffickers and the big kingpins of the drug Mafia, but rather to repress the righteous struggle of the people of Mexico and of the indigenous people of Chiapas in the southeast of our country, and to murder innocent men, women, and children.

We don't receive any aid from foreign governments, people, or organizations. We have nothing to do with national or international drug trafficking or terrorism. We organized ourselves of our own volition, because of our enormous needs and problems. We are tired of so many years of deception and death. It is our right to fight for a dignified life.

At all times we have abided by the international laws of war and respected the civil population.

Since all the other compañeros of the Zapatista National Liberation Army were more modest, El Sup stole the spotlight. He was unquestionably *la estrella*. And his enigmatic identity began to obsess people. His education, some said, is obviously extensive. He must be a product of the Distrito Federal, the Mexico City of the early eighties. Was he overwhelmed by the outpouring of public affection? "I won't put much stock in it," he told one interviewer.

I don't gain anything from it, and we're not sure the organization will, either. I guess I just don't know. About what's going on. I only get an inkling of what's going on when a journalist gets angry because I don't give him an interview. I say, "Since when am I so famous that they give me a hard time about being selective, and the lights, and I don't know what all." That is pure ideology, as they say up there, no? We don't have power struggles or ego problems of any kind.

Being selective: *el discriminador*. But his ego, no doubt, is monumental. He courted attention relentlessly. By 1995, stories circulated that internal struggles within the Zapatistas were growing, fought over El Sup's stardom.

Meanwhile, unmasking El Sup became a sport. Who is he? Where did he come from? I, for one, thought I knew, though not through any feat of journalistic prowess. I haven't been to the Chiapas jungle since the Zapatistas launched their rebellion. And if he is who I think he is, I haven't spoken to him since long before his communiqués began streaming from the Lacandonian rain forest.

The clue to his identity came in early 1995, after Salinas had ceded power to his successor, Ernesto Zedillo Ponce de León, in the aftermath of a series of political assassinations that had rocked the PRI, the governing party. The enemy grew restless. El Sup had become too dangerous. And too popular! He was better known than any politician. He commanded more attention than any of the soap operas on Mexican TV, the opiate of the Mexican masses. Enough was enough. It was time for him to go.

Desenmascarar. What the Mexican government performed was an ancient ritual at the heart of the nation's soul: the unmasking. Quetzalcoatl was unmasked by the Spaniards, Sor Juana by the Church, and Pancho Villa by a spy. To unmask can mean to undo, or to destroy, but it can also mean to elevate to a higher status: every six years, as the country prepares to receive its new president, the head of the PRI literally unveils his successor before everyone's eyes.

In the public eye—El Sup's own terrain—Mexican government revealed his true self: Rafael Sebastián Guillén Vicente, a thirty-seven-year-old former college professor. A revelation, indeed, which El Sup immediately disputed . . . before vanishing into the night. Just like that, he disappeared. Off the TV screens. Out of the spotlight. He became a nonentity: *un espíritu.* Other Zapatistas replaced him in the high command of the Zapatista army.

In Mexico, of course, the government is always wrong; that is, since it promotes itself as the sole owner of the Truth, nobody believes it. And yet, El Sup might well be Guillén. I personally have no trouble equating the two. They sounded the same, right down to their rhetoric language, which I learned at the Xochimilco campus of Mexico City's Universidad Autónoma Metropolitana (UAM), the decidedly radical school where Guillén taught. In discussing his communiqués with several old college friends, we were struck by the similarities between his postmodern tongue and the often-hallucinatory verbiage at Xochimilco, full of postscripts and qualifications and references to high and low, from modernist literature and academic Marxism to pop culture. El Sup said his idols were the nationally known "new journalists" Carlos Monsiváis and Elena Poniatowska, whom my whole intellectual generation deeply admired and whose own works trespass intellectual boundaries with glee. When asked to describe the books that influenced him, he would cite the seventies writings of Octavio Paz,

Julio Cortázar, Mario Vargas Llosa, and Gabriel García Márquez, although he would be careful to distance himself from the right-wing politics of Paz and Vargas Llosa.

El Sup mooned journalists with his writings. His speeches, like the authors we studied at UAM, seamlessly mix fiction with reality, becoming masterful self-parodies, texts about texts about texts. In a reply to a letter from the University Student Council of the Universidad Nacional Autónoma de México (UNAM), he writes that with great pleasure the Zapatistas have received the students' support. He asks them to get organized following the pattern of the Zapatistas and concludes:

> If you accept this invitation, we need you to send some delegates so that, through an intermediary, we can arrange the details. We must organize everything well so that spies from the government don't slip through. And if you make it down, don't worry about it. But keep up the fight over where you are, so that there can be justice for all Mexican people.
>
> That's all, men and women, students of Mexico. We will be expecting a written response from you.
>
> Respectfully,
From the mountains of the
Mexican Southeast.

P.S.: El Sup's section: "The repeating post-script."

Another postscript follows, and then more and more.

> P.P.S.: As long as we're in the P.S.'s, which of all the "University Student Councils" wrote to us? Because back when I was a stylish young man of twenty-five . . . there were at least three of them. Did they merge?

> P.S. to the P.S. to the P.S.: In the event that you do (whew!) take the Zócalo, don't be selfish . . . Save me some space where I can at least sell arts and crafts. I may have to choose between being an unemployed "violence professional" and an underemployed one, with underemployment wages (much more marketable that way, under NAFTA, you know).

P.S. to the nth power: These postscripts are really a letter disguised as a postscript (to hide it from the Attorney General's Office and all the rest of the strongmen in dark glasses), and, but of course, it requires neither an answer, nor a sender, nor an addressee (an undeniable advantage of a letter disguised as a postscript).

Nostalgic P.S.: When I was young (Hello, Attorney General's Office. Here comes more data), there used to be a lightly wooded place between the main library, the Facultad de Filosofía y Letras, the Torre de Humanidades, Insurgentes Avenue, and the interior circuit of Ciudad Universitaria. We used to call that space, for reasons obvious to the initiates, the "Valley of Passions," and it was visited assiduously by diverse elements of the fauna who populated at 7 P.M. (an hour when those of good conscience drink hot chocolate and the bad ones make themselves hot enough to melt); they came from the humanities, sciences, and other areas (are there others?). At that time, a Cuban (Are you ready, Ambassador Jones? Make a note: more proof of pro-Castro tendencies) who used to give lectures seated in front of piano keys the color of his skin . . . and who called himself Snowball, would repeat over and over, "You can't have a good conscience and a heart . . ."

Final fortissimo P.S.: Have you noticed how exquisitely cultured and refined these postscripts are? Are they not worthy of the First World? Don't they call attention to the fact that we "transgressors," thanks to NAFTA, are striving to be competitive?

"Happy Ending" P.S.: Okay, okay, I'm going. This trip is coming to an end, and the guard, as usual, is still asleep and someone is tired of repeating "Is anybody out there?" and I tell myself, "Our country" . . . and what is your answer?

El Sup's unconventional style was a commonplace at UAM in the early eighties. I was a student there at the time, the same time that Guillén, about five years my elder, was teaching. Some of my friends took classes with him, remarking on his sharp intellect and infectious verbosity. Crossing paths with him in hallways and cafeterias, I remember him as bright and articulate.

Well known as an incubator for Marxist, pro-Cuba, pro-Sandinista activity, UAM's Xochimilco campus had been built by the government in the early seventies. UAM included two other campuses in far-flung corners of the city. It was built in an attempt to dilute the massive student population at UNAM, the oldest institution of higher learning in the country.

In her book *La noche de Tlatelolco*, Poniatowska chronicled the protests of 1968. It was UNAM's student body, some thirty thousand strong, who led the protests, which were brutally crushed in the massacre at Tlatelolco Square. El Sup, although not Guillén, was born during that massacre—a ritual birth, an origin in which his whole militant odyssey was prefigured. If the revolution couldn't be won in the nation's capital, he would join the unhappy peasants in Chiapas and the Yucatan—he would become an urban exile.

When Xochimilco opened, it immediately superseded UNAM in anti-government militancy. It became a magnet for subversive artists, would-be guerrilla fighters, and sharp-tongued political thinkers. The place was known for its unorthodox educational methods, and fields of study often lost their boundaries. Professors not only sensitized us to the nation's poverty and injustice, they encouraged us to take action. Friends would take time off to travel to distant rural regions and live with the indigenous people. Most eventually returned, but many didn't—they simply vanished, adopting new identities and new lives.

Injustice, inequality, freedom of speech—we wanted changes. "Down with the one-party system!" We would take advantage of cheap fares and travel to Havana, to become eyewitnesses to the profound transformation that had taken place in a corner of the Hispanic world. The Sandinistas in Nicaragua captured our attention and love. We admired their courage and identified with intellectuals like Julio Cortázar, Ernesto Cardenal, and Sergio Ramirez, who had put their literary careers on hold to work for the Nicaraguan government or who had orchestrated international campaigns to support the Sandinista fight. We were excited—and we were blind. Our personal libraries were packed full of Marxist literature. Our writers were busy fashioning a style in which art and politics were inseparable. We disregarded any argument that tried to diminish our utopian expectations.

Indeed, finding bridges between political theory and activism became a sport. Those of us who studied psychology embraced the antipsychiatry movement and were expelled from asylums for allowing patients to go free. I, for one, worked with a metropolitan priest, Padre Chinchachoma, who devoted his ministry to homeless children. He believed that to help the children he needed to live among them, in Mexico City's garbage dumps—foraging with them for food, making and selling drugs for money, and occasionally engaging in acts of vandalism. I read Padre Chinchachoma's books with great admiration. He was my messiah, my Sup before El Sup.

Xochimilco—exciting, contradictory. Our teachers were dissatisfied middle-class Mexican leftists, exiled Argentinean intellectuals, and other Latin American émigrés. Our idols were Che Guevara, Félix Guattari, Antonio Gramsci, and Herbert Marcuse. Wealthy professors urged us to agitate among peasants in the countryside. And, what's more aware that the government perceived our radicalism, our animosity, as productive.

In fact, it wanted our hatred. Its rationale was clear: if adolescents in the Third World are always full of antigovernment feeling, they should be provided with a secluded space to vent their rage. They'll scream, they'll organize, but as long as they're kept in isolation, nothing will come of it. And so we did, investing our time and energy in countless hopeless insurrectionary projects. But it wasn't a waste of energy. Something great did come out of it: El Sup.

I left Mexico in 1985, but I often look back at my years at UAM as a turning point. Between the pen and the sword, I thought I was wise for choosing the pen. But El Sup was even wiser: he chose both.

My politics and artistic views have changed somewhat. I have become a critic and scholar and have adopted a new language. In the process, I acquired a new mask of my own: I became part Mexican and part North American—at once both and neither.

Evidently, El Sup is also an academic, although a less reticent one. I was the coward, the egotist. He was the hero. We are both bridges across cultures, across social classes. I chose the library as my habitat, while he made Mexico itself his personal creation.

So what if he is Guillén, and vice versa? Simply that his unmasking has served its purpose: El Sup has faded away from public attention. His once-omnipresent visage now appears infrequently, if at all, a haggard reminder of the still miserable conditions in the south.

Now there's talk of him, El Sup, becoming a leftist candidate in national politics. But history has little room for heroes shifting gears and even less for legends who undress themselves. Besides, no career is more discredited in Mexico than that of a politician. Better to vanish: only then will his trademark become truly indelible. Or better still: to become a novelist. After all, Latin America is depressing in its politics but vivid in its imaginings. Viva El Sup, the intangible—a giant of the imagination.

[1996]

¡LOTERÍA! OR,
THE RITUAL OF CHANCE

*L*OOOOH-TEH-REE-AH . . . THE SOUNDS STILL RESO-
nate in my ears. Pepe and Lalo Gutiérrez, a charismatic set of siblings who
lived next door to my childhood house in Colonia Copilco, in the southern parts of Ciudad de México, often organized impromptu tournaments
of la lotería, a board game somewhat similar to bingo. These took place
on weekday afternoons. Pepe, the younger of them, enjoyed stretching the
syllables, especially the first one. His pronunciation foreshadowed an afternoon of clamor and competition in their dining room. A small purple box
would be taken from a kitchen cabinet, where it was religiously stored after
each session. Soon every neighbor—there are approximately eight players per session—would have a *tabla* (i.e., a carton board) in front of them
and a pile of blue and yellow chips the size of a nickel to its side, ready to
be placed in the right spot. The group guide, appointed by majority (usually Lalo was the chosen one), would pick up a card, immediately hiding
it from everyone else. Then he would chant a brief riddle: for example,
"¡Pórtate bien, cuatito, si no te lleva el coloradito!," loosely translated into
English as "Behave properly, my friend. Otherwise the Little Red One will
sweep you away!" The first one to guess the answer would immediately
shriek, "¡El diablo!" (The devil!). Or another riddle: "Para el sol y para
el agua" (For the sun and for the water). The answer: "El paraguas" (The
umbrella). Anyone with the correct image on their tabla would place a chip
on it, regardless of who answered the riddle.

An hour or so later, each neighbor would be called home to finish home-
work and have dinner. The winner—the one with the most images covered—would be awarded a sack full of five cent coins. The order of the
afternoon had been about envy, frustration, genuflection, perhaps even

anger. In how many games was I a loser? Too many to count. It was the goddess of Fortune (with capital F) who had been courted, but the courtship, in my own case, was hardly ever fruitful. Noticing my dismay, Pepe and Lalo's uncle, who lived with them, would always say: "¡El que de suerte vive, de suerte muere!" (He who rises by luck, falls by luck, too!).

The term *lotería* has the Teutonic root *hleut*, which was adopted into the Romance languages: in French it evolved into *loterie*, in Italian *lotto*, and in English (which is Romance influenced) it is the source of *lot*, a method used in ancient times to solve disputes by appealing to chance. The lots, according to the *Diccionario de la lengua española de la Real Academia*, were placed in a receptacle—in Homeric Greece, a helmet—with an element (a sign, a letter) that tied each of them to a participant. The receptacle was then shaken, and the victorious lot was the one that fell out first. Every country, from Scandinavia to Africa, has one or more varieties of games of chance, and Mexico is no exception. Or is it?

As with most things popular, the game has a complex, mostly unexplored history. According to the chronicler Bernal Díaz del Castillo, Hernán Cortés was an assiduous cardplayer. In La Nueva España, as Mexico was known during the viceroy period, there were public stands where the dwellers of Ciudad de México could play cards and a handful of fixed board games. As a collective pastime, La Lotería Nacional was established in 1769 by King Charles III of Spain. It quickly traveled across the Atlantic and since then has flourished like virtually no other Mexican institution: almost free of corruption (with a brief exception in 1838), with philanthropic tentacles that support schools and hospices. To this day the variegated tickets are like currency, with the peculiarity that they become worthless as soon as the contest is over.

The designs remain beautiful, though. The anonymous designers in charge of producing them are an inspired cast. The pictures represented on the tickets include the Mexican flag, an emblem of the nation's sovereignty; a group of Aztec hieroglyphics; and the angel symbolizing Mexico's independence from Spain. They have a standard size that doesn't change: four inches by eight inches. What distinguishes not only one edition from another, but also a single ticket from the rest, are the numbers, randomly organized: 4135428201, 2566494, 040761 . . . Why buy a particular ticket and not another? The response, of course, is simple: intuition. Fortune is ruled by intuition.

Along with the tickets, La Lotería Nacional produces large quantities of publicity material: posters, calendars, matchboxes, and special toys. The momentous weekly lotería contest, late in the afternoon on Mondays and Wednesdays, mesmerizes the entire nation. A bounty is awarded to a single individual. The selection makes no distinction across racial, class, religious, or ideological lines. Everyone is eligible as long as the individual invests at least one peso in a single ticket. The results are publicized in the late evening and next morning through radio, TV, and newspapers.

When I was little, my father's business frequently took him to El Centro, the bustling downtown section. I often accompanied him. We would start the day with a stop for breakfast at the Sanborn's in Casa de los Azulejos, on Calle Madero, and then do the rounds on adjacent streets where he needed to visit clients and creditors. It was in the Edificio de la Lotería Nacional, near the statue known as El Caballito in the intersection of Avenidas Reforma and Benito Juárez, that on occasion he would stop to buy a ticket. My own grandfather, Zeyde Srulek, an immigrant from the Ukraine, arrived in Mexico penniless in the early part of the twentieth century. He began by selling shoelaces and razor blades. After a short time, he invested the little money he had saved in a lotería ticket—and hit the jackpot. The experience made him forever grateful. Fortune had smiled. Mexico had opened its arms to him.

I remember vividly the back streets behind El Caballito as a full-scale ant colony: vendors pulling chariots with rags and cages filled with parakeets; señoritas swinging their miniskirts while being greeted by adventurous swindlers; *tragafuegos* vomiting flames at intersections; desperate police-men running after a thief; automobiles and buses making their horns heard incessantly while bicycles artfully sneaked through the fumes—and, amid the hullabaloo, *marchantes* selling tickets while screaming ingenious slogans constrained only by endless exclamation marks: "¡¡¡¡¡¡Gane sus millones hoy y despreocúpese mañana!!!!!!" (Win your millions today and forget about tomorrow!!!!!!).

Were the weekly national contests of la Lotería Nacional and the indi-vidual sessions in Pepe and Lalo's house that riveted our attention on those tablas before us unlike one another? Not really: they are fundamentally the same game, played on different scales.

La lotería is a favorite *entretenimiento* not only in Mexico but in the western and central parts of the United States. From Oregon to Texas, it is ubiquitous in *ferias* attended by migrant workers and sold in *mercados* in the versions manufactured since 1887 by the French entrepreneur Don Clemente Jacques, widely known as the principal promoter of the game in manageable containers that include ten boards, eighty cards, and a joker, known as *un naipe*. Jacques's commitment to the game is still shrouded in rumor, but the development of the pastime might owe more to him than anyone.

It is said that in the central state of Querétaro, he built, in the late nineteenth century, a prosperous canned-food and ammunition business. (The former has flourished; fortunately, the latter is gone.) At the time of the Mexican Revolution, around 1912, aware of the long hours of duress soldiers were subjected to, he decided to attach a small lotería board to his products so that the men could "pass the time." But it was when the *soldados* returned home after the battle that the demand for lotería boxes notably increased. In response, Jacques, using the same press he used to create food labels, increasingly printed more . . . until the brand and the game became synonymous. (Nowadays the division of Don Clemente Jacques devoted to the manufacture of the game is called Pasatiempos Gallo.)

I still keep an old set made by his company in a closet: it includes cards that feature, among other characters, the drunkard, the hunchback, and the Indian. Over the years I've studied these images almost to exhaustion. And I've also become acquainted with other designs. For instance, the lampoonist José Guadalupe Posada made his own set, which included one of Posada's recognizable calaveras, a skeleton poking fun at . . . what else, but death? There was a plethora of sets designed for kids, as well as kits depicting heroes in Mexican history (Huitzilopochtli, Cuauhtémoc, Hernán Cortés, Father Miguel Hidalgo y Costilla, Porfirio Díaz), famous themes (Indian slavery), events (the independence movement of 1810, as well as the Battle of Puebla, in which the fateful date of Cinco de Mayo became the occasion for a clash between the armies of the United States and Mexico), and sites (Mitla, the castle in Chapultepec, et cetera).

Then there is the ecclesiastical lotería set with depictions of priests, biblical scenes, and the Seven Deadly Sins. But whatever design one might come across, its power isn't reducible to its graphics. The poetic participation of the players is equally essential. At Pepe and Lalo's house the sessions would frequently become—especially when Lalo was the group guide—a sort of poetry slam. He would recite his improvised riddles, known in Mexico as *acertijos*. He would also use other forms of popular poetry: *colmos*, *tantanes*, *refránes*, and *trabalenguas*—conundrums, corollaries, aphorisms, and tongue twisters. Sometimes these poetic capsules had the length of a single line. Others involved entire stanzas, rhymed in easy patterns like *abab* and *aabb*. Pepe used to describe the sum of his brother's lyrics as a *cancionero*, a medieval term used to describe a compilation of ballads.

Today these images and the poems they were accompanied by might appear racy and even awkward, but they were commonplace at the time I was growing up. And through them, to some extent, millions of other children, young adults, and I learned to understand the way Mexican people behave: the way they eat, drink, think, dream, dance, and make love. The Mexico of the 1960s and 1970s was controlled by a corrupt single-party system, which might explain our obsession with chance. The reality that surrounded us was tight and undemocratic, with little space to debate ideas in any meaningful fashion, at least at the political level. It was in the private sphere where individual spontaneity was championed. And it was also in that sphere where a person's future might be challenged and, along with it, the future of the country as a whole. For all of us felt that in command of our lives was not a savvy, coherent government with enough knowledge to lead; instead, our fate was in the hands of a bunch of disoriented politicos without a clue as to how to feed approximately 80 million stomachs. Ramón López Velarde (1888–1921), the nation's most susceptible, heart-torn poet, in "La suave patria," roughly understood as "sweet homeland," wrote about the randomness of la lotería as Mexico's *manera de ser:*

Como la sota moza, Patria mía,
en piso de metal vives al día,
de milagro, como la lotería.

Here is the English version of Margaret Sayers Peden:

Like a Queen of Hearts, Patria, tapping
a vein of silver, you live miraculously,
for the day, like the national lottery.

To us the images of lotería cards and boards weren't types but prototypes and archetypes in the nation's psyche. To play a single game was to traverse the inner chambers of *la mexicanidad*.

Mysteriously, I've been transported back to the boisterous sessions in Pepe and Lalo's dining room through the recent rendition of *¡Lotería!* by artist Teresa Villegas. This modernized interpretation is the product of her journey to San Miguel Allende, in the state of Guanajuato, filtered through a modern sensibility and a north-of-the-border view of life. I became hypnotized by it after learning of an installation she built of the total fifty-four cards, rendered—"reappropriated"—by her brush. I've found myself

enthralled, for instance, by the frequency in the game of gastronomic motifs (churros, nopales, *horchata*, posole), religious symbols and amulets (ex-votos, *milagros*, *polvo mágico*, la Virgen de Guadalupe), and also pop icons and the media (El Santo, Subcomandante Marcos, TV soaps, comic strips). And I'm spellbound, too, by how the dichotomy of sexes is turned upside down: machos like the street-corner fire breather on one side and, on the other, dignified females like Sor Juana Inés de la Cruz and the *independentista* Josefa Ortíz de Domínguez. Is this still the Mexico of my past? Not quite: much has changed, though much remains the same.

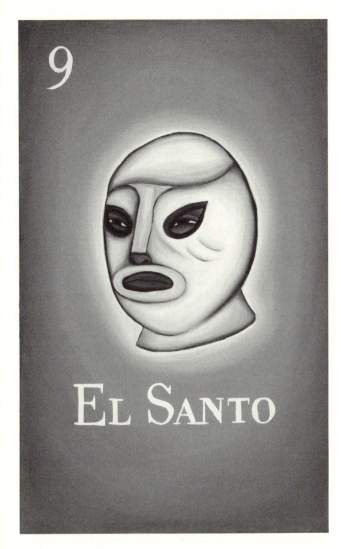

9

EL SANTO

Figure 4:
Teresa Villegas,
"El Santo," part
of *La Lotería: An
Exploration of Mexico*.
© Teresa Villegas,
2004. Reprinted
by permission of
the artist. www.
teresavillegas.com

Villegas's images have inspired me to recreate the riddles that populated my yesteryears, hopefully in a mood that is akin to our present era. These riddles of mine, a total of twenty-seven, which the artist herself has selected, pay homage to Lalo's talents. Hopefully they contain the same dose of irony and fatalism that infused his words. Indeed, his cancionero always seemed to distill a skeptical philosophy: Is love truly redemptive? Does the food we eat have any connection with our emotions? Is there magic in the world? What is the value of freedom? In hindsight, those competitions in Colonia Copilco taught me early on some fundamental lessons in the art of living:

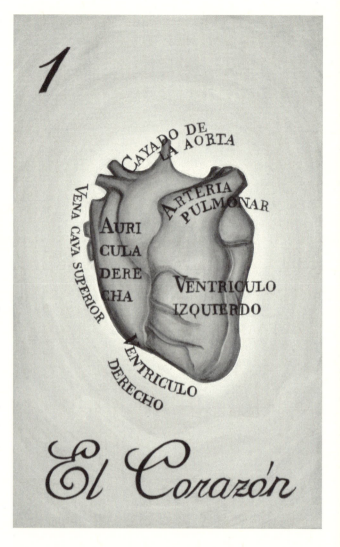

"¡El que de suerte vive, de suerte muere!" I learned that things are not what they seem and, also, that our existence is shaped by sheer chance. Every single decision we make, no matter how insignificant, represents a forking path before us. To choose one alternative among many is to say no to the other ones—to say no to the other selves we might have been.

Albert Einstein once said: "God doesn't play dice with the universe." That isn't true. With us He plays *Looooh-teh-ree-ah*.

[2004]

SANTA
SELENA

SAINT, *n.* A dead sinner revised and edited.
—AMBROSE BIERCE, *The Devil's Dictionary*

*D*URING A RECENT TRIP I TOOK TO SOUTH TEXAS, A dignified old man told me Selena had died because heaven was desperate for another cherub. He described her to me as "a celestial beauty whose time on earth was spent helping the poor and unattended." In San Antonio, a mother of four has placed Selena's photograph on a special altar in her home, surrounded by candles and flowers, just beneath the image of the Virgin of Guadalupe. "Please, Selena," her prayer goes, "let me remain a virgin . . . just like you." (This despite the fact that, at the time of her death, Selena was married to Chris Perez, her guitar player.) The collective imagination is stronger than anything reality has to offer: a young lady from Corpus Christi who spends a good portion of her days singing "selenatas" swears she sees the singer's ghost appear on her TV screen every night— after she's switched the set off. And a Spanish teacher I know in Dallas who recently lost her job has begun selling a poem of her own creation, "Adiós mi linda estrella," to make money. She sent me a copy of the poem, a tribute to the pop star she considers her angel protector:

Do not cry for me, do not suffer for me
Remember I love you with all my heart
I know if you listen and do as I ask
I will be content because

I have completed my mission here on my beautiful earth
and
I can continue to sing to Our Father in Heaven.
Listen, Heaven does not thunder
The sun begins to hide
Our father has given us a new light
Look up to Heaven
The light comes from a divine star
That lights up all of Heaven
It is the Angel Selena
The most beautiful star of the world and now of Heaven.
Goodbye, my lovely Star.

Welcome to *la frontera*, the painful wound dividing Mexico and the United States, a land of kitsch and missed opportunities where outlandish dreams and workaday life intertwine. Encompassing 12 million people, la frontera has as its capital Tijuana, where *El Día de los Muertos* is the most popular holiday: an opportunity for the living to spend a wild night carousing in the cemetery at the sides of their dearly departed. The flag of the region is red, white, and blue, but at its heart is an eagle devouring a writhing snake. La frontera is where NAFTA and Kafka cohabit, where English isn't spoken but broken, and where *yo* becomes I and I becomes *ay, carajo*—a free zone, autonomous and self-referential, perceived by Mexicans as *el fin del mundo* and by Anglo Americans as a galaxy of bad taste.

Since her tragic death, Selena has become omnipresent in la frontera, the focal point of a collective suffering—a patron saint, of sorts. Tender señoritas cannot bring themselves to accept the idea that she is no longer with us. On radio call-in shows, her followers bemoan the injustice of her disappearance. A movie is in the works, several instant biographies have already been published (in Spanish and English), and more are on their way to the printers. Countless imitators mimic her style, her idiosyncratic fashion, her smile: an upcoming national contest in Corpus Christi will soon crown the girl who impersonates Selena most perfectly, who loses herself in Selena's chaste yet sexy persona. In fact, the whole of Lake Jackson, Texas, Selena's hometown, has already become a kind of Graceland: pilgrims come to weep at her birthplace and to pay homage at the places she graced with her presence—her home, the neighborhood rodeos where she sang at intermission, the arenas where she entertained the masses. Her grave at Seaside Memorial Park is inundated daily with flowers, candles, and mementos, and the cemetery keeper has trouble disposing of the colorful offerings. Amalia González, a radio host in Los Angeles, says Selena had sojourned on earth in order "to unite all creeds and races."

Elvis, John Lennon, Kurt Cobain, and Jerry Garcia . . . roll over: there's a new kid in the pop star firmament, one who gives voice to the silenced and the oppressed. This until-yesterday-unknown Tejana, née Selena Quintanilla—awarded the Grammy for Best Mexican-American Album for a work titled, ironically, *Selena Live!*—has instantly become the unquestioned queen of mestizo pop, part wetback and part *gabacha*.

Selena's life may have been tragically short, but death has given her an imposing stature. At 1:05 PM on Friday, March 31, 1995, she became immortal: just short of her twenty-fourth birthday, she ceased to exist as a pop

Figure 6:
Ester Schlimper,
Selena's Shrine.
© Ester Schlimper.
Used by permission
of the artist.

singer of modest means but high ambitions, poised to cross over to a mainstream market, and became not only Madonna's most fearsome competitor (her album *Dreaming of You*, which included a handful of songs in English, sold 175,000 copies in a single day), but also a cult hero, a Hispanic Marilyn Monroe, an object of relentless adoration and adulation. She has joined Eva Perón in the pantheon of mystical and magical Hispanas, protectors of the *descamisados*, immaculate personification of eternal love.

How many of us from outside la frontera had heard of her before the murder? Not many. But even if we had heard some of her songs on the radio, we could not have fathomed her appeal: her music is *cursi*—melodramatic, cheesy, overemotional. Tejano rhythms, which Selena was in the process of reinventing, are a jumbled fusion of rock, jazz, pop, and country seasoned with a hint of rap—an endless addition resulting in a subtraction. She was beginning to master them all when she died. But that's not the point: her conjunto pieces, as well as the mental imbalances of Yolanda Saldívar, the administrator of her fan club and her killer, are only props in a theatrical act in which Selena is the star regardless of her talents. She was a symbol, not a genius.

Selena's father, Abraham Quintanilla Jr., whose family has been in South Texas for at least a hundred years, forced her to learn Spanish in order to further her career. She debuted at age five with Los Dinos, her father's group. (He was a vocalist.) Less than twenty years later, with a sexy public persona built around a halter top and tight pants, she was worth more than $5 million dollars. Since she passed just as her crossover dreams were beginning to materialize, her legend was never—will never—be forced to confront the conundrum of assimilation: she will go down as a brave, courageous Chicana, perhaps ambivalent toward, but never ashamed of, her background. "You'd see her shopping at the mall," people in South Texas say, wistfully. "And you'd see her working at home. A real sweetheart." Some even recalled how accessible she was—*una de nosotros*: Selena never turned up her nose at Mexican popular entertainment, performing in variety shows like *Siempre en domingo* and the melodramatic soap *Dos mujeres, un camino*, starring Erik Estrada. Small parts, no doubt, but the real *sabor*. Had Selena been visited by the angel of death only a few years later, it would have been a very different story: she would have been an American star, and her tragedy would not serve to highlight the plight of la frontera.

Now Selena is ubiquitous: on TV screens and CDs, on book covers and calendars, on velvet slippers and plastic bracelets, on shampoo bottles and make-up advertisements, on designer clothes and piñatas. She is a present-day Frida Kahlo: a martyr whose afterlife *en el más allá* promises to be infinitely more resonant than whatever she managed to achieve *en el más acá*. In la frontera, she has been made into a heroine, an ethnic mass-market artifact. "Thanks to her Tejanos are being heard," a disc jockey from Houston told me. "She put us in the news—and on the front page." And so she did: Rosa López was merely a bit of Hispanic seasoning in the O. J. Simpson mix, but Selena has turned la frontera—whose children, adopted and otherwise, include film director Robert "El Mariachi" Rodriguez, performance artist Guillermo Gómez-Peña, and novelists Laura Esquivel and Cormac McCarthy—into a banquet of possibilities for the media. The trial and sentencing of Saldívar alone has catapulted Selena to eternity, winning more newspaper columns for Latinos than the Zapatista rebellion. Even Texas Governor George W. Bush, whose knowledge of Tejano culture is close to nil, was quick enough to declare April 16, 1995—Selena's birthday and Easter Sunday—El Día de Selena. There's even a motion to put her face on a postage stamp.

Selena's was a life quilted by sheer coincidence but which, studied in retrospect, shows the deliberate design of a well-patterned tapestry. The murder itself (which, strangely, took place on Cesar Chavez's birthday) is already legendary, rivaling the Crucifixion for pathos and histrionics: Saldívar—whose much-lauded punishment is life in prison—comes out of room 158 of the Corpus Christi Days Inn on Navigation Boulevard with a .38-caliber revolver. Selena stumbles ahead of her, wounded, bleeding, and crying for help. She names her assassin and then dies, in close-up. Cut! Roll the commercial. The next scene takes place minutes later, as Saldívar seals herself in a pickup truck and, holding the pistol to her temple á la O. J., threatens to commit suicide and keeps the police at a standstill for nine and a half hours. Blood, tears, desperation—the recipe lacks not a single ingredient. Saldívar had been a good friend of the singer and her business partner in Selena, Inc., the company that managed the singer's boutiques and beauty salons in Corpus Christi and San Antonio. So what went wrong?

You might find the answer in cyberspace, where a Selena home page on the World Wide Web has kept her *admiradores* up to date since a few weeks after her death. Or simply tune in to *El show de Cristina*, starring the Spanish-speaking Oprah Winfrey, which was among the first TV programs to capitalize on Selena's tragedy by devoting several episodes to her family's sorrows. Or you might give up on investigating the logic and become a *selenamaníaco* and start building up your pile of collectibles: nightgowns, hats, purses, money holders, sleepers, umbrellas, and a lot more, all sporting her beautiful photograph. Or if you are ready for a deeper investment, keep in mind the seventy-six-page special issue of *People*, which retailed at $3.95 and now sells for more than $200.00. There is also, of course, the notorious April 17, 1995, issue of the same magazine, which appeared in two different versions: 442,000 copies with Selena on the cover, for sale in Texas, and 3 million issues featuring the cast of the TV show *Friends* for the rest of the country. A single copy of that Selena issue has auctioned for more than $500.00. My own favorite item is the advertisement for the colorful T-shirt on sale at Selena, Inc. ($10.99), which is marketed as a sign of loyalty: "Tell the world of your love for Selena and her music with one of several full-color designs." One size fits all.

For those inclined to read more about it, an illustrated tribute to La Virgen Selena is now available, complete with photos of her grave, third-grade class, and mourning mother, plus a snapshot of the singer and her killer cavorting at a fan club appreciation party at the Desperados Club in San Antonio during the Tejano Music Awards in 1993. Or you might want to bring home the most complete of Selena's thirteen biographies (at this writing), titled *Selena: Como la Flor* and written by Joe Nick Patoski, a senior editor at *Texas Monthly* and coauthor of the bestseller *Stevie Ray Vaughan: Caught in the Crossfire*. Patoski's definitive report on the life of *la reina* will tell you how many hours a day she exercised to keep up her figure, the names of her favorite stores, the shoes she was wearing at the time of her death, and all the skinny you will never find in the *National Enquirer*. The newspaper's anti-Hispanic bias has forced its editors to ignore Selena's story from A to Z.

Never fear: Selena will survive all aggressions, and her apotheosis is not yet complete. That apex will most surely be reached with the release of the Hollywood movie by director Gregory Nava (who brought you *El Norte*, a film about the plight of poor Guatemalan immigrants in *el otro lado*, as well as *La Familia*, a transgenerational melodrama to end all melodramas). From the moment Selena's body hit the hotel floor, a pitched battle has raged over securing the movie rights to her story. (Patoski devotes several pages of his biography to the wrangling.) By all accounts, her father is firmly in command of choosing the screenwriter and, more important, who gets to play his daughter. (He also chooses who gets to play himself; unidentified sources claim that he rejected Edward James Olmos as too ugly.) Selena will surely do wonders for Nava's career. She has already granted so many miracles—one more shouldn't be a problem. Victor Villaseñor is next in line for redemption, a Chicano writer known for his *Roots*-esque family epic, *Rain of Gold*, who is under contract to write the "official" companion to the film.

Although the second book of his family saga was almost unreadable, it will be hard to go wrong with Selena for inspiration.

Inspiration is what she is all about. Just when Latinos were convinced no one cared for them, along came Selena. As long as la frontera remains a hybrid territory, hidden from the sight of Anglo America and ignored by the Mexican government, people north and south of the Rio Grande will continue to pray to their new Madonna. They have realized that the best way to conquer the mainstream culture of the United States is by media storm, a subversion from within. They are confident that sooner, rather than later, all gringos will make room for Latino extroversion and sentimentality. Sooner, rather than later, the *National Enquirer* will publish a report on her return to earth in a UFO. A new, darker-complexioned Elvis is here to capture the imagination of a nation: SELENA IS ALIVE.

[1996]

THE NOVELIST
AND THE DICTATOR

$\mathcal{D}$OES THE CURRENT CROP OF LEFT-WING CAUDILLOS IN Latin America like Hugo Chávez inspire the type of animosity their military counterparts once did? And will it end up metamorphosed into larger-than-life characters in novels of the type of Gabriel García Márquez's *The Autumn of the Patriarch?* Has the literary intelligentsia finally given up the foolish practice of using fiction to pretend to force tyrants out of their thrones?

These aren't rhetorical questions. For centuries the literature from the former Spanish colonies on this side of the Atlantic has sought to define itself, in part, as resistance to autocratic rulers, as if what justified writing was a quest to fight oppression and be free in a totalitarian state. That, of course, is a reason, but not the sole one, although it might be difficult to guess it from the plethora of *novelas del dictador*, narratives, mostly gargantuan in scope, in which a narcissist tyrant serves as protagonist and at times as the narrator, too.

Exactly how many have appeared altogether is anyone's guess, among other reasons because some items on the bookshelf are closer in length to a novella—for instance, Esteban Echeverría's *Slaughterhouse* (1838), an attack against Juan Manuel de Rosas, who mercilessly imposed himself over Argentina from 1835 to 1852. Or Elena Poniatowska's *Massacre in Mexico* (1971), which is neither a novel nor about a dictator, but, in its journalistic quest to uncover the motives that led to the massacre of students on Mexico's Tlatelolco Square in 1968, denounces the despotic regime of then president Gustavo Díaz Ordaz, the head of the nasty ruling party, PRI, that held Mexico under a tight fist for over seventy years.

In other words, literary historians like Julio Calviño Iglesias and Conrado Zuluaga are evasive, for an array of reasons, in confining the parameters of the novela del dictador. What is unquestionable, however, is that for decades respectable novelists in the region felt the need to fashion their own avatar. The key to success is to find a worthy foe—arrogant, dogmatic, overbearing, if possible misogynistic, maybe even a voodoo practitioner—and God knows that, from the first search of independence the colonies engaged in at the dawn of the nineteenth century onward, there was no scarcity of them. Take your pick: Juan Domingo Perón in Argentina, Rafael Leónidas Trujillo in the Dominican Republic, Juan Vicente Gómez in Venezuela, Anastasio Somoza in Nicaragua, José María Velasco Ibarra in Ecuador . . . the catalog is plentiful!

Indeed, as Renaissance Spain was a fertile ground for the chivalry novel—the most illustrious, as well as its most subversive, example of which is Cervantes's *Don Quixote of La Mancha*—in the Americas this tradition might be said to have started with Domingo Faustino Sarmiento, whose *Facundo: Civilization and Barbarism* (1845), written against Rosas while the author was in exile in Chile, is part biography and part essayistic pastiche on the perils of repression. *Facundo* rallied public opinion against Rosas, and Sarmiento eventually became president of Argentina, thus modeling the paradigm of the intellectual whose pungent fight against absolutism brings in a democratic change.

His odyssey summons the polarities at stake in the novela del dictador: the dinosaurs versus the free thinkers, the forces of obscurantism against the conduits of liberty. Needless to say, life was never that simple, but for artistic purposes it's always safe to counter the good with the bad guys. Totalitarianism, after all, is a system of government with little patience for the novel, which symbolizes liberalism, openness, and democracy. And democracy, as far as the cadre of dictators goes, is like a Mexican tamale: it tastes better after it cools down.

The most commendable models don't attack a clear and present danger; instead, they build their structure historically, as is the case of Augusto Roa Bastos's *I, the Supreme* (1974), about José Gaspar Rodríguez de Francia y Velasco, who dominated Paraguay for thirty-six years in the first half of the nineteenth century, soon after its independence from Spain (he was praised by, among others, Thomas Carlyle); in its dense 467 pages, it feels like a behemoth. The author was, obviously, taking a metonymic approach: wasn't Rodríguez de Francia a sit-in for Alfredo Stroessner, who dominated Paraguayan politics from 1954 to 1989?

In between and around these examples are *The Caudillo* (1921) by Jorge Borges, who was Jorge Luis Borges's father (Borges *hijo* was apolitical, or in any case conservative, which stopped him from indulging his talents in such an ideology-driven genre), as well as Miguel Ángel Asturias's *El Señor Presidente* (1946), Alejo Carpentier's *Reasons of State* (1974), and Mario Vargas Llosa's *The Feast of the Goat* (2000). The hope behind these projects was to articulate the ancient equation of the pen and the sword in a new way and to pose intellectuals as freedom fighters. But fashions are ephemeral. García Márquez once promised not to write again until Augusto Pinochet renounced power in Chile. For a while the stance helped sell books. But Pinochet couldn't have cared less. And García Márquez wasn't really serious about interrupting his illustrious career. In the end, it was the writer who gave in to pressure.

Remember: the novela del dictador is testosterone filled; not only are the dictators almost all male (the extremely rare exception is the domineering Isabelita, aka María Estela Martínez Cartas de Perón, Perón's third wife, although she is known as a *presidenta* from 1974 to 1976), and so are the authors—a list of the latter includes less women than might be counted with a single hand, among them Luisa Valenzuela and Marta Traba. (Curiously, among Latinos in the United States, Julia Alvarez carries the torch with *In the Time of the Butterflies* [1994]. The novel has strong feminist undertones, an attribute almost completely absent in the tradition.)

Shouldn't Hugo Chávez be at center stage in one of these artifacts? He has the three *i*'s: he is irritating, impulsive, and intolerant. How about Nicaragua's Daniel Ortega? Or Bolivia's Evo Morales? Why haven't the larger-than-life left-wingers who populate the Latin American political stage nowadays inspired novelistic silhouettes? There are, once again, plenty to choose from. And though, as a rule they don't resort to torture and death to eliminate their adversaries, like their right-wing counterparts did, and their regimes aren't controlled by vengeful police bodies, their *caudillaje* is just as palpable: the constant rewriting of constitutions to perpetuate themselves as supreme leaders, the triumphant embrace of a populist oratory that condemns materialism and ridicules individuality, and the alignment with an anti-imperialist (often a synonym for anti-American) stance that classifies them as supporters of the downtrodden.

The answer to these questions is quite simple. To understand them, it is important to consider that the Latin American intelligentsia habitually embraced Communism. To be a novelist was tantamount to being anti-establishment. This nefarious attitude didn't mean, at least not regularly, that you needed to be a bohemian to be considered serious. It was about a self-professed nearsightedness of judgment. It was based on the belief that power corrupts and the excess of power corrupts excessively. It was grounded in the trust that Latin America since 1492 was at once a mental asylum and a garbage dump for Western civilization. It was centered on the conviction that the road to the region's redemption was to be found by rejecting foreign ideologies that helped root capitalism but not those that supported Communism, because Communism was about the collective goodness and those values were already known by the pre-Columbian dwellers in these lands, meaning that Communism was in some sense a vindication of the Indian past.

The facile Communist hurrah was pervasive in the sixties, in response to the impact the Cuban Revolution had on the entire continent. The majority of writers came from middle-, upper-middle-, and upper-class backgrounds, but on the road to self-definition and out of peer pressure, they categorically rejected their class origins. To shake Pinochet's hand, as Borges did, was a heresy, and he paid dearly for it, perhaps even giving up the Nobel Prize, as has been rumored, since as a rule the more vocal an author was against a tyrant, the heftier his accolades were not only in Stockholm but in Barcelona, Paris, and New York. Nothing better than an entertaining and enlightened *subversivo*. Borges was among a handful of exceptions to the norm. A couple of years before he died in 2005, Roberto Bolaño, who came of age reading magical realism, said that "the best lesson Vargas Llosa ever offered was to go out jogging every morning." As it happens, Vargas Llosa was by then a neo-liberal, post-Reaganite thinker, having renounced, in no tentative terms, his loyalty to the Cuban Revolution.

To some intellectuals, the nearsightedness became indefensible as Fidel Castro's government became crueler and he became a prime candidate for a protagonist role in a *novela del dictador*, soon becoming an island onto himself on the bookshelf of this literary tradition. As time went by Castro became the subject of books ranging from, for instance, Reinaldo Arenas's memoir *Before Night Falls* (1992) to, more recently, Norberto Fuentes's *The Autobiography of Fidel Castro* (2004), a colossal fictionalized life story—the Spanish original was published in two volumes—about . . . well, about El Comandante's oversized ego. Still, absurd as it might be, in some quarters Castro continues to be defended today, as if his censorship stance and his incarceration of dissidents and homosexuals were ignorable in comparison to his alphabetizing efforts and his mandate to make health care available to every Cuban. In regards to Communist tyrants, Latin American writers often *se hacen de la vista gorda*, as the Spanish expression goes: they see what they want to see.

So is it the left-leaning sympathy that keeps writers from turning Hugo Chávez into a novelistic ogre? Yes, but there's another reason. Latin American writers no longer command the kind of attention they once did in the so-called Age of Revolution. At the time of El Boom, as the rejuvenating aesthetic movement that brought Cortázar, García Márquez, Vargas Llosa, and others to the attention of international audiences was known, these celebrities symbolized the collective spirit. They were the voice of the voiceless. But the voiceless are now anesthetized through TV, soccer, and other idol-worshiping, consumerist indulgences. Literature has become inconsequential.

Add to this the fact that many Latin American writers have given up on Latin America, which is, I trust, a healthy, natural move. It was "the duty"—ah, that painful command!—of intellectuals to target their attention in their immediate surroundings to allow others, i.e., foreigners, to see the sorrowful state of things in the Third World. In the nineties young stars, part of the generations known as McOndo and El Crack, rejected this responsibility. Why couldn't their books be about the making of the atomic bomb or the climbing of Mount Everest? And while their quest produced worthy books, the region lost its defenders in world forums. A result of this de–Latin Americanization of the Latin American writer is that a political position is currently seen, among the up-and-coming, as unappealing, a rejection that, to some old folks, amounts to taking the sweetness out of sugar. The *escritor de moda*, the fashionable auteur, meets his fans at Starbucks, spends hours at the gym, vacations in the Bahamas, and teaches at American universities.

In short, the novela del dictador doesn't ridicule left-wing caudillos, not because these politicos are less appealing, although it is true that writers from the region have a softness for Communist suckers, but because Latin American literature—happily, I might add—has ceased to be mindlessly virile.

[2010]

THE RIDDLE OF
CANTINFLAS

In everything that can be called art there is a quality of redemption.

—RAYMOND CHANDLER

*C*ULTURE IN MEXICO IS GOVERNED BY TWO OPPOSING
sides, sharply divided by an open wound: on the one hand, a highbrow,
Europeanized elite dreams of inserting the nation's creative talent into a
global stream of artistic consciousness; on the other, native art, a hybrid
that results from ancient and borrowed elements, is produced by and for
the masses. High-brow: Frida Kahlo; the painters Rufino Tamayo, José
Clemente Orozco, Diego Rivera, and David Alfaro Siqueiros; the globe-
trotting opera singer Plácido Domingo; even the Russian and Spanish
filmmakers Sergei Einsenstein (*¡Que viva México!*) and Luis Buñuel (*Los
olvidados*), who greatly influenced the nation's self-understanding through
powerful cinematic images. Lowbrow: the popular wrestler El Santo; the
ranchera movies of the thirties and forties with Pedro Infante, Jorge Negrete,
Blanca Estela Pavón, and Lupe Vélez; the archfamous children's songwriter
Francisco Gabilondo Soler, aka Cri-Cri; and the romantic balladist Juan
Gabriel. Don't worry if you're unable to recognize the latter references: the
nation's cultural exports are invariably Westernized products, hardly any
proletarian items.

A common belief has it that lowbrow Mexican culture is kitschy.
Nothing is further from the truth. The terms *kitsch* and *camp*, which
Webster's dictionary defines as "artwork characterized by sentimental, often
pretentious bad taste" and "something so outrageously artificial, affected,
inappropriate, or out-of date to be considered amusing," don't even have an

equivalent in Spanish; *cursi*, meaning parodic, self-referential, inbred with intentional exaggeration, or perhaps misrepresentation, of human feelings, is the closest in aesthetic terminology Spanish gets to them. But American icons like *The Lawrence Welk Show*, Barry Manilow, and the Bee Gees are cursi; native art in Mexico, instead, is nothing but rascuache, a south-of-the-border colloquialism ignored by the Iberian standardizer, the *Diccionario de la lengua española de la Real Academia*, yet often used in Mexico to describe a cultural item of inferior quality and proletarian origin.

Rascuache has no English cognate: the pachuco fashion style in Los Angeles, for example, was rascuache; the musician Agustín Lara; the porcelain replicas of smiling clowns and ballerinas known as Lladrós, sold at department stores; imitations of Yves St. Laurent and Ralph Lauren clothing; T-shirts of the music group Menudo; and native sodas such as Chaparritas and flavored Tehuacán. Tamarind and coconut, in spite of their global recognition (or perhaps as a result of it), the *novelistas* Laura Esquivel, responsible for *Like Water for Chocolate*, and Paco Ignacio Taibo II, known for dirty-realist thrillers that have private detective Héctor Belascoarán Shayne as protagonist, are somewhat rascuache as well. While Mexico's highbrow society uses and abuses the term in order to establish a distance, to distinguish itself from cheap, lowborn inventiveness, rascuachismo, with its trademark of authenticity, is also a source of pride and self-respect among the dispossessed. It is applied by the bourgeoisie to *alguien más*—"someone else" judged to be outside the demarcations of approved taste and decorum; to be rascuache is to be inferior, undeserving. But the lower classes assume its aesthetics with a happy smile: a rascuache item is truly, unequivocally Mexican and therefore a magnet of self-satisfaction. Throughout the decades, rascuachismo has acquired something like a logic of taste, a consistent sensibility that can be crammed into the mold of a system. Avant-garde bourgeois art, even when addressing the most vulgar and tasteless, will by definition never descend to such low esteem. But the ruling class always maintains a kind of "negotiating relationship" with it; it uses it to establish a bridge across economic and social lines, to create an image of the nation's collective psyche, and to benefit the tourist industry.

As proven by the case of the early-twentieth-century engraver José Guadalupe Posada, occasionally a proletarian artist can be "saved" from his rascuache background through the help of enlightened, upper-class artists. Posada died poor and forgotten and was buried in an anonymous grave in 1913, as the Socialist revolution was sweeping the country. His lampoons ridiculed Porfirio Díaz's dictatorship (1876–1911) and commemorated holidays and natural disasters. But he would have remained anonymous had Jean Charlot, a French immigrant to Mexico and a friend of muralists Rivera and Orozco, not shown Posada's prints around and written about him in the context of the European style cubism. Charlot brought him to international attention, thus redeeming him from the imprisonment of rascuachismo and turned him into a veritable artifact of highbrow culture. In other cases, nonetheless, a rascuache artist will be used by the intelligentsia to promote a certain "official" vision of the country, only to be dropped when such a vision becomes either unnecessary or obstructive. Popular arts and crafts endure and grow because they fulfill certain functions within nationalism and capitalist reproduction and because they offer a valuable mirror through which to sell an accepted, convenient image of society as a whole. For example, the anthropologist Néstor García Canclini, author of *Transforming Modernity: Popular Culture in Mexico*, has written eloquently on the values of rascuache art, folklore, and aboriginal souvenirs for a certain government regime interested in sponsoring the production of export artifacts among the lower classes for purely touristy purposes. They sell and they offer an image of Mexico as intimately connected with its pre-Columbian roots: a nation with a historic past and a non-Western philosophy of life, a civilization thirty splendorous centuries in the making.

The art critic Tomás Ybarra-Frausto, in a stimulating 1990 essay, explains in more detail this attractive concept, rascuachismo:

Propriety and keeping up appearances—*el qué dirán*—are the codes shattered by the attitude of *rascuachismo*. This outsider viewpoint stems from a funky, irreverent stance that debunks convention and spoofs protocol. To be *rascuache* is to posit a bawdy, spunky consciousness, to seek to subvert and turn ruling paradigms upside down. It is a witty, irreverent, and impertinent posture that recodes and moves outside established boundaries.

While pertaining to Mexican culture in general, Ybarra-Frausto's study is centered on the Chicano community of the Southwest, where, to distinguish itself from its Mexican past, rascuachismo becomes something of an insider's private code. "Very generally," he argues, "rascuachismo is an underdog perspective—a view from *los de abajo*, an attitude rooted in resourcefulness and adaptability, yet mindful of stance and style. . . . It presupposes the worldview of the have-nots, but is also a quality exemplified in objects and places (a rascuache car or restaurant) and in social comportment (a person who is or acts rascuache)." Ybarra-Frausto suggests a random list of rascuache items akin to the Mexican American community: the Royal Chicano Air Force, paintings on velvet, the calaveras of Posada, and the movie by Cheech Marin *Born in East L.A.* He then distinguishes levels of *medio* and *muy*, low and high rascuachismo: Microwave tamales, the comedian Tin Tan, shopping at Kmart, flour tortillas made with vegetable oil, pretending you are Spanish, and portraits of Emiliano Zapata on velvet slippers (*chanclas*) belong to the first category; to the second, frozen *capirotada*, flour tortillas made with lard, being bilingual and speaking with an accent in both languages, shopping at JCPenney, portraits of Pancho Villa on velvet chanclas, and Cantinflas. Which brings me back to kitsch and camp, two terms implying a sense of parody and self-consciousness never found in rascuachismo. A rascuache artifact will not become emblematic of lowbrow Mexicanness until the sophisticated elite, always an alien force, says so—that is, until it is rescued to become a souvenir, a Mexican curiosity in the universal archives of Western civilization.

Of the whole rascuache galaxy in Mexican lowbrow culture, Cantinflas, Ybarra-Frausto's last entry, is of particular interest to me. In spite of his incredibly high profile south of the border, today he is virtually unknown in Europe and the United States, which, I am sure, is directly related to the lack of sympathy with which the Mexican sophisticated elite views him nowadays. Indeed, this most revered Spanish-speaking comedian, admired at first by the middle class and the ruling intelligentsia, aside from the masses, of course, illustrates the never-ending rivalries between high and low culture, between elitist and rascuache perspectives in Mexico and the Hispanic hemisphere at large. His fame and decline show what's hot and cold, in and out, south of the border—and why.

Cantinflas, whose real name was Fortino Mario Alfonso Moreno Reyes, was the *peladito* par excellence—a lumpen, streetwise itinerant citizen, the master of *mal gusto*, bad taste. He's slightly abusive, often disoriented, never totally happy, in total control of *la pelade̹*, with an irreverence that at once highlights and eases the tension between upper and lower classes in Mexico. Cantinflas's rascuachismo is also Mexico's. When he first appeared on stage, in the late thirties, the sophisticated elite championed him as a crystalline expression of the native soil. But by the time he died, at the age of eighty-one, he had become a casualty in the struggle to find an identity that suited the ruling party's desire to be part of the industrialized world. His mannerisms, his simplicity, while still adored by the populace, are today

Figure 7: Arsenio J. Gárate Jauffred, *Cantinflas Chow*. © Arsenio J. Gárate.
Used by permission of the artist. www.cheniofolio.blogspot.com

largely ignored by highbrow Mexican culture. Obviously, a drastic change of heart had taken place in the nation's mood.

A symptom of such a change is the fact that when Cantinflas passed away, on April 20, 1993, he never received an obituary in *Vuelta*, Octavio Paz's literary monthly, probably the best cultural thermometer south of the border by which one can understand the ups and downs of the Latin American literati. The magazine is a sideboard of cosmopolitanism and finesse, a catalog of bourgeois taste, a promoter of Europeanized ways of thought and conduct. Everybody's favorite rascal, Cantinflas, on the other hand, symbolizes the rough-and-tumble slapdash in poor barrios, the treacherousness of the illiterate, the vitality of the dispossessed, the obscenity of working-class people. By the midnineties his appeal had certainly passed, at least for the ruling class. Determined to sell NAFTA, the North American Free Trade Agreement, to Canada and the United States, the Partido Revolucionario Institucional (PRI), led by President Carlos Salinas de Gortari, was interested in selling an altogether different image of Mexico, not as a perfidious and disloyal neighbor, but as honest, stable, trustworthy, a country made by a growing, money-oriented middle class hypnotized by the American Dream.

Cantinflas: an unpleasant face to be hidden. Cantinflas: an arbiter of low taste in the process of eradication. But he was viewed this way only among the wealthy and socially mobile because half a century after the splash he made as the ultimate master of rascuachismo, among the poor and dispossessed he still typifies, as least for the masses, Mexico's true heart and soul. It's the ruling class and the intelligentsia that have changed: first love, then rejection. The transformation is not surprising. Others have suffered a similar fate. Cantinflas's early achievements were rapidly capitalized by a segment of the Europeanized Mexican intelligentsia who saw him as the champion of the forfeited, a magnetic representative of the underdog with a larger-than-life charisma. In 1948, for instance, Tamayo painted his portrait, *Retrato de Cantinflas*, and three years later, Rivera placed him at the center of his mural in Teatro de los Insurgentes, in Mexico's capital. But around 1968, when the regime of President Gustavo Díaz Ordaz ordered a massacre of students in Tlatelolco Square, just as the Olympic Games were about to take place, the country underwent a deep identity crisis. Goodbye to the disoriented peladito. No more disjointed, disheveled heroes. It was obvious that the PRI was starting to implement a less rascuache, more modernized image of Mexico. The nation was ready to abandon the Third World, to cease looking south to Latin America and begin looking north: to emulate Uncle Sam. The transformation would take place over a period of decades, and, in the end, Cantinflas and other similar lowlife symbols would become a mishap.

As a result of this increasingly incurable allergy to rascuachismo and pop art, the intellectual elite has generated almost no bibliography about Cantinflas, neither panoramic nor reflective. The index of Carlos Fuentes's *The Buried Mirror: Reflections on Spain and the New World* makes no mention of his incomparable contribution to Hispanic humor. Here and there, some marginal references to him are made by others. The poet Salvador Novo, for instance, described his intrepid ascendance in *Nueva grandeza mexicana*; the playwright Xavier Villaurrutia praised him in the magazine *Hoy*; and Jorge Ibargüengoitia, the comic novelist responsible for *The Dead Girls*, does refer to him in passing in an essay included in his 1991 collection, *Autopsias rápidas*. Perhaps the only serious, thought-provoking interest in Cantinflas can be found in Carlos Monsiváis, a practitioner of New Journalism *a la mexicana* attracted to the cultural manifestations of the underclass. A text of 1988 states: "The smiles and laughter that Cantinflas's performance still generates among Mexican and Latin American audiences are not incidental. . . . What is being applauded? His incoherence is the incoherence of the masses, the aggression that is ignorance among the ruling class, the memorizing joke that is certified to be repeated, time and again, with success." And Monsiváis adds:

> Cantinflas, programmatic mumbling and conditioned reflex. He shows up, he moves, he begins a verbal twist, he puzzles his listener, he makes fun of the knowledge never captured in linguistic chaos . . . and his audience is bamboozled, is entertained and feels happy, finds inspiration in everyone's joy. . . . Cantinflas is a true Son of the People, the idiosyncratic expression that will become our tradition. This powerful asset allows the comedian-impresario to overcome the numerous mistakes of his films and generate permanent admiration through the gag in which there's much talk but nothing is said. What's humorous in Cantinflas: his image and voice; his comic message; his silhouette. The myth, a function of memory.

The only available biography of Cantinflas is a second-rate, "official" one written in 1994 by Guadalupe Elizalde: *Mario Moreno y Cantinflas . . . rompen el silencio*. Full of innuendos, repetition, unverified information, typos, and spelling mistakes, it encapsulates, in its quality, the comedian's rascuache spirit: it confuses and deceives. It details the tense relationship he had with Mario Arturo Moreno, his illegitimate son, and the scandalous suicide of one of Moreno Reyes's lovers, the United States model Marion Roberts. But the biography does succeed in delivering an image of him as an institution: photographs of Cantinflas alongside every single Mexican president, from Díaz Ordaz to Miguel de la Madrid Hurtado, as well as with Lyndon Johnson and Richard Nixon, invade the volume. It discusses also his liaison with Mexico's actor's union, ANDA, which once accused him of mishandling the organization's money and of abusing his fame during a benefit performance for the Red Cross by embezzling donated funds. But if studies about his life and oeuvre are almost nonexistent, his influence in Hispanic art is far-reaching. His name is invoked every day on TV, the radio, and in the printed media. His movies are shown everywhere from Ciudad Juárez to Buenos Aires. Performance artists summon his ghost. Musicians sing to his legend. Take the case of Luis Valdez, the legendary Chicano playwright and funding director of El Teatro Campesino in California and responsible for *Zoot Suit*, *La Bamba*, and other plays and films. His 1973 epic play *La carpa de los rascuaches* follows a Cantinflas-like protagonist from his crossing of the border into the United States to the subsequent indignities he undergoes. Even if the name Cantinflas is never mentioned, the play is a direct homage, a tribute to this most durable and beloved comedian.

Lewis Jacobs once said of Charlie Chaplin that his importance lay, not in what he contributed to film art, but in what he contributed to humanity. Cantinflas had a less universal, if equally ambiguous, pact: he remains an archetype, a model, a bottomless well of inspiration personifying the plight suffered by a preindustrial Mexico struggling to assert itself in the twentieth century. His adventures allow his audience to understand the transition from a rural to an urban setting that many poor, uneducated campesinos have been forced to make in Latin America to earn only a few pesos. This means that, in spite of his cultural eclipse among the powerful, Cantinflas is an invaluable map to his nation's psyche, a compass pointing to a rascuache aesthetic, an invaluable tool to understand the clash between haves and have-nots in his society and culture. Through him we see, hear, and feel the Mexican self better. Posterity refuses to incorporate Moreno Reyes's villainous aspect; it prefers to remember him in an undiscriminating, uninformed, uncritical way—as the one and only peladito.

∽

Born on August 12, 1911, in Santa María la Redonda, a poor neighborhood in Mexico City, Moreno Reyes was the son of a mailman, the sixth of thirteen children. A born entertainer, he charmed passersby with his dancing and rapid-fire jokes and wordplay. As a teenager, he became, by turns, a bullfighter, a shoe-shine boy, a taxi driver, and a successful boxer before joining up with a *carpa*, an itinerant sideshow that combined circus acrobatics with slapstick comedy from the turn of the century to the advent of mass media in the forties. The carpa was a favorite gathering point for the disenfranchised mired in elemental struggle. A mixture of clowns, acrobats, and stand-up comedians, the *carperos* contributed a unique sense of weltanschauung to lowbrow culture south of the border: they emphasized rapid corporeal movements interlaced with slapstick action, pratfalls, and verbal virtuosity. Tin Tan, Clavillazo, Mantequilla, and Resortes were all acclaimed comedians in the forties and fifties, with large followings. Tin Tan in particular offered a different picture of *lo mexicano*. As John King, the British film and literary critic, argues in his book *Magical Reels*, "His Mexican-American pachuco, the zoot-suited, upwardly mobile con man, could talk and dance his way out of any difficult situation in a mixture of Spanglish idioms and border-music rhythms."

The pachuco image had to be modified to suit the popular taste of the time, but the origins of Tin Tan—the border towns such as Ciudad Juárez, the mass migrations (legal and illegal) across the border, the Americanization of Mexican culture—were all to become an irresistible part of the Mexican experience. In *El rey del barrio* (King of the Neighborhood, 1949), his most memorable film, the verbal patter is exhilarating, as are the spectacular dance situations with Tongolele (Yolanda Montes).

One night, the story goes, Cantinflas had to stand in for a sick master of ceremonies and made the audience laugh without end. The first thing he did was pee in his pants. Afterward, nervous, virtually out of control, he became incoherent, his sentences tangling one another up, ridiculous. Instead of getting him boosted off the stage, his muddled patter was greeted with applause. Accident became routine. But the name Cantinflas only came into being when someone in the audience shouted "¡En la cantina tu inflas!" (You tank up in the cantina! You're drunk!). The words conflated in Moreno Reyes's mind into a name: Cantinflas. It became his nom de guerre and ultimately entered the *Diccionario de la lengua española de la Real Academia* as a verb, *cantinflear*, which means to blather on and on and say nothing; as a noun, *cantinflada*, something done by an adorable clown; and as an adjective, *cantinfleado*, which means dumb. The combination produces the following dog-Latin expression: "Cantinflas cantinflea cantinfladas," or "Cantinflas blathers cantinflanisms." Cantinfladas are heard everywhere in Mexico. The ear grows so accustomed to them, it quickly ceases to pay attention. An example of an eponymous one is the famous joke about one of Mexico's former presidents, Luis Echeverría Álvarez. In a legendary speech detailing the ruling party's political ideology, he is said to have explained: "No somos de la izquierda, ni de la derecha, sino todo lo contrario" (We are neither of the left, nor of the right, but entirely the opposite).

Cantinflas began as a supporting actor in 1937 and then married Valentina Zubareff (she died in 1966), the daughter of the owner of the carpa where he worked. It was she who suggested that Cantinflas appear in advertisements for products made in Mexico. The commercials were a success, so Moreno Reyes decided to found a film company, Posa Films, whose exclusive product would be movies starring Cantinflas. By 1941, the company had a couple of major Latin American hits, and Moreno Reyes was well on his way to becoming a legend. During World War II, he met Miguel M. Delgado, who directed him in one hit film after another, such as the parodies *Romeo y Julieta* (1943) and *Gran Hotel* (1944). During those years, Moreno Reyes shaped the identity of his alter ego. Eventually, his creation would be recognized by visual and spiritual features: a dirty, long-sleeve T-shirt; a rotten tie; baggy, patched pants always covering only half his buttock; a robe used as a belt; old, broken shoes; on his head a hat several sizes too small; a sparse mustache and short, uncombed hair. He is the Spanish Golden Age's *pícaro* reincarnated: a scoundrel, a knave. When Cantinflas walks, he seems to be loose in his posture. When Cantinflas talks, he takes his hat off, switches it from one hand to another, and often hits the furniture or a friend with it to accentuate his anger or discomfort. Social mobility is taboo in Mexican society: once indigent, always underprivileged. Since classes are dogmatically rigid and unchangeable, Cantinflas ridicules the abyss between social groups and allows for relaxation and acceptance. He often goes from oppressed to oppressor, but no explosive conclusion is drawn. His movies lack an ideologically charged message inviting the unhappy to rebel. They open a space in which discomfort and complaints are dealt with through healthy laughter. This explains why the Mexican government endorsed Cantinflas when his image was useful: he makes the agitated masses happy; his subversive spirit works in the abstract, never upsetting the status quo. As Jonathan Kandell, a *New York Times* reporter, argues, Cantinflas "was riotously effective at deflating the rich and pompous, the staid and conventional. . . . [He transformed the] apprehension of the burgeoning urban poor into laughter."

Mexicans constantly use verbal puzzles that demonstrate the cleverness of the speaker and challenge the wit of the audience. They are akin to *adivinanzas* and *rompecabezas*, riddles and brainteasers, often obscene; they utilize as well proverbs, unexpected rhymes, humorous naming, folk poetry, and shrewd puns. Through humor the nation handles collective and individual catastrophes and shortcomings. Only a few days after Pancho Villa was assassinated, in Hidalgo del Parral, in 1923, thousands of riddles and jokes circulated among the population. The same thing happened following the tragic 1985 earthquake in Mexico City. Whenever a group of Mexicans gets together at a friendly gathering, they invariably spend ten, fifteen minutes, perhaps longer, cracking jokes about politicians and television stars, food and habits. Such jokes have a linguistic edge personified by Cantinflas. A scene in the film *Ni sangre ni arena* (Neither Blood nor Sand, 1941) exemplifies his linguistic bravado, his verbal virtuosity, and the often insurmountable difficulty of making him available through translation. Cantinflas is selling cigars—in Spanish, *puros*, a word also meaning "only" and "pure"—outside a bullfighting arena. "¡Puros! ¡Puros!" he says. Confusion takes place, and he ends up selling tacos as well. "¡Puros! ¡Tacos! ¡Tacos! ¡Puros!" More confusion takes place, and Cantinflas is left without cigars, only with tacos. The humorous sequence concludes as he shouts: "¡Puros tacos! ¡Tacos! ¡Tacos puros!" Both rolled tacos and puros have the same shape, except that the former is a symbol of Mexico's lower class, whereas the latter exemplifies the highbrow European aristocracy. By mixing them up, the comedian offers a sample of his worldview: social extremes south of the Rio Grande are based on cultural paraphernalia that, when scrambled, loses its power and invites laughter. Replace a rich white man's cigar with a taco, and you get an average mestizo.

What is remarkable is the fashion in which Cantinflas's rascuachismo brought world literature to Mexico: his films adapted, or subverted, Shakespeare's *Romeo and Juliet*, Cervantes's *Don Quixote*, and Alexandre Dumas's *The Three Musketeers*. As in vaudeville art, a single theme recurs in all of Cantinflas's films (available on VHS from Arkansas Entertainment, without subtitles): the mistaken identity. He is often confused with somebody else: a rich entrepreneur, a hotel bellboy, a corrupt policeman, Don Quixote. Plots circle around comic misunderstanding that allows for linguistic irreverence and pyrotechnics. One enters his universe without aesthetic pretension and invariably leaves it with a sense of fulfillment: we have attended an enlightening rendezvous through the twisted behavioral paths of underprivileged Mexicans. He is the ultimate satirist, making fun of the macho husband, the virginal female, the abusive priest, the naive foreigner; but he also promotes the image of Mexicans as lazy, siesta driven, immoral, and treacherous. Does he somehow perform a disservice to his people by poking fun at Hispanic mannerisms? He brings forth a sense of relaxation that allows for Mexican culture to cope with its tragedies and digest its shortcomings. Therefore, he proves (if proof was ever needed) that humor, while universal, is distinctly local: there is nothing more difficult than translating it from one language to another, from one entourage to the next. Whenever

Cantinflas ignites a hearty laughter, it's usually about something nonnatives would find unappealing, even insensitive. His oral jokes need to be explained, redesigned, and reformulated for foreigners to understand.

From 1939, when his first fifteen-minute-long films, *Siempre listo en las tinieblas* (Always Ready in Darkness) and *Jenjibre contra dinamita* (Ginger against Dynamite), were distributed, to 1981, when *El barrendero* (The Garbage Man), his last movie, was produced, he was the protagonist of a total of forty-seven films. Every single one was a huge box-office success, turning him into a millionaire. His comic talents were appreciated worldwide. Chaplin, for instance, is reported to have said, after watching a Cantinflas movie, "He's the greatest comedian alive . . . far greater than I am!" In Mexico and elsewhere in Hispanic America he was repeatedly the subject of innumerable homages and retrospectives and inspired a celebrated comic strip, many TV cartoons, and a weekly magazine called *Ahí está el detalle*. He was sought by diplomats and artists alike and was the symbol for the 1986 Soccer World Cup. Furthermore, rumors have it that since World War II, nobody else has been the runaway winner in every national presidential election, simply because the electorate knows its vote is ultimately irrelevant in a system plagued by fraud. Thus, Cantinflas becomes a much-beloved *subversivo* through which the population manifests its unhappiness with the undemocratic, repressive spirit it lives under. A magnetic, insurgent figure, Cantinflas is a proud ignoramus and a master in the lack of refinement. Ignorance is his weapon. He hides his illiteracy, stupidity, and lack of knowledge about the importance of science and technology in the modern world by pretending he was a consummate master in just about everything, from quantum mechanics to Shakespeare. In that respect, he symbolizes twentieth-century Mexico's unfulfilled desire to be a contemporary of the rest of humankind.

His authentic talents, visual and verbal, cinematic and linguistic, are also the areas in which his country's art has reached higher distinction: pictorial and literary. While in politics Mexico has always been unimaginative, the artistic legacy, from the Aztecs to Octavio Paz's 1990 Nobel Prize, is unquestionable. When attempting to find an equivalent in the English-speaking world, the obvious choice might appear to be Charlie Chaplin's wistful Little Tramp. Both use pantomime; both poke fun at social types; both are unredeemed romantics, championing love as the true medicine of the human spirit; both refuse to approach film as a malleable, experimental art. But the similarities between the two are only superficial. Chaplin's creation was essentially a hostile character. His was a socially conscious message, inserted in the tradition of Jewish European liberalism, and his left-wing views often placed him at the center of heated controversies. A product of the era of silent cinema, which he refused to let go of even when talkies were already dominating the market, Chaplin achieved the apex of his career from the twenties to the forties, in films such as *The Gold Rush*, *Modern Times*, and *The Great Dictator*. Cantinflas's main strength is in speech—his tongue is his main weapon. He twists and turns it; he talks nonsense ad infinitum to confuse and disorient. As critic Rosa-Linda Fregoso claims in her 1993 study *The Bronze Screen*, he emerged as the unchallenged master of *cábula*, using "the subversive (and pleasurable) play with language . . . [he] satirized a rhetorical tendency of Mexican politicians known as *pura palabréria*, the excessive usage of words that said either 'nothing' or very little." He filled the vacuum of his solitude with verbs and adjectives, if only not to feel aloof and lonely. While Chaplin's switch to talkies was challenging and ultimately unsuccessful, his mute hero, because of his unspecified background, achieved universality. Cantinflas, on the other hand, spent his energy exploring the intricacies of the Mexican collective self. Consequently, his art was overwhelmingly regional and parochial, and only through that particularity he achieved universality. Cantinflas's true Hollywood equivalents might be the Three Stooges, with their humorous vaudevillian sketches that captivated their audiences in the late thirties; or, even better, the Marx Brothers. Their film debut took place in 1929, and as Guadalupe Elizalde claims, in spite of his miserable English, Cantinflas was their loyal fan. Groucho's humor is based on funny looks and a caustic sense of laughter that uses ridiculous statements to philosophize about politics and daily life. W. C. Fields used to call the Marx Brothers "the only act I could not follow," and many Spanish speakers often say the same about Cantinflas. While he uses (and abuses) sighs, shrugs, and grimaces, language is his strength—his aggressive weapon, his defense mechanism, his true forte, the crucial expression of his convoluted self. He conjugates verbs erroneously, invents adjectives and adverbs, and consistently fails to complete his sentences. In short, he reinvents the Spanish language, makes an idiosyncratic hybrid, a Mexican jargon, a rascuache code. Indeed, his verbal pyrotechnic is at its best when Cantinflas talks to the educated: he takes detours, repeats sentences, gets lost, starts all over again. The message is clear: in Mexico, high- and lowbrow cultures live misunderstanding each other; they misrepresent, misquote, deceive, distort, and slant each other. The following transcription, representative of his convoluted style, comes from an interview published in the newspaper *Excelsior* on October 20, 1938:

Vamos por partes: ¿Usted me pregunta que cual ha sido mi mejor interpretación? ¿Y yo le tengo que responder que . . . ? ¿Qué le tengo que responder? ¿O usted me responde? Bueno, pero qué relajo es este? A ver, otra vez: usted quiere que le diga cuál ha sido, es, y será, a través del devenir histórico-materialista-dialectico, la mejor de mis interpretaciones proletarias. Y yo creo que hasta cierto punto, y si no, de todos modos, porque usted sabe que, al cabo y que, y como quiera que, la mejor de todas mis interpretaciones ha sido la interpretación racional y exacta del universo conforme al artículo tercero . . . ¿Qué? ¿Eso no . . . ? Bueno, ¿pues usted de qué habla?

An inevitably raw, insufficient translation. The reader should know that in Spanish, *interpretación* means simultaneously "performance" and "interpretation":

Let's see: You're asking me which has been my best interpretation [i.e., performance]? And I have to answer that . . . ? What do I have to answer? Or is it you who should answer? OK, but what mess is this? Again, let's see: you want me to tell you which has been, is, and will be, throughout historical-materialistic-dialectical, the best of my proletarian interpretations. And I believe that up to a certain point, and if not, in any case, because as you know, notwithstanding, and in spite of all, the best of my interpretations has been the rational and exact interpretation of the Universe, according to article 3 . . . What? It isn't true . . . ? OK, so what are you talking about?

Not long ago, during a one-day tribute at Lincoln Center's Walter Reade Theater, I had *Ahí está el detalle* (That's the Deal, 1940), his most famous movie, shown as part of a retrospective on modern Mexican cinema. The response was intriguing. Whereas the rest of the films, a product of contemporary artists, attracted a cosmopolitan, intellectually sophisticated audience, Cantinflas brought a large number of lower-class Hispanos anxious to recapture a certain sight, a charming laughter of a native culture left behind. It was impossible to get a subtitled copy, which forced us to use simultaneous translation. Richard Peña, the Harvard educated executive director of the New York Film Festival and a native Spanish speaker of Puerto Rican background, took upon himself the impossible task of translating the comedian. Seeing him after the show was saddening: he was empty of all energy, humorless, completely mute. To understand his plight, imagine for a minute doing a simultaneous translation of Woody Allen into Hebrew or German while retaining its New York sense of Jewish comedy.

In the forties the Mexican film industry underwent a tremendous transformation. From small studio productions to blockbusters, movies were delivered at an amazing speed and had successful runs throughout Hispanic America. Jorge Negrete, María Félix, Dolores del Río, and Pedro Infante populated the screen with peasant heroes, ignorant and naive in the ways of the industrial world. As John King puts it: "The success of Mexican cinema in the forties was due to a series of circumstances: the added commercial opportunities offered by the war, the emergence of a number of important directors and cinematographers, and the consolidation of a star system resting on proven formulae." Cantinflas, in spite of his rascuachismo, worked with internationally renowned figures in Mexico: the Russian émigré Arcady Boytler, a pupil of the theater director Konstantin Stanislavsky; the musician Silvestre Revueltas; the filmmaker Chano Urueta; the screenwriters Salvador Novo and Pepe Martínez de la Vega; and the cinematographers Jack Draper, Alex Phillips, and Gabriel Figueroa.

Figueroa is of special importance. His work always leaned toward exteriors or sequences of the countryside. Together with Emilio "El Indio" Fernández, responsible for the movies *Flor silvestre* and *María Candelaria*, he inaugurated a black-and-white aesthetic view of Mexican lowlife, particularly the peasantry. He worked with John Ford and John Huston. His liaison to Cantinflas is another intriguing connection between high- and lowbrow art. Figueroa photographed a total of seven films of his, including *Los tres mosqueteros* (The Three Musketeers, 1942), *Un dia con el diablo* (A Day with the Devil, 1945), and *El bombero atómico* (The Atomic Fireman, 1950). Their work together marks the time in which Cantinflas was not only adored by the masses, but highly respected by the middle class and the intellectual elite. He personified Mexican street wisdom. "In my view," Figueroa wrote in a 1990 autobiographical essay, "Mexican cinema has excelled above all in the dramatic genre, and in the antics of Cantinflas. Mario Moreno's early performances were brilliant, a marvelous portrayal of the Mexican *peladito*." The thirties, when Cantinflas began his acting career, were a period of intense search for the clues to the nation's psyche. In 1934, Samuel Ramos, a philosophy professor at Universidad Nacional Autónoma de México, inspired by Sigmund Freud's and Alfred Adler's theories, published his influential *Profile of Man and Culture in Mexico*, a collection of interrelated essays in which he analyzed the personality of *el pelado*, as well as the urban and the bourgeois Mexican. Ramos believed Mexico was incapacitated for progress, owing to a paralyzing inferiority complex. The best way to examine the nation's soul, he argued, was through el pelado mexicano. He described him as "less than proletarian and in the eyes of intellectual, a primitive. . . . [His] explosions are verbal and his lexicon is nasty and aggressive."

> We shouldn't be deceived by appearances. The pelado is neither a strong person nor a brave man. The physiognomy he exhibits is false. It's a camouflage to deceive him from those that interact with him. One could indeed establish that, the stronger and braver he behaves, the bigger the weakness he is trying to hide. . . . He lives with continual fear of being discovered, doubting himself.

Other thinkers afterward, including Octavio Paz in *The Labyrinth of Solitude* and Roger Bartra in *The Melancholy Cage*, have expanded this argument. Although unmentioned, the early Cantinflas is always in these writers' (and their readers') minds: a rogue, a cunning devil, an awkward citizen, a parasite. He incarnates the chaos of modern Mexican life. Can he put aside his complexes to work toward progress? Not quite: his convoluted self will always make him walk on the edge of an abyss, neither falling down nor moving away to safety. Cantinflas's Mexico: a mirror of confusion.

By the next decade, the Mexican film industry had pretty much exhausted its talents, but it was precisely in 1950 when a Spanish émigré, Luis Buñuel, produced a most astonishing film, one that would reevaluate the whole era: *Los olvidados*, a study of orphans in Mexico City pushed to a low life in crime. Buñuel was already in his late forties; the film established him, a Surrealist enfant terrible, as an international figure. Astonishing in numerous ways, it retains an intriguing link with Cantinflas, its cast of astute rascals openly emulating him, which, in the end, results in a masterful metamorphosis of rascuachismo into highbrow culture and in one more cultural theft by the haves of the have-nots. *Los olvidados* is Cantinflas for the politically sensitive, which helps explain why Cantinflas's vicissitudes beyond continental borders, particularly in the United States and Europe, are almost nonexistent. In 1956, already a monumental hero south of the Rio Grande, he was cast as Passepartout, opposite David Niven, Buster Keaton, Frank Sinatra, and Marlene Dietrich, in *Around the World in Eighty Days* (directed by Michael Anderson). But the multistellar Hollywood movie was a total disaster. Soon after, George Sidney directed him in *Pepe* (1960). The cast included Shirley Jones, Edward G. Robinson, Zsa Zsa Gabor, Janet Leigh, Jack Lemmon, and Kim Novak. But again, the success was limited. Although Cantinflas made the cover of *Life en español*, in Mexico and elsewhere in the southern hemisphere he was sharply criticized. His performances, people argued, were a death stroke to his comic capabilities. Vulgarity was his nature, why escape it? I must agree: what's remarkable about him is found in the humorous situation in the legendary *Ahí está el detalle*, where he acts as his own lawyer against a prosecutor ready to put him behind bars for a crime he didn't commit.

In his mature years, he was famous for his wealth. He had witnessed the modernization of his own country and had played a crucial role as therapeutic instrument and as millionaire. At the time of his death his personal fortune was estimated at $25 million. He loved luxury, owning five mansions, the one in Mexico City containing an art gallery, a swimming pool, a jai alai *frontón*, a theater, a barbershop, and a beauty parlor. His private jet flew him to his thousand-acre ranch, La Purisima, where he practiced his favorite hobby, bullfighting. He was a philanthropist and each year distributed $175,000 to the homeless waiting outside his door on his birthday. He built apartment houses in the Granjas neighborhood in his nation's capital and sold them to the poor for a fraction of their worth. His high-ranking contacts in the ruling party, and he himself, often went out of their way to assure his audience that Moreno Reyes's fortune had nothing to do with drug trafficking and corruption. In *Cantinflas: Aguila o sol*, a commemorative illustrated volume published by the government's Consejo Nacional para la Cultura y las Artes in 1993, shortly after his death, critic Carlos Bonfil time and again portrays him as an honest, self-made man, a humble, dignified Mexican—an image the state, for obvious reasons, is obsessed with safeguarding. In old age, however, Moreno Reyes was known to have close links to members of Mexico's drug cartel and to corrupt union leaders. Several million Mexicans attended his funeral ("¡El rey ha muerto!"). As time went by, Cantinflas, his creation and theirs as well, had become an immobile feature in the Mexican landscape. Like Superman and Little Orphan Annie, he never aged: his features were exactly the same from the forties to the eighties. (Moreno Reyes did gain considerable weight, but his movies never addressed this transformation.) It became obvious, at least to the ruling class, that Cantinflas could not continue as the idol of the Mexican poor simply because he had switched classes, becoming immensely rich. Rich and obese. Indeed, the whole country had grown in size: from 1938 to the early 1980s, Mexico underwent drastic changes—a massive overpopulation, growing political corruption, social injustice, the institutionalization of authority, and a student massacre. In his movies Moreno Reyes hardly acknowledged this metamorphosis. His Mexico was ahistorical, immutable. His protagonist was static, uninvolved, apolitical. Occasionally he does ridicule an adolescent for wearing long hair or a union leader is brought to justice for incompetence, but nothing more serious or dangerous. The total government support he enjoyed early in his career translated into his own complacent silence: laughter without criticism, suffering sublimated into comedy.

By the early sixties his aesthetic contribution—his championing of rascuachismo—had been accomplished, and what followed was mere repetition: Cantinflas imitating himself in movie after movie. The status quo grew accustomed to him. His verbal usage, his civil subversion, his tasteless self, his cheap attitude were antielitist, antiprogress, perhaps even anti-Mexican, but never against the establishment: comedy without meanness, mass appeal without aggression. Unlike Chaplin, he never exhibited any form of leftism. In fact, his canonization probably was a result of his apolitical stand: ridicule, but not aggression. So when Mexico needed to revamp its collective identity, when it looked northbound to sell another image of itself to the world, Cantinflas's rascuachismo was put aside: it became useless—an obstacle. Technology and education, not apathy and confusion, were now on the nation's agenda; consumerism and political stability were the accepted values, not improvisation and anarchy.

His life cycle is better understood as one realizes that when Mario Moreno Reyes entered the national scene, during the hypernationalistic period of President Lázaro Cárdenas, from 1934 to 1940, the government was preoccupied with selling an image of a peasant country in search of its pre-Columbian roots. Cardenas expropriated foreign-held properties and oil companies, distributed land to campesinos, and instituted social reform to benefit Indians and Mexican workers. Cantinflas at the time was an irreplaceable expression of lo mexicano. But as the nation south of the Rio Grande moves into the twenty-first century looking northward instead of southward in search of economic, social, and political stability, another image of the country's collective spirit has emerged: enchanted with modern technology, in an eternal shopping spree, enchanted with its media image, and dressed up like the rest of Western civilization. While Cárdenas, before he was elected Mexico's president, was a general in the revolution of Pancho Villa and Emiliano Zapata, a leader in touch with the masses, contemporary presidents and their cabinet members, particularly under Carlos Salinas de Gortari's and current President Ernesto Zedillo Ponce de León's regimes, are Ivy League–educated, English-speaking dealmakers. Cárdenas has ceased to be a role model; the new inspirations are magnates and neo-conservatives north of the Rio Grande, known for fortune and stability, not populist visions. And thus, Cantinflas's art, if not always remarkable in film-making terms, but at least always authentic, has lost the favor of the sophisticated elite, which I guess only serves to highlight the utilitarianism of the highbrow Mexican culture.

But culture is a composite, a united effort, a mosaic—the production and reproduction of symbols and motifs by upper and lower levels of society. If anything, the aesthetics of rascuachismo highlight the enmity, the tension between rich and poor in Mexico, between Europeanized and native viewpoints. Cantinflas might be too harsh, too confronting, too conflicted an image for the bourgeoisie to accept: unwillingly, he denounces his own and everyone else's laziness, his intellectual confusion, his immature strategies to deal with modernity. Overall, he promotes a negative stereotype of el mexicano and might nurture fear and uncertainty toward Mexico among foreigners and "potential investors" who somehow manage to understand his verbal agitation. It's a matter of fashion, of course: to reject him, to deny his importance is to ignore the tattered, shattered, broken world of proletarian Mexico, perpetually ruptured, yet constantly stitched together and proud of itself. To discard Cantinflas, to portray him as a ruffian or parasite is to neglect one of the two halves of the Mexican self.

[1995]

MARIO VARGAS LLOSA

Civilization versus Barbarism

$\mathcal{T}$HE DECISION TO AWARD THE 2010 NOBEL PRIZE IN
Literature to Mario Vargas Llosa is a triumph of reason over the forces of
chaos in Latin America. At a time when the region has moved from dictatorship to fragile civilian government marred by corruption, illiteracy, violence (particularly against women), and an abysmal gap between the haves
and have-nots, the author of classics like *The Green House, Conversation in
the Cathedral*, and *Aunt Julia and the Scriptwriter* is an invaluable defender
of freedom and democracy. In not just his fiction but also in his newspaper
column, he holds them out as the only viable path for the future.

The choice, while long overdue, is surprising. In recent years the Nobel
committee has at times used recipients—some obscure, even dusty—
as mere puppets to expound its left-leaning politics. At age seventy-four,
Vargas Llosa isn't only center right, he is also a favorite target of radical
demagogues in Latin America, especially in Cuba and Venezuela. He has
repeatedly challenged the government policies of those countries, as well as
all who believe the army is the best response to popular unrest. And in his
native Peru, segments of the population detest him. The reasons are manifold, including Vargas Llosa's aristocratic persona and, more prominent,
the outcome of his failed presidential campaign in 1990, when, after he and
his neoliberal, Thatcherite platform were defeated by the then-unknown
Alberto Fujimori, he left the country for Spain, where he was immediately
granted citizenship. While he keeps a home in Peru, he lives mostly abroad.
The noun *traidor*—traitor—often follows his name.

That is not necessarily unwelcome to Vargas Llosa, who thrives on
polemic. Controversy, he has held, is good for reflection, even if it means

that the writer needs to be in the eye of the storm. Indeed, he has been a participant in some of the most significant political and aesthetic debates defining Latin America in the second half of the twentieth century. A member of the generation of writers of El Boom, he has challenged Hispanic literary conventions. As important, he is a distinguished representative of the intellectual tradition that sees literature, not as entertainment, but as an instrument of change.

Change isn't always physical. It starts in the mind. What Vargas Llosa has contributed to Hispanic civilization is in his capacity to think things through. He has raised questions, for example, about the conflicting motives of so-called progressives who argued against prosecuting former dictators like Augusto Pinochet. What opponents of prosecution feared was that bringing such tyrants to justice would "open the door for other dictators—whatever their politics—to be investigated and punished for their crimes," he wrote a few years ago. He also analyzed the case of Vladimiro Montesinos Torres, Fujimori's right-hand man, whose own corruption, when revealed, helped bring down his mentor by showing the Peruvian people the extent of Fujimori's political excesses. In Vargas Llosa's reflections, Montesinos's actions, outrageous as they were, offered a precious opportunity for Peruvian democracy "to cleanse and reform" itself.

Further, the author has made Latin America less provincial, more cosmopolitan, emphasizing its bridges with the rest of the world. He has reflected, for instance, on the importance of literary classics like *Heart of Darkness* and *Tropic of Cancer* and has meditated publicly on the British philosopher Isaiah Berlin's concept of "negative liberty," the absence of restraints on the individual, and what it means for encouraging literature—and a critical spirit—in a region where reading novels has been an elitist endeavor.

If, in those endeavors, and in his caution against fanaticism, the author has courted anger, it has only been as an antidote to brutishness. In other words, Vargas Llosa, even when detested, has consistently forced Latin America to think about how to live in pluralist societies.

His is a restless mind, given voice, as one member of the Nobel committee graciously said, by a "divinely gifted storyteller." Vargas Llosa's oeuvre covers enormous territory, from his first novel, *The Time of the Hero*, about the military academy in Lima where he was sent by his tyrannical father in order to become a true man, to a religious rebellion in rural nineteenth-century Brazil in the epic *The War of the End of the World*, to Trujillo's totalitarian state in the Dominican Republic in *The Feast of the Goat*. He has delved into the erotic novel (*In Praise of the Stepmother*), into detective fiction (*Who Killed Palomino Molero?*), and even into "minority" literature to explore Jewish relations with indigenous peoples (*The Storyteller*). He has written lucid monographs about such diverse writers as Gustav Flaubert and Juan Carlos Onetti and has studied "conflict zones" like the Middle East, where he has taken the Israeli government to task for excesses in Gaza.

Even his most fervent detractors, and there are scores of them, admire his Renaissance curiosity and his forceful voice. That voice, to legions of readers in the 400-million-plus population of the Spanish-speaking world, offers a cornucopia of possibilities. One is in awe of the magic of his language. Vargas Llosa's ear for various registers and tonalities allows him to reproduce the parlance of vastly different segments of society, be they middle-class *Limeños* or exiled Bolivians. The countless pages he has produced in more than fifty years of writing have made the language of Cervantes more elastic.

This time around, the Nobel award is well deserved. It goes to an *hombre de letras* adored and detested in almost equal measure, and that duality is a statement of where Latin America finds itself today. In fact, the entire continent—torn at its core between light and darkness—is being celebrated. And maybe the prize is proof that the Stockholm committee, ready to endorse a literary giant who is also a conservative, is growing up as well.

[2010]

THE ART OF THE
EPHEMERAL

Our fine arts were developed, their types and uses were established,
in times very different from the present, by men whose power of
action upon things was insignificant in comparison with ours. But
the amazing growth of our techniques, the adaptability and precision
they have attained, the ideas and habits they are creating, make it a
certainty that profound changes are impending in the ancient craft
of the Beautiful. In all the arts there is a physical component which
can no longer be considered or treated as it used to be, which cannot remain unaffected by our modern knowledge and power. . . . We
must expect great innovations to transform the entire technique of
the arts, thereby affecting artistic invention itself and perhaps even
bringing about an amazing change in our very notion of arts.

—PAUL VALÉRY, *La conquête de l'ubiquité*

$\mathscr{E}$ARLY ON IN A VISIT I MADE TO EL SALVADOR SHORTLY
after the civil war of 1980–1992, a reporter told me, rather dismayed, that
the majority of the people in the country got their news, not from traditional media outlets—TV, radio, newspapers—but from spontaneous
messages posted in outdoor spaces. "Such channels," he added, "lead to
anarchy." As I traveled around the capital and some rural areas, the sheer
number of examples overwhelmed me. Brushed on buses, brick walls, and
garage doors, on visible surfaces of public squares and parks, these messages
inveighed against the old corrupt dealings of Roberto d'Aubuisson and
his conservative party, the National Republican Alliance (ARENA), and
the extremism of the left-wing Frente Farabundo Martí para la Liberación

Nacional (FMLN). I was also exposed to accusations of incompetence against President Alfredo Cristiani and the San Salvador mayor, Armando Calderón Sol. There were further references to the martyrdom of Bishop Óscar Arnulfo Romero and to the massacre in El Mozote, as well as eulogies to the Jesuits who had been murdered in 1989. On a market fence I even came across a line by poet Roque Dalton, author of *Small Hours of the Night*: "Poetry like bread," it stated.

The messages were succinct, targeted, their syntax ranging from the inconsistent to the egregious. They posed an aesthetic challenge to an environment seeking order. And they were anonymous. This last quality intrigued me. The authors didn't seek recognition. The messages were expressions of discontent voiced by a disenfranchised segment of the nation's population. In a region where the foundations of democracy have been shallow at best, these postings served as a thermometer by which one could read the political temperature of the land. Moreover, a number of questions needed to be asked: Who was responsible for the messages—age, class, gender? When and how were they conceived? Where did the paint and brushes come from (i.e., who provided the tools)? And how did the authorities react? The answers invariably split along political and ideological lines: disaffected FMLN members, said some; foreigners seeking to destabilize the peace process in El Salvador, claimed others. The postings materialized in the dead of night and, for the most part, were erased as mysteriously a few days later by what I was told was a *comando de limpieza urbana*, a cleaning battalion hired by the municipality. Some appeared in particularly troublesome areas and hence lasted longer, sometimes a week, or perhaps an entire month.

Not every posting had a partisan bias. I came across numerous advertisements for music, sports, and U.S. movies (obscenely, one of Sylvester Stallone's *Rambo* films was playing). But there were other kinds of messages, too. Victimized as the nation had been through years of armed struggle, people still found the spirit and strength to impulsively express their emotions—love, primarily. Signs like "María y Pedro se aman" (Maria and Pedro love each other), circumscribed in a big heart crossed from left to right by an inclined arrow, were ubiquitous. Some were risqué: "Petronila, quiero ser el padre de tus hijos" (Petronila, I want to be the father of your children). Others were ingenuous: "Deja las llaves bajo el tapete" (Leave the keys under the carpet). Still others were frankly sexual: "¿Cuando meta mi espada en tu vaina?" (When am I putting my sword inside your scabbard?) There were also numerous messages that had been posted by organized gangs. These were surely forms of graffiti: the hieroglyphics marked a particular turf as belonging to one band and not to another. As it turns out, the graffiti in El Salvador was linked even then to immigrant gangs in Los Angeles, where numerous Salvadoran refugees had fled.

"People don't think the newspaper classified section does the trick," the reporter added. "One would imagine that, given the dangerous atmosphere, they would steer away from acts of defiance. But the dialectic between expression and repression is attractive. At a time when pluralism is at its shakiest, there is magnetism in the tension between expression and repression. Why not use an answering machine? No, the entire country is a switchboard."

El Salvador as a whole seemed to have become a larger-than-life canvas, filled with miscellaneous texts. To the question "Who is in charge?" the answer was clear: no one. This type of lawlessness wasn't alien to me. I came of age in the Mexico of the 1970s. My family lived in the southern part of the capital, adjacent to the Universidad Nacional Autónoma de Meéxico (UNAM), the country's largest publicly funded university. The student population in the area ensured a constant flux of unprompted information via flyers, street messages, and the like. "¡Muerte al PRI!" (Death to the PRI!) read a perennial notice. In others the animosity was directed toward the present: "Libertad a los presos políticos del '68. ¡Muerte al Rector Salmeron!" (Freedom to the 1968 political prisoners. Death to Chancellor Salmeron!). I had always understood these pronouncements as a symptom on the road toward equality, a decidedly unfinished process in Latin America. As its countries struggled to find a balance between the model of industrialized society, imported from without, and the aboriginal past, roadblocks loomed: Is our path to be the same as that taken by Europe? Is capitalism the system to emulate? How to cure the schism left behind by colonialism? With a population of some 5.5 million, El Salvador appeared to me to be a miniature replica of Mexico, which was twenty times more populous. Yet the difference was more than one of scale; I wasn't prepared for the sheer number of messages. Is this what war does? I asked myself.

As fate would have it, my attention in El Salvador was drawn to a feature of the urban landscape I had become intrigued by: posters. Late one afternoon I was invited, through an acquaintance (a FMLN member), to the hacienda of a wealthy entrepreneur, whose career in the diplomatic service had come to an abrupt end at the beginning of the war. Over the last few years he had spent considerable time, energy, and money assembling an archive of approximately sixty to seventy posters, maybe more, reflecting

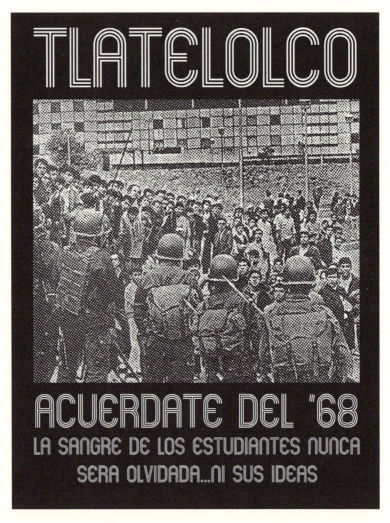

Figure 8: Jesus Barraza, *Tlatelolco: Acuérdate del '68.* © Jesus Barraza. Used by permission of the artist. www.dignidadrebelde.com

various national backgrounds and ideological persuasions. An inveterate connoisseur, he turned on a pair of spotlights and, with pride and affection, carefully displayed his collection on an outsized dining-room table.

What my eyes took in left a lasting impression. I saw images by the legendary Alfredo Rostgaard and Rafael Patiño; anonymous placards from Peru (among them one about Abimael Guzmán and the Shining Path); tributes from Chile to Salvador Allende and Pablo Neruda; and a placard for the

Cuban film *Lucia* by Humberto Solás. There were images addressing agriculture, imperialism, and education; depictions of Omar Torrijos, Augusto César Sandino, Nelson Mandela, Evita Perón, Mao Zedong, Fidel Castro, and, especially, Ernesto "Che" Guevara.

My gaze fell upon a poster of Jesus Christ, portrayed as a guerrilla fighter, juxtaposed against one vilifying Richard Nixon. Others featured profiles of Jose Martí, Ernest Hemingway, Pablo Neruda, and Marilyn Monroe, and there were placards manufactured by the Cuban agencies Instituto Cubano de Arte e Industria Cinematográficos (ICAIC) and Organización de Solidaridad con los Pueblos de Asia, Africa y América Latina (OSPAAAL), including one by Gladys Acosta (female artists are a rarity, not only in Cuba but in Latin America generally), as well as posters from Peru, Panama, Guatemala, Puerto Rico, and, naturally, El Salvador. One of the images made reference to the CIA; another showed an adolescent girl carrying a rifle. The posters were filled with flags. Flags and weapons. Weapons of all sorts: knives, machetes, pistols, M16s, machine guns, hand grenades, and so on. Unlike the impromptu messages on the street, however, the posters were aesthetically compelling and methodically executed. I was entranced by their bright, mottled colors. Their purpose was simple, unambiguous: to enlist people in a cause, to focus the viewer's attention on a particular issue. Although they often depicted the United States as an imperial aggressor, it was nonetheless apparent how significantly they drew on the imagery and style of U.S. pop culture. As I recollect them now, the posters seem to validate the notion of "retro art": they belong to the ages of *Dr. Strangelove* and of disco.

"Politics is always messy," I remember my host saying. "But the art that comes out of it is pure!"

I had never before paid attention to posters. Now, they caused me to think of writings by Paul Valéry (*La conquête de l'ubiquité*) and by Susan Sontag (on pornography) that I had recently been reading. Art in the age of mass culture poses unique challenges to interpretation. Artistic expression has changed dramatically in the last hundred years, as a result not only of the emergence of new techniques but also because new channels of communication became available (photography, TV, comic strips, the Internet). These channels mix drawings, mechanical reproductions (cameras, engravings, photocopies), and text in ways previously unexplored. Consequently, our understanding of Beauty, with a capital "B," has been transformed. It is no longer the exclusive domain of the educated elite, and human expression may now be seen in a different light. The highbrow and the popular have gradually intermingled. Is a hologram of an ET or the face of Elvis Presley on a teacup an artistic form?

The entrepreneur who first introduced me to poster art had, with his statement, generated a difficult question: Is popular art pure? For centuries art was perceived as a cleansing agent for the spirit. Artists were seen to possess superhuman qualities: they were able to appreciate life in a clearer, less adulterated fashion than the rest of humanity. But once art is democratized, once it is designed for substantial numbers of people, does it still retain its purifying qualities?

These thoughts ran through my mind that day in El Salvador as I admired the impressive array of posters. At one point, after looking at several images inspired by a portrait of Emiliano Zapata, my host walked toward an armoire. Behind a glass door stood numerous bottles of wine with a variety of shapes. "I have a tequila collection too—one of the contributions to taste by your country, my friend," he said. "For several years I lived in the neighborhood of Polanco, near extraordinary restaurants." Obviously, he was more than an art connoisseur; he was also a dilettante. After tasting several brands and settling on an *añejo*, he and I wandered into the garden, where he posed a question: "In the promotion of tequilas, companies like Sauza and Cuervo declare their product to be *auténtico* . . . But what about authenticity in popular art?"

Although I've forgotten my answer to his question, I clearly remember that it made me burrow more deeply into the issue. Popular art is often manufactured for great numbers of people. Unlike elite art, it has an impersonal quality to it: popular artifacts aren't unique; often they aren't even signed by the artist. In appreciating a replica of Flemish painter Hieronymus Bosch's *The Garden of Earthly Delights*, is the viewer able to have the full aesthetic experience? With this example, however, at least there is the knowledge that Bosch's original, done in 1500, is available. But what of a work of art produced for the masses? Is there authenticity without an original?

Since my trip to El Salvador, I've become fascinated by poster art in Latin America. The word *poster* is of fairly recent use. *Placard* used to be the term in vogue, which the *Oxford English Dictionary* defines as "a notice, or other document, written or printed on one side of a single sheet, to be posted up or otherwise publicly displayed." It offers a long list of spellings, among them *placquart, plakart, plagart, playcart*, and *plagard*, and includes two synonyms: *bill* and *announcement*. Etymologically, *poster* probably reflects the fact that placards were originally placed on sidewalk posts. A more utilitarian definition of the artifact embraces its function and content: posters are items used to disseminate information, as well as to advertise and sell. There are individually made posters, whose creation is left to the artist's inspiration, and their mass-produced counterparts, which vary in size and treatment, depending on their purpose. In Latin America, posters (also known as *afiches*, from the French *affiche*) are a byproduct of modernity, that is, the conquest and colonization by Europeans. While the use of hieroglyphics and color graphics by elements of the pre-Columbian population, working in *amate* and other types of paper, reveal an aboriginal culture immersed in forms of written communication often displayed in public spaces, studies of the Maya, Mexica, Toltec, Olmec, and other aboriginal peoples do not suggest any concerted effort to bridge the gap between the individual and society, as occurred in Europe through the design and use of placards.

The European origins of the tradition are traceable to the Roman praetors, charged with using wooden slabs painted in white to publicize legal matters. During the Middle Ages, the Holy Office of the Inquisition used placards as public invitations to an auto-da-fé. Subsequently, with the invention of the printing press, knowledge ceased to be the exclusive property of a small elite. The masses now acquired a measure of power and, as a result, a number of public services began to be implemented: roads, sewers, a police force, and an incipient transportation system. Freedom of enterprise became a commodity, bringing a constant need for public announcements. The open exchange of information posed risks for the established order, so much so that a royal edict was issued in France in 1653 prohibiting the production of placards unless manufacturers were granted Crown approval. Yet such edicts could not stem the tide; by the late eighteenth century, as a revolutionary spirit swept Paris, streets were covered with political boiler sheets exhorting people to action: "Liberté! Egalité! Fraternité!" Posters, however, were used for more than ideological persuasion. Increasingly in the nineteenth century, lithographs done by artists like Jules Cheret, Alphonse Mucha, Paul Berthon, and Henri de Toulouse-Lautrec and advertising plays, concerts, and dance hall performances became de rigueur. Art and commerce had forged a partnership.

The repeated use of the word *public* in the preceding paragraph was not accidental: afiches make the individual a part of the collective and vice versa. In fact, we are able to use them as a kaleidoscope through which to appreciate the entire history of modernity. In this respect, consider the following examples: the Japanese art of Utagawa Kunimasa, the building of the underground trains in London and New York and their public advertisements, the production of Soviet propaganda, and the work of twentieth-century masters like Pablo Picasso, Oskar Kokoschka, Joan Miró, and Salvador Dalí. Consider also the Nazi Olympics, the Allied machinery during World War II, mass media in the fifties, Elvis Presley and the Beatles, the student uprisings in Prague, Berkeley, and Mexico in 1968, the protests of the Vietnam years, and the postings of 9/11. Consider Hollywood from the silent era of Charlie Chaplin to Alfred Hitchcock and *Star Wars*, and consider, finally, the countless siblings of poster art: magazines, stamps, calendars, long-playing records (LPs), children's books, museum shops, and sports paraphernalia. Politics, business, entertainment, and sports all march hand in hand.

As a result of my Salvadoran sojourn, my interest gravitated toward poster art within the Hispanic world and, specifically, that segment of Latin American poster art that is defined by its political message. Unfortunately, no thoroughgoing critical history of the genre has been written, so a number of important issues remain unaddressed: What are the most significant moments in the tradition? Should one talk of distinct national subtraditions or of a single continentwide tradition? Who are its most significant artists? What are the representative artistic movements? Is style defined by national background? Is anonymity a recurrent practice? What is the rationale? Are anonymous artists unknown to the public but not to their peers? Are signed placards more valuable than unsigned ones? What kind of influence did European posters exert or those of the Soviet school? What about the influence of placards from the Spanish Civil War, in particular those of the International Brigades and the Council for the Defense of Madrid? Who pays for manufacturing posters? Who consumes them? Where are they posted and by whom? On average, how many copies of an individual poster are created? Have there ever been training schools? What kinds of collecting efforts have taken place? Is the Cuban Revolution the main source of creativity? Although not all of these questions may have definitive answers, they help open a wide field of discussion worth exploring.

Afiches first registered their influence south of the Rio Grande during the age of independence (1810–ca. 1830). Padre Miguel Hidalgo y Costilla, a leader of the 1810 uprising in Mexico that sought to break ties with Spain, used the image of the Virgin of Guadalupe to great effect in public meetings. Anti-Rosas placards, according to Domingo Faustino Sarmiento's *Facundo: Civilization and Barbarism*, were displayed on streets in Argentina. In José Joaquín Fernández de Lizardi's *The Itching Parrot*, which is considered the first modern novel produced in Spanish America, the protagonist, with a growing sense of frustration, comes across chapbooks, advertisements, and educational material meant for the masses. And to judge by the oeuvre of Rubén Darío, known as the father of *modernismo*, placards served as a major graphic device through which symbolism, Parnassianism, and other French literary and cultural fashions were imported to the Spanish-speaking Americas at the end of the nineteenth century. In this regard, it is important to note that modernism and modernismo are not the same thing. Modernism was a European-based movement, which sought to forge connections with primitive, subconscious forms of expression in a way that was consonant with the scientific and technological changes of the day. Modernismo, on the other hand, represented an attempt in Latin America (and to a lesser degree in Spain) to find a legitimate, authentic regional artistic voice. Several prominent modernist painters, among them Joaquín Torres-Garda, Tarsila do Amaral, and Xul Solar, as well as successors like Wifredo Lam and Roberto Matta, experimented with posters in order to bridge the gap between fine and popular art. This experimentation also took place in the literary world. Writers such as Jorge Luis Borges, Pablo Neruda, and César Vallejo wanted to make their poetry available in public spaces, and they often used posters to do so. For example, in the early 1920s, Borges, along with Eduardo González Lanuza, Norah Lange, and Francisco Piñero, belonged to a futurist movement called *ultraísmo*. As a means of declaring its purpose, the movement launched a short-lived magazine (only two issues) entitled *Prism*. Designed as a "mural journal," the magazine was not distributed through newsstands but, instead, was posted on walls across the length and breadth of Buenos Aires. Borges once described how he and his associates would wander the city, glue and brushes in hand, in order to disseminate the ultraist principles and program.

It was also in this general period—the latter years of the nineteenth century and the first decade of the twentieth—that the work of Mexican engraver José Guadalupe Posada left its mark. A craftsman of very limited means, yet a foundational figure in Latin American poster art, Posada was a lampooner, with a workshop in downtown Mexico City, who specialized in the visual representation of freaks, miracles, and disasters. He also enjoyed ridiculing politicos, revolutionaries, and the incipient Mexican bourgeoisie. He popularized the calavera as a satirical symbol, making the skeleton into a national archetype. What would the tradition of the Día de los Muertos be, it is fair to ask, without Posada?

Another significant early moment in the history of poster art in Latin America is the Mexican Revolution. Or more properly, its aftermath, for the most memorable images of the revolution do not reside in placards.

On the contrary, only a handful of black-and-white afiches survives from the 1910–1917 period in Mexico. It is not that the posters have been lost or have disintegrated but, rather, that the tradition was simply not part of the armed struggle. That little energy seems to have been invested in the production of revolutionary posters is explained by several factors. Skirmishes took place primarily in the countryside. The soldiers were illiterate peasants, and mass culture had yet to become a feature of Mexican society. Thus, the best visual record of events surrounding the revolution is to be found in photographs. In this connection, the photojournalism of Agustín Víctor Casasola, a freelancer and personal portraitist of General Porfirio Díaz, who took his camera—despite its size and weight—everywhere he could, is preeminent. Casasola's images, which attest to the loyalties of different segments of society, aren't meant to persuade people to action, in the manner of posters. They are simply a visual narrative of the upheaval. It was the *tres muralistas*, Diego Rivera, José Clemente Orozco, and David Alfaro Siqueiros, who from the 1920s onward turned the unkept promises of the revolution into an engine of art. Sponsored by the government and the private sector, they painted, in both Mexico and the United States, ideologically motivated epic murals designed to instruct and to agitate. While the muralistas did occasional placards, they did not perceive themselves to be primarily poster makers. Still, their importance to the tradition is unquestionable, and their use of open spaces in order to reflect on history and politics became a hemispheric benchmark.

It is vital to keep in mind that, at a time when the reach of television was still limited, afiches were used as consensus builders in governmental campaigns. The rise of Juan Domingo Perón in Argentina and of Lázaro Cardenas in Mexico shaped a singular aesthetic during the 1930s and 1940s. Peronism serves as a striking paradigm, one later replicated in Chile during the Augusto Pinochet years. Although Evita's charisma may have emanated from her radio appearances, her voice would have been depersonalized had those broadcasts not been accompanied by visual images, including posters. Populist military regimes, such as that embodied in Peronism, used posters in the same way that Hitler employed them in Germany and Stalin in Russia, namely, to enshrine and advance government strategies. Parenthetically, it is worth noting that the Catholic Church in Latin America appears generally to have kept away from producing posters, although two interesting examples to the contrary are the Cristero uprising in Mexico during the late 1920s (about which Graham Greene wrote in *The Power and the Glory*), when posters were freely used by religious advocates, and in 1970s Central

America, when Liberation Theology priests also engaged in channeling popular disenchantment through graphic art.

Unquestionably, the most sustained effort to create a school of poster art in Latin America occurred in Cuba after the triumph of the revolution in 1959. With the establishment of a Communist regime, aligned with the USSR from the early sixties to the breakup of the Soviet Union in 1989, placards became the instruments of organized propaganda. The images that emerged from the Caribbean island dealt with sugar, literacy, and rural education; resistance against U.S. imperialism coupled with expressions of solidarity toward other Third World revolutionary movements; sports (mostly baseball); and equality for women and blacks. A number of institutions, notably Comité Central del Partido Comunista Cubano (CCPCC), Comisión de Orientación Revolucionaria (COR), Instituto Cubano de Arte e Industria Cinematográficos (ICAIC), Organización Continental Latinoamericana y Caribeña de Estudiantes (OCLAE), Organización de Solidaridad con los Pueblos de Asia, Africa, y America Latina (OSPAAAL), and Unión de Periodistas de Cuba (UPEC), included staff devoted to poster making. The result was an immense archive of images that span several decades. Within that period, a number of themes repeat themselves, reflecting events with international impact (the Bay of Pigs in 1961 and the fall of the Berlin Wall in 1989, for instance), as well as matters internal to the country. The great majority of these posters are characterized by the use of hand-cut silkscreen stencils, mixed-media techniques (full-color photographs are seldom used), and photo-offset methods of reproduction. On average, between two hundred and fifteen hundred copies of a single poster were printed.

Cuban artists achieved a degree of individuality not witnessed before. The most celebrated names include Valencia-born Eduardo Muñoz Bachs, whose best work as a poster artist was done for the ICAIC but who also achieved fame as a children's book illustrator; Luis Martínez-Pedro, widely known as an abstract painter of the so-called third (Cuban) generation in the fifties; René Mederos Pazos, famous for the poster art he created when he was sent to Vietnam, whose posters became images on Cuban postage stamps; and the Cuban-Chinese-Dutch-Jamaican artist Alfredo J. González Rostgaard, who served as art director of OSPAAAL from 1960 to 1975 and whose majestic oeuvre is exhibited internationally. The sustainability of Fidel Castro's government has made it possible for artists to develop a craft in a way that is unimaginable elsewhere in the region. The influence of Cuban artists is seen everywhere in Latin America, extending from the popular graphic art surrounding Salvador Allende's presidency in Chile in 1971–1973, to the posters of the Sandinista revolution in Nicaragua in 1978–1979, to the visual images that accompanied the Zapatista uprising in Chiapas, led by Subcomandante Marcos in 1994.

In the attempt to understand Latin American poster art in context, another significant moment—although one slightly out of geographical context—is the United Farm Workers' struggle that was led by activist Cesar Chavez in Delano, California, and in parts of the Southwest during the years 1966–1978. Chavez used nonviolent strategies, inspired by Mahatma Gandhi and the Reverend Martin Luther King Jr., to protest the deplorable labor conditions that grape pickers were forced to endure. The unrest associated with these protests coincided with Chicanos reasserting their self-identity within the broader civil rights movement. Nor did Chavez's marches, negotiations, and hunger strikes take place in the fields alone. They were also conceived as a media relations effort. As such, theater groups like Luis Valdez's Teatro Campesino performed *actos* and *pastorelas*. Poetry readings (called *florican-tos*) also took place, where works such as "I Am Joaquín/Yo soy Joaquín" by Rodolfo "Corky" Gonzales were recited. What is more, posters were displayed in Mexican American areas, deployed as part of an effort to recruit supporters. Some of these posters were makeshift, but others were excellent works of art created through a variety of techniques. The posters done by Yolanda López and Ester Hernandez, two leading Chicana artists, epitomize this variation, as each approached the medium from different perspectives. López often used self-portraits, inserted in a religious halo familiar from the iconography of the Virgin of Guadalupe. She thus announced not only that the Mexican matron saint sympathized with the farmworkers' quest, but also that Catholicism was an integral part of the struggle and of the art that sprang from it. Conversely, Hernandez used another type of pop culture image, a manipulation of a well-known sun-dried raisin box cover, onto which she inserted a typical Posada calavera. The imagery, evocative of Andy Warhol, suggested that California grapes were deadly because of the working conditions under which they were picked.

In addition to the creation of afiches, consideration must also be given to context. In general, political afiches in Latin America appear in milieus wherein a certain response is expected. Visual and textual material are harmonized and made to fall within the realm of the predictable. In other words, the overall content might be rebellious but not subversive. Imagine, for instance, a placard of Che Guevara clothed in a tuxedo and promoting Viagra. Anarchy is never endorsed by tradition. That kind of dissidence is left to the advertising industry.

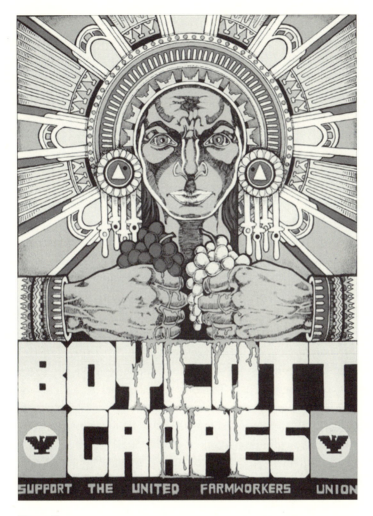

Figure 9:
Xavier Viramontes, *Boycott Grapes*. © Xavier Viramontes.
Used by permission of the artist. www.xavierviramontes.com

There is also the issue of consumption and the various questions attendant upon it. Whom do the posters target? What is considered a "successful" poster? What about authenticity? Might an artist be unworthy of producing placards? These questions came home to me not long ago in a dialogue I had with a graffiti artist whom I met at a reception. He knew of my interest in Hispanic popular culture. Over hors d'oeuvres and wine, our topics of conversation ranged from carpa comedians, like Cantinflas, Resortes, and

Tin Tan, to Nuevo Latino cuisine and from activist movies like *Salt of the Earth* to the graphic novels of the Brothers Hernandez. He then proceeded to describe for me in rich detail the graffiti world of the late 1970s—the theft of aerosol paint, the use of color, the special codes employed by different artists, and so on. He invited me to visit a railway station in the Bronx where abandoned freight trains still displayed graffiti paintings, done a couple of decades ago, which had traversed the nation from Seattle to Florida. He also introduced me to retired aerosol artists, mostly Nuyorican, with whom I discussed the "Golden Age of Graffiti" and the way in which it had been "corrupted" by gallery owners interested in exhibiting their work. "It was suicide," said my friend. "Can you be applauded by the same people you're eager to bring down?"

Apparently, it had happened to him. After gaining a reputation as an enfant terrible, who through the graffiti pieces he left on subway cars had infuriated not only the entire New York Metropolitan Transportation Authority but Mayor Ed Koch personally, the artist was offered an exhibit of his own in a Greenwich Village gallery. TV, radio, and newspaper reporters flocked to the opening, interviewing him about his ideas, career, and future plans. He was applauded by critics eager to be part of the limelight. His former graffiti friends, on the other hand, repudiated the entire endeavor and rejected him as an Uncle Tom. (Several Latinos even nicknamed him El Diablo.) The dilemma is hardly new: artists like Van Gogh, Picasso, and Gauguin found their unique vision while being treated as pariahs, only to be converted—either while still living or posthumously—into stalwarts of the status quo (a conversion to which some, as it happened, gladly acquiesced). For in art, as in politics, rebels invariably end up becoming either martyrs or consensual figures. Such has occurred even with graffiti masters like Crash.

My intention, however, is not to compare graffiti with posters: their medium and their purpose are divergent. At issue, though, are the same dilemmas: Is popular art on display in an exhibit space still popular art? Has it entered the terrain of the haves and abandoned that of the have-nots? If so, what are the consequences of this journey? The answer points to relativism as a philosophy that permeates everything we do. No cultural artifact is ever looked at out of context. That context—the juncture of three coordinates: space, time, and disposition—necessarily shapes our reaction. A kitchen utensil used by the Yanomami in the Amazon jungle becomes an anthropological object the moment it is transposed to another setting. Likewise, a viewer in Camagüey in 1971 looking at an afiche depicting Fidel Castro has a different response from someone in Tallahassee, Florida, viewing it at the very same moment. The dilemma becomes more acute when posters are displayed in an exhibit space. They weren't designed for this purpose. Indeed, for the most part, political posters are not conceived to be viewed in groups. While some notable exceptions exist, such as the Solentiname posters done under Catholic priest Ernesto Cardenal in Nicaragua (and turned into a celebrated story by Julio Cortázar), the Vietnam series produced by René Mederos, and certain of the albums produced in Mexico by members of the Taller de Gráfica Popular, artists more typically imagine political posters as autonomous, self-sufficient units. A stylistic empathy might be inferred, but it is not emphasized.

I now return to my days in El Salvador. What did I take away from the experience? The impression that war, for all the devastation it brings, can also be a source of inspiration. I spoke with numerous people about their desire to move forward, and I sensed a widely shared belief that democracy offered the only escape from the quagmire. The scribbles that I saw painted on fences, trucks, and bridges were proof that people were wholeheartedly engaged, that their social environment was, as the reporter believed, a kind of "disorganized mind at work." They were a counterpoint to the exhilarating afiche collection I had been shown at the hacienda by the entrepreneur-collector. In the placards, the chaotic world outside found coherence, even unity. The posters were anything but muddled. Rather, they were artistic expressions grounded in logic. The British poet W. H. Auden once said that a poem "doesn't do anything," that is, that art is incapable of changing the world. Poster artists would clearly disagree. Their captivating, colorful figures (always appreciated vertically) aim not only to be aesthetically pleasing but also to agitate, to transform, to revolutionize.

"Ah, the art of the ephemeral," the entrepreneur said as he sipped the last drop of tequila. "How long do you think it will take for propaganda of this kind to be auctioned at Sotheby's?"

[2006]

SANDRA CISNEROS

Form over Content

*O*FFICIALLY ANOINTED LA GIRLFRIEND BY THE English-speaking media, Sandra Cisneros is considered a living classic. She is the most sought-after Latina writer of her generation and a guest impossible to ignore in any multicultural fiesta. The black-and-white photographs used to promote her work are colored by an overwhelming sense of theatricality. They make her look like a sweet, light-skinned *india* with a European flair, a natural beauty out of a Sergei Eisenstein film. Her enigmatic smile hides the ancient mysteries of her people, and her cowboy boots, tiny miniskirts, idiosyncratic Mexican shawls, and hairbands inject the needed exoticism into her ethnic roots.

Her status as the voice of a minority has not befallen by accident. Born in 1954 in a Chicago barrio and educated in the Midwest, Cisneros acquired her distinct Tejana identity when she settled in San Antonio in the mideighties. She has since turned the U.S.-Mexican border into her habitat. She proudly parades around under a hybrid facade that is part nativist Spanish and part antiestablishment American. She is constantly asking her audience to approach her as the star of a cross-cultural bildungsroman where mestizas, ignored and underrepresented for ages, end up baking the cake and eating it all. Indeed, Cisneros describes herself as "nobody's wife and nobody's mother" and "an informal spokeswoman for Latinos." Her imposed profile is that of an eternal sympathizer of lost causes, a loose woman, a south-of-the-border feminist outlaw happily infuriating anyone daring to obstruct her way. "They say I'm a bitch," a poem of hers reads,

Or witch. I've claimed
the same and never winced.

They say I'm a macha, hell on wheels,
viva-la-vulva, fire and brimstone man-hating, devastating,
boogey-woman lesbian. Not necessarily,
but I like the compliment.
By all accounts I am a danger to society. I'm Pancha Villa.
I break laws
upset the natural order,
anguish the Pope and make fathers cry.
I am beyond the jaw of law.
I'm la desperada, most-wanted public enemy.
My happy picture grinning from the wall.

Her artistic talents are clear but overemphasized. In fact, what truly attracts readers is not her compact prose, which she perceives as "English with a Spanish sensibility," but her nasty, taboo-breaking attitude. Her works are pamphleteering. They denounce rather than move; they accuse rather than educate.

Responsible for several poetry collections, a children's book, and a couple of volumes of fiction, Cisneros hit high into the firmament with her 1984 novel *The House on Mango Street*, a chain of interrelated vignettes widely read from coast to coast and repeatedly assigned to undergraduates. The plot is unified by the voice of Esperanza Cordero, a preteenage girl coming to terms with her impoverished surroundings and her urge to write her life. Cisneros's second published book, with the imprint of Arte Público Press, a small nonprofit house at the University of Houston devoted to minority literature, *The House on Mango Street* came out just as she was celebrating her thirtieth birthday. The match between writer and publisher seemed ideal: a simple, cliché-filled coming-of-age tale by and about Hispanic women, uncomplicated and unapologetic, with the potential for enchanting a broad audience of young school girls, and a federally funded press whose mandate had been to place in bookshelves the fiction by Latinos that mainstream New York publishers refused to endorse. In a short time both parties benefited greatly, the unknown Cisneros becoming, without any major reviews, an incipient version of the *bandida latina* that would later blossom, and her title turning out to be one of the fastest selling in the house's catalog.

That all happened when diversity and the politics of inclusion were still in diapers. By the late eighties, multiculturalism had become a national obsession, and a spokesfigure for the brewing Latino minority was urgently needed. Richard Rodriguez, whose autobiography *Hunger of Memory* had appeared in 1982, was already an illustrious presence, but his antibilingualism, often confused with anti-Hispanicism, seemed repugnant and xenophobic to the liberal establishment. Since Rodriguez stood alone, an unopposed male, a right-wing intellectual whose soul not even the devil could buy, a female counterpart was quickly sought. Cisneros seized the opportunity: Susan Bergholz, a Manhattan literary agent making a niche for emerging Latinos literati, took her as a client; soon after, Vintage agreed to reprint *The House on Mango Street* and Random House to publish another collection of stories, *Woman Hollering Creek*. A sudden metamorphosis occurred. Talented and outgoing as she was, Cisneros *la marginal* became Cisneros *la atractiva*. With the help of the right promotional machinery, she moved to center stage, and the applause hasn't stopped: from a Before Columbus American Book Award to a MacArthur Fellowship, she basks in the spotlight, sporting fancy sunglasses to reduce the glare.

But the problem, paraphrasing Gore Vidal, is that Cisneros wants to be, not good, but great, and so she is neither. Her style shows signs of maturity; her tales are not prepubescent anymore, and her sentimentality has mellowed down. *Woman Hollering Creek*, for instance, offers a gamut of pieces of self-discovery, set primarily in southern Texas and Mexico, often overstyled, on the role of women in our collective psyche: Rachel, narrating "Eleven," tells what it is like being a girl of that age; Inés Alfaro, who in "Eyes of Zapata" runs away with Mexican general Emiliano Zapata, talks about how his machismo destroyed her life; Cleófilas Enriqueta de León Hernández, the character at the heart of the title story, follows her husband to the United States, where she realizes the extent of her own oppression—to cite only three among many other "suffering souls." These tales are neither fully original nor groundbreaking. Race and gender is their stuff, which Cisneros, by an act of cultural fiat, recycles with just the right ingredients to call attention to Hispanics as instinctual and exciting and interesting. For what they are worth, a handful are actually commendable, but the public has embraced them with far less ardor than it had *The House on Mango Street*, which isn't a good novel. It is sleek and sentimental, sterile and undemanding. Its seductive flavor, I guess, is to be found in its primitiveness. What Cisneros does is tackle important social issues from a peripheral, condescending angle, drawing her readers to the hardship her female characters experience but failing to offer an insightful examination of who they are and how they respond to their environment.

Since its republication by Vintage, *The House on Mango Street* has sold close to a quarter of a million copies. It might seem fine for seventh graders, but making it required reading in high schools and colleges from coast to coast, where students should have more substantial fare, is saddening. Its impact in the United States, obviously, has resonated worldwide. It has appeared in a dozen translations, including the unrefined Spanish one made by Elena Poniatowska, another one of Susan Bergholz's clients and Mexico's most important femme de lettres. Cisneros builds her narrative by means of minuscule literary snapshots, occasionally as short as half a page. Esperanza Cordero, whose name in Spanish means "hope," thinks aloud. She describes what she sees and hears in poetic terms, focusing on the women who surround her and the way they are victimized by men. The image of the house, a ubiquitous motif in so-called Third World fiction, becomes the central leitmotif: Esperanza's poor house embarrasses and pains her; she dreams of a larger, embellished one, a signature of the better times she yearns for herself and her family. Men in her neighborhood are by nature evil; women, on the other hand, particularly the untraditional ones, are saintly, and she seeks a handful of them (Minerva, Alicia, Aunt Guadalupe) as role models. At one point Esperanza is raped as she accompanies her friend Sally to a carnival. At another, Sally is beaten by her father as punishment for seeing boys. The cast is presented as real folks but, in truth, it is Manichaean and buffoonish. Together they introduce a risky rhetoric of virtue that utilizes the powerless victim to advance a critique of the Hispanic idiosyncrasy but that fails to explore any other of its multiple facets.

Cisneros seasons her plot with the type of "magical realism" readers have grown accustomed to in Latin American masterpieces. This is done to make her work ethnic enough; it validates its authenticity. A witch woman, for instance, reads Esperanza's cards to unravel her destiny, and what she finds is "a home in the heart." Her identity quest is dissociated into alternative selves, all related to the various names she dreams of possessing. But her main concern is with the female body. Her descriptions of Esperanza's nascent sexuality are built upon the recognition of the opposite sex as a bestial monster ready to attack. A distant resemblance can be found between Cisneros's novel and Alice Walker's *The Color Purple*. Clearly Walker is much more concerned with relevant historical issues; she tackles slavery from a female perspective and reaches a level of high melodrama as her protagonist, Celie, undergoes a transformation from passive acceptance to self-assertion and human dignity. The epistolary structure of her book, as well of her use of dialect, give it a depth absent in Cisneros. Nonetheless, both writers resort to the same manipulative devices: their novels depict men within an ethnic minority as patently evil and detail the psychological development of female characters who only through conversion can receive redemption. First you learn to understand the injustices of the environment, and then you become your own master.

Does the book deserve its current status? The answer is no. True enough, Latino fiction in English is still green, but turning *The House on Mango Street* into obligatory reading, presumably because of its accessibility, is wrong. It ratifies the image of Hispanics as sentimental dullards, and, equally worrisome, it celebrates the Latino intellectual as pubescent protester. I do not mean to blame Cisneros for a wrong she is not responsible for. Hers is a first novel, a debutante's first turn around the dance floor. What is disturbing is the uncritical deification that surrounds her book. Scholars date the origins of the genre back to 1959, when José Antonio Villarreal published *Pocho*, a tale of revolution and assimilation, about a young Mexican American kid facing discrimination and finding his rightful place in America. Since then a lot of what is published today by Latino fiction writers is realistic and semi-autobiographical. The field is clearly awaiting a major breakthrough that will push its boundaries from conventional immigrant literature to a more sophisticated world-class writing, the type of transition carried on by Philip Roth and Saul Bellow in Jewish letters in the United States. Whenever such reformulating takes place, a recognition of earlier nontraditional voices will be crucial. Few, for instance, regard the pre-postmodern novelistic exercises by an Iberian, Felipe Alfau's *Locos: A Comedy of Gestures*, published in 1936, as a Latino ancestor, if anything because Alfau was a conservative fellow, unconcerned with ethnic envies, and also because, as a Spaniard, he automatically suits the profile of the oppressor. His novel, though, in the line of Luigi Pirandello and Italo Calvino, is light-years ahead of the immigrant-handles-it-all fiction we have grown accustomed to from a considerable segment of the Latino intelligentsia.

But the pantheon is vastly expanding, and high-caliber figures like Oscar Hijuelos, Julia Alvarez, Aristeo Brito, and Cristina Garcia have already delivered commanding and mature novels, at once multifaceted and far-reaching, volumes that go far beyond easy stereotypes. Their understanding of what fiction ought to be—an investigation into the obscure aspects of humanity—makes Cisneros, by comparison, a far less demanding artist. Her messages come in sound bites and often have the taste of stale political sloganeering. She makes social protest the foundation for utopia. Trapped in her condition as Hispanic and woman, her creation, Esperanza, can only rely on her words and imagination to escape. She vows not to grow up tame, which makes her perceive poetry as the door out—her way of escape to an alternative life, her device to reject the ugliness of the outside world. So what type of literary model is La Girlfriend? Confrontational yet whole-heartedly anti-intellectual, she uses her pen just as a weapon to incriminate. Nothing new in this, of course; after all, Cisneros is part, indirectly at least, of the illustrious genealogy of Latin American writers qua opponents to the system, from José Martí to Rosario Castellanos and Elena Poniatowska herself. But her readymade U.S. odyssey, her "making it" in the American Dream, is curiously harmless. Hers is a domesticated form of belligerence. Rather than position herself as opponent to the powers that be, she courts them, feeds them with the dose of animosity they need, and in turn is fed lavishly by them on a diet of awards and prizes. Her forte lies in her articulation of words, not in her display and knowledge of ideas. She offers neither surprises nor profound explorations of the human spirit. The ethnocentrism that gives her legitimacy transforms her complaints into bourgeois mannerisms—transistory temper tantrums that society is ready to accept simply because they present no real subversive threat. Her tales are flat and unoriginal and thrive on revising moribund stereotypes.

In short, the acclaim granted by the liberal establishment to *The House on Mango Street* and to this nineties version of the flamboyant Mexican artist Frida Kahlo as the classic Latina writer of her generation is, to me at least, a form of collective nearsightedness and one more piece of evidence of how exoticism pays its dues. What forces us to give simplistic, overly accessible novels, fiction cum caricature, to the young? Are they allergic to more complex readings? Or could it be that our research into the archives of Latino literature has not gone far enough? By endorsing Cisneros's attitude and no one else's, we run the high risk of falsifying the role of Latino intellectuals. All serious literature, by definition, is subversive, but in our MTV age, not all of it needs to be foulmouthed and lightweight.

[1996]

CIVILITY
AND LATINOS

*M*Y PURPOSE IN THE FOLLOWING PAGES IS TO MED-
itate on the concept of civility as it relates to the Latino minority in the
United States. Before I start, I'd like to make a brief etymological reflection
and also offer a general introductory comment.

There is no equivalent for the noun *civility* in Spanish. A number of
approximations are available: *urbanidad, buena crianza, decoro, afabilidad,
atención,* and, in the proper context, *educación,* as in "Esa persona tiene
buena educación." None of these words—in English, they can be translated
as "urbanity," "well-bred," "decorum," "affability," "attention," and "education"—have the connotation of *civility,* which Merriam-Webster defines
as "a polite act or expression." I found a Spanish dictionary that includes
the cognate *civilidad,* but I've never heard it used. In fact, to me it sounds
like Spanglish.

Truly, the meaning in English of the word *civility* is roughly the equivalent of the Spanish word *cortesía,* which in English translates as "courtesy." Hence, a question begs itself on us: is civility in English the same
thing as courtesy? Merriam-Webster states that *courtesy* is "behavior marked
by polished manners." It equates it with consideration, cooperation, and
generosity.

Anyway, by mentioning the fact that Spanish has no word for civility I'm
not implying, of course, that Hispanics (a term I use to refer to people anywhere in the Hispanic world, from the Iberian Peninsula to Latin America
and the Caribbean Basin to the United States) aren't civil. It does imply that
the Hispanic understanding of civility is somewhat different. And therein
lies the core of my argument.

Now to my general introductory comment. It is often said that nowadays we live in rough-and-tumble times in which people no longer act civilly toward one another. Whenever one hears a statement such as this, it is pronounced with a dose of regret. Respect, courtesy, and politeness are passé. The collective mood now is insolent, vicious, cruel. This cutthroat attitude manifests itself in mainstream culture in multiple ways. The bombardment of media images we experience on a daily basis has as its most tangible consequence a numbing of the senses and a disregard for the well-being of others. One can sense this unkind (my twenty-year-old loves the word *nasty*) outlook in hip-hop music, say, gangsta rap, as well as in the plethora of reality shows on TV, like *Jersey Shore*, where civil law seems to have been replaced by another type of law: the law of the jungle.

Judging from these examples, I'd say our current climate appears to be more selfish than at any time in the past. By selfish I mean less mindful, more insensitive to the public good. According to this worldview, rudeness and cold-bloodedness are in fashion. A fashion that's here to stay. Well, maybe so, but, in all honesty, whenever I hear these types of statements, my "anti-wistfulness" antennae go on alert. I'm suspicious of anything smelling of nostalgia. Nostalgia is what drives the vision that the past was always better than the present, which isn't true. Were the olden days more civil than the present? It depends on what scale is used. Brusqueness is an essential part of human behavior. Steven Pinker might want us to believe that violence is on its way out, or at least on its way down, but to me that viewpoint seems fishy. Is the world more gentle today than during World War II? The movie *Life Is Beautiful* drew smiles when depicting the Holocaust, but that's because it was an antidote to reality. How about Vietnam? The Balkan War? The genocide in Uganda? Guantánamo? Abu Ghraib? Does anyone think that Arabs might love Jews a little bit more sometime soon? Gentility and unfriendliness go hand in hand. Like darkness and light, one can't exist without the other.

Especially in the city. I mentioned the word *urbanity*. The urban landscape is synonymous with sophistication. The city is elegant, cultured. It is also mean-spirited, brutal. A few years ago, I read in the *New York Times* that the word *zoo* had lost its meaning. It no longer described a park in which living animals were kept in captivity. Instead, *zoo* was used to refer to cities. Ah, what a zoo! Clearly, urban centers have changed dramatically in the last century, as a result of a number of factors. One of these factors is overpopulation. There are far more people alive at present than ever before, and the majority are concentrated in cities. Many of these cities have insufficient food, plumbing, electricity, and transportation. They aren't quite livable.

Another factor redesigning the contemporary city is immigration. Almost every major metropolis on the globe has experienced a demographic increase as a result of immigration. Here I want to focus exclusively on the United States. The American city has always been the theater where newcomers test their capacity to survive. New York, Boston, Chicago, Miami, Los Angeles were never really kind, peaceful places to arrive. Ask Jacob Riis, the Danish immigrant who in 1890 produced an invaluable photojournalistic depiction of the living conditions of the poor in New York City slums. It was called *How the Other Half Lives*.

Immigration to the United States today is quite different from what it was when Riis was taking his pictures. The vast majority of present-day immigrants to American cities don't trace their origins to Europe. Europe (Ireland, Italy, Germany, Scandinavia . . .) was the prime feeder of newcomers to the United States approximately up to World War II, perhaps the fifties. After that, the sources have been Asia, Africa, and Latin America. This isn't to say that people from non-European areas of the globe didn't settle here before. Obviously, the African slave trade is an essential ingredient in colonial America and beyond. Hispanics and other groups were also part of the nation's early mix, numerically less significant than blacks yet indispensable as well.

I mentioned Europe as the source of immigration until 1950 because civility is often perceived as a feature—as well as a fixture—of civilization. Civilization as a concept is traced to Europe. The word comes from the Latin *civilis*, which is related to *civitas*, meaning city or city-state. Our model for civitas is the Greek and Roman city. All this to say that perhaps what we're experiencing now isn't the collapse of civility but its redefinition. As the United States recognizes its multiethnic identity and as the white population sees its pivotal role diminished, different types of social behavior are likely to compete for acceptance. The nation's changing face comes along with a revamping of our collective conduct. In other words, I'm saying that our understanding of civility has Europe as its source and that it is different in non-European cultures—for instance, in the Arab world, Asia, Africa, and Latin America. As the United States becomes more multiethnic and, as part of this transformation, more Hispanicized, that understanding will undergo—indeed, is already undergoing—radical changes.

If you think of it, you might agree with me: civility is a contradictory practice. It seeks the moral good by asking individuals to perform social conventions that are not always in accordance with their family, class, ethnic, and religious values. That is, these social conventions are often at odds with their personal interests. An act of politeness is performed on the premise that those around us deserve the same respect that we do because they are individuals whose intrinsic value is equal to ours. To paraphrase a famous biblical quote, one must do unto others what one hopes others will do unto you. The eleventh-century French rabbi known as Rashi, who authored a comprehensive commentary on the Talmud, put it in even more perplexing fashion: If I am not for myself, then who will be for me? And if I am only for myself, then what am I?

Immigrants to the United States must come to terms with the concept of the public good. This is not to say that the rest, meaning those who aren't immigrants, don't need to do the same. But for immigrants it has a special undertone because they've come here in search of a better life. A better life *for themselves*. Moving from one place to another isn't just an act of geographic relocation. When that movement is permanent, it involves a radical reformulation of the person's character. In order to "make it," immigrants arriving to the new country undergo a dramatic learning process. They adapt to a new schedule, a new diet, a new dress code, a new hierarchy of emotions. This isn't done from one day to the next. Depending on the immigrant's age and the support he receives at home and in the community, the acquisition of these new aspects implies a reinvention that takes years, if not decades. A new self is being gestated.

That process I'm referring to is known as *assimilation*. Sociologists toy with various synonyms: *adaptation, accommodation, acclimatization, acculturation, transculturation,* and so on. The more emblematic of these synonyms is *naturalization,* meaning "to make someone feel natural in the new place." Theories are built around these variations of the word *assimilation* to explain why one individual has an easier time becoming a natural than the other. The standard definition of *assimilation* is "the process whereby an individual as well as minority group gradually adopts the customs and attitudes of the prevailing culture." Years ago, this definition was seen as a one-way street: immigrants giving up their immigrant culture to embrace the modes of the welcoming country. The favorite metaphor around this mechanical effort was the melting pot, first used by Israel Zangwill in 1908. Immigrants jump into the pot as outsiders, and they jump out as insiders. The purpose of the pot is to melt identities so that they resemble the receiving nation's standard way of being.

The melting pot, as everyone knows, is out of fashion. That is to say, the metaphor has become trite. Scholars today have replaced it with alternative models, particularly the mosaic and the salad bowl. In each of them, the newcomer no longer surrenders anything. Instead, the immigrant becomes part of a larger picture in which the individual is part of the whole. The motto "E pluribus unum," or "Out of many, one," is interpreted to mean an elasticity of the public sphere that allows for a cultural distinctiveness that comes from addition, not subtraction. Not a one-way but a two-way street: the immigrant assimilates to mainstream culture, while the mainstream assimilates to the immigrant's culture.

For decades I have been studying the cultural patterns of Latinos, as Hispanics living in the United States are commonly referred to. This isn't a detached subject of study for me, for I'm a Latino myself, born and raised in Mexico. I'm an immigrant, too. Not all Latinos are immigrants. In effect, every Latino is different. It sounds like a redundant statement, but the country tends to collapse us all into a Platonic proto-Latino, a one-size-fits-all kind of person. Some Latinos are mestizo. Others are black, white, Asian, and so on. There are rich Latinos, middle class, poor. A huge number of Latinos live in California, Texas, and Florida, but there are plenty in New York, New Jersey, Illinois, Colorado, New Mexico, practically everywhere in the nation, including Alaska and Hawaii. According to the U.S. Census Bureau, the United States has a population of more than 50 million Latinos. The number of undocumented immigrants, which remains unsettled, isn't part of this total. While the flux back and forth across the U.S.-Mexican border has diminished in recent years, there might be some 12 million undocumented immigrants here now. The total would then be beyond 60 million.

By the way, I like the anachronism at the heart of the expression "undocumented immigrants." Should those who are undocumented be described as "immigrants"? Perhaps that's why some people prefer to describe them as "illegal aliens." In many cases, yes, although the intolerant wing of the Republican Party, which, unfortunately, is more than a wing, responds with a robust no. At any rate, for the purposes of my argument I won't count undocumented immigrants because it is easier to make my case that Hispanics have a different understanding of civility by using as models those Latinos who *are* counted by everyone. My argument won't fall apart when a solid segment of the undocumented population is allowed a path toward citizenship, which I hope happens quite soon. Our nation still believes in the public good, doesn't it?

Fifty million, as I said, is a conservative number. Consider for a second the demographic connotations of that number. There are more Latinos in the United States than Spaniards in Spain. There are also more Latinos here than Canadians in Canada. In 2009, California was home to 13.7 million

Latinos, Texas to 9.1 million. In contrast, that same year El Salvador, to give one example, had a total population of fewer than 6 million. What's more, Latinos in the United States are the second largest concentration of Hispanics worldwide, after Mexico, which has a population of around 112 million. (Because of its Portuguese background, I'm not counting Brazil as part of the Hispanic world.) Behind the United States comes Colombia, with more than 45 million, and Argentina, with more than 40 million.

The demographic growth of Latinos in the United States is simply astonishing. Hispanic surnames in the country ranked among the fifteen most common in this country for the first time a decade ago. In 2000, García was the most frequently used Latino last name, placing eighth on the national list. How to account for this growth? I have the impression as if suddenly the Almighty shook the hemispheric carpet, and the south took over the north. Something along similar lines has taken place in Europe, where in the past few decades the African immigrant population, above all the Arab minority, has expanded exponentially. Europe is no longer the Europe of old. Nor is the United States what it used to be. This, as far as I'm concerned, is all for the good.

You probably have the same reaction I do when it comes to demographics. Why is it that when talk of Latinos is at hand, the size of this minority is invariably invoked? Quantity might be a way to look down at the Latino revolution we've witnessed: a human revolution, meaning a profound change of self. Isn't it time to talk about quality, not quantity? Yes, it is, so let me move my argument in that direction. One can't really avoid numbers, but one can use them to dig deeper.

I said before that there's no one Latino type (although there *is* one stereotype). For every ten Latinos, there are six Mexicans. And each of the ten Latinos is unique. Smaller national groups include Cubans, Dominicans, Colombians, and so on. And Puerto Ricans too, but aren't Puerto Ricans Americans? Should Puerto Ricans be talked about as immigrants? In any case, each of these national groups has distinct characteristics, and the individuals belonging to these groups are individuals, not numbers. Every one of the twenty-four Latin American countries is generously represented in the United States through the millions of immigrants it has sent north. This picture is all the more complex when one remembers that Mexican immigrants come from every one of the thirty-one Mexican states. Those states— say, Chiapas, Jalisco, Sinaloa, and Nuevo León—are as different from one another as Utah is from Maine. Therefore, the word *Latino* is not only an umbrella term but also a buffer zone, a neutral area where separate forces, at times hostile to one another, come together. I say "hostile" because to speak of Latinos as a harmonious minority is utopian. *Utopia*, by the way, comes from the Latin "nowhere."

Internal strife in the Latino minority isn't new. We're not always civil to one another. There's a rooted distrust based on our differences. Costa Ricans dislike Nicaraguans. Chileans and Peruvians have long-standing misunderstandings that have led to war. The current political tension between Colombia and Venezuela is also grounded in history. Likewise, Puerto Ricans are suspicious of Cubans. Mexicans are suspicious of Puerto Ricans. And everyone is suspicious of Mexicans. So there you have it: a nice picture of the dysfunctional family. Much like yours . . .

Intriguingly, while tensions exist within the minority, if and when Latinos perceive themselves threatened by the outside world, we become tightly knit. Let me put this another way. Dysfunctional families often display a survival mechanism whereby a threat to the group makes the various individuals seek a truce. In the case of Latinos, the good of the minority, which is quite similar to the good of the community, becomes a priority. That good comes before the good of society as a whole. That is, Latinos are likely to defend each other first before they defend someone from another ethnic background.

This is a crucial point. For Latinos, the value of our own community is decisive, superseding even the value of the individual. Yes, we Latinos are community minded. We cherish the family as a nuclear unit in ways that might appear old-fashioned, especially in times like today, where the nuclear family in the United States is frighteningly vulnerable. We also cherish the gravitational power our culture exerts on us. Through socialization, Latino children are taught that the community good—that is, your life as a Latino among Latinos—is a priority that supersedes even your own personal dreams. I'm always amazed at how, when there's a family emergency, my Latino students, chiefly in the case of women, are twice as likely to drop everything they're doing and run home than my non-Latino students are. I'm generalizing, of course, but generalizations are based on truth.

So how do more than 50 million Latinos travel the two-way street we know as assimilation? Patiently, I guess. Unlike the cases of other immigrant minorities, the wave of Latino immigration to the United States doesn't have a specific starting moment as well as a moment of closure, like, say, the way Ashkenazi Jewish immigration generally began in the 1850s and ended in the 1930s. Latinos have been coming to this country for centuries. Some of us have ancestors who have been here even before the *Mayflower* Pilgrims arrived. Others arrived just yesterday. Culturally, Latinos have been quite an infrastructure. Univisión and Telemundo are the fastest-growing television networks in the nation. For that reason, they are stunningly influential when it comes to politics. There are more Spanish-language radio stations in the state of California than in all of Central America together. Ask any presidential candidate of the last two decades what is at peril if these networks are ignored. There're also Latino food factories here, advertising agencies, athletic leagues, and so on.

My reference to the two TV networks has a purpose. I'm fascinated by the language of Latinos. In and of itself, that language is the perfect kaleidoscope through which to appreciate the two-way-street process of assimilation I mentioned before. Just as the term *Latino* is an umbrella, so is the language we use on a regular basis. You will hear that gorgeous language on Univisión and Telemundo. Some Latinos speak Spanish, some speak English. Some of us are monolingual, some are bilingual. And then there's Spanglish, a hybrid, mestizo language, incorporating elements of Spanish and English. Again, things are far more complicated. There isn't one type of Spanish in the United States, nor is there one type of Spanglish. The Census Bureau reports that the number of U.S. residents five and older who speak Spanish at home is 38 million. This means that 12 percent of the country's population speaks Cervantes's tongue; that is, roughly one out of every eight people. It also means that approximately two out of every three Latinos here speak some form of Spanish. Indeed, 76 percent of Hispanics five and older speak Spanish at home. And, according to the Census Bureau, more than half of these Spanish speakers speak English "very well."

Semantically, the Spanish language has a number of indicators enabling us to understand how authority is conceived for Latinos. Among the most significant ones is the pronoun *usted*. This formal form is used in most Spanish-speaking countries to denote respect. The difference between *tú* and *usted* might be the equivalent of *you* and *thou* in English, except that *thou* was never as current in all levels of society as *usted* is. It's common to hear *usted* in the Iberian Peninsula or Latin America, mainly in conversations where the age difference among speakers is apparent. Seniors are addressed by means of *usted*. Curiously, the *tú* form is more commonly used to communicate with God than *usted*.

Deference, respect, obsequiousness, and reverence have been essential features of the Spanish language since this code of communication evolved from Vulgar Latin to become a powerful Romance language, as well as the language of the Spanish Empire, around the thirteenth century. From 1492 onward, Spanish was used as a tool of colonization—is *colonization* a less benign synonym of *assimilation?*—in the Americas. For the Iberian con-quistadores, soldiers, explorers, and missionaries to implement Spanish to the local population in the colonies across the Atlantic (or, shall I say, "to teach it"?) was a shrewd political move. After all, the quest of the Spanish Empire was not only about appropriating large portions of territory that were economically exploitable, but also—and here the duty of the evangeli-cal Catholic Church plays a crucial role—to "civilize" the Indians, that is, to make them suitable for receiving the Eucharist.

Here comes the word *civilization* again. It surely has a troubled his-tory in Latin America. The number of Hispanic American foundational books debating this term—What does it mean? What kind of baggage did it have in the fifteenth century? How is it understood today?—is substan-tial. Among missionaries like the Dominican Fray Bartolomé de las Casas, one of the key theopolitical questions was how to perceive the natives. Were they monkeys, meaning that they belonged to the animal kingdom? If not, how could it be proven that they were humans? Las Casas was known as the "defender of the Indians." He is responsible for spreading the so-called Black Legend, the bad rap pointing to the miserable treatment of the aborig-inal population the Spaniards were engaged in: physical and mental abuse, torture, death.

In the middle of the nineteenth century, Domingo Faustino Sarmiento, who eventually became president of Argentina, wrote *Civilization and Barbarism*, a political treatise through which he wanted to persuade his fel-low citizens to "whiten" the country's population. To whiten it, Sarmiento proposed opening the doors of European immigration to Argentina. For it was in the arrival, and eventual assimilation, of those Europeans that Argentina's future as a modern country depended. In his view, the nation was a pendulum between two extremes: the European model of civiliza-tion—which Sarmiento understood to mean the Greek and Roman legacy, the concept of the city as harbinger of reason, progress, civility—and the other extreme, represented by the title's other noun: barbarism.

For Sarmiento, barbarism was personified in the gauchos who lived in the pampas. Argentina didn't have as sizable an Indian population as Mexico or Central America did. The gauchos were dwellers of the grass-lands who raised cattle and, at least in the popular imagination, were cow-boy types devoted to a free, unattached mode of life. In *Civilization and Barbarism*, published in 1842, Sarmiento described different types of gau-chos, some good, *gauchos buenos*, and some bad, *gauchos malos*. In his eyes, these gauchos malos were a threat to the future: disruptive, rowdy, bad mannered. They were not only beyond contempt but unlikely to be improved through educational reform.

If immigration was the answer to spread the gospel of European civilization in a country like Argentina, located "at the end of the world," as Argentines describe their homeland, the way for Sarmiento to deal with the gauchos malos was . . . well, to annihilate them. This sounds like an extreme measure now, but at the time it was seen as rational. In 1872, one of Sarmiento's fellow Argentines, José Hernández, wrote the poem *El gaucho Martín Fierro*, in part to counterattack Sarmiento's misrepresentation of the gaucho. The book was an instant best seller. Today it is the equivalent of *Leaves of Grass* in the United States: a national book.

I don't have space to rehearse here other vicissitudes of the words *civilization* and *barbarism* in the Hispanic world. As I stated before, they are many and quite colorful. I do want to mention one more, albeit briefly. It has to do with Shakespeare's last play, *The Tempest*. In it Prospero, the protagonist, is advised by two characters: Ariel and Caliban. One represents idealism, the other materialism. One is dreamlike, the other instinctual. The question of how Shakespeare, who never left England, came across the term *Caliban*, a reference to the Carib tribe, is, in and of itself, fascinating. I shall leave it for another occasion, though. The fact is that nowadays Ariel and Caliban are seen in Latin America as the forking paths of the region's attitude toward life as a whole. Prospero symbolizes the New World. Latin America likes to portray itself as Ariel. It also likes to see the United States, the mean, powerful brother, as Caliban. If all this sounds like a series of crisscrossed animosities, they surely are. Culture functions that way: what means one thing for a particular person or collectivity is turned upside down by another.

If the term *civilization* is muddled, language is too. The world's third most popular language (after Mandarin and English), Spanish is used today by almost half a billion people, the majority of them in the Americas. As I said earlier, it was already a fixture there by the late seventeenth century. With it also came a distinctive worldview that depicts a hierarchical society based on honor, class, and ethnicity, all elements dating back to the Middle Ages. More than five centuries later, expressions such as *Sí, patrón* (Yes, boss), *Mande usted* (At your orders), and *Para servirle* (Pleased to serve you) are widely common, particularly among Mexicans and Central Americans. They are conduits through which to understand the way authority is perceived in the Hispanic world.

In his book *The Labyrinth of Solitude*, Octavio Paz includes a telling anecdote. He talks of a maid he and his wife once had. One night they heard her sneak into the kitchen. She was hungry and was looking for food. When he heard noises, Paz asked from his own room: "Who is it?" The maid answered: "It's no one, señor. It's me . . . !" The psychology of this anecdote is complex. The maid acknowledges she is in the kitchen. But her answer denotes a negative self-image: I'm nobody. (The line reminds me of Emily Dickinson's "I'm Nobody! Who are you?") That is, she first sees herself as unworthy. Only later does she affirm her own individuality.

The relationship between the house owners (Paz and his wife) and the maid is part of a tapestry of interconnecting identities. Paz is the one asking the question, which emphasizes his role as authority. After all, it's his house. A thief might be in their midst. When he doesn't recognize the sounds he hears in the kitchen, he inquires who might be making them. The maid, in turn, is a subaltern. The house isn't hers. She's there on a temporary basis. Moreover, she herself might be seen as part of the owner's property. How did she become the maid? In other words, could these roles be reversed, Paz becoming the subaltern and vice versa? Not if one sees language as a deep expression of the collective self. The maid has no sense of herself—again, she's a nobody—whereas Paz is a somebody.

Something similar might be extracted from the Spanish sayings, all expressions of civility, I mentioned three paragraphs ago. "Sí, patrón" is an assenting statement connoting the speaker's sense of inferiority. "Para servirle" assumes that the role of the working class is defined by its dependence on its upper- and middle-class counterparts. And "Mande usted" is frequently used in response to someone calling: "Luis . . ." "¡Mande usted!" It assumes that the listener is always ready to take orders from an authority figure.

Again, these expressions are ubiquitous, especially in Mexico and Central America. Other types of responses are present in the Caribbean and South America. It would be good to discuss them as well, but I need to select here some examples, and I've chosen these. Given that, as I stated before, six out of every ten Latinos in the United States is of Mexican descent, and if we expand that to include Central Americans the equation might be seven out of ten, it becomes clear that what we have at hand is a generalized disposition permeating millions of people in the country.

I'm talking about *servitude*. The word might sound extreme, yet I can't avoid invoking it. It's defined as "a state of subjection to an owner or master." The definition suggests that it's an economic model that drives the relationship. There's a master and a servant. One depends on the other. That dependence implies a reduction in freedom as well as the partial renunciation of individuality. In this economic model, the servant is a lesser being—meaning, less worthy—than the master.

Servitude and civility are opposing models of behavior. Servitude is based on inequality. It isn't quite a synonym of *slavery*; still, it is based on discrimination. I don't want to say that everyone in Mexico and Central America uses these types of expressions. My argument is that expressions don't belong to a person in particular but to a culture. As such, they are a tool through which one might be able to understand the social and psychological traits of that culture. The tension between the haves and have-nots in the region is profound. To ease it, a dramatic overhaul is required, not only at the political level, although it often starts there, but in the way people relate to one another on a regular basis.

I also don't want to say that other civilizations, in this case the United States, are freed from any form of servitude. Servants are a fixture all over the country. Yet the inferiority that servitude engineers isn't a psychological trait here. A person working at Dunkin' Donuts isn't perceived as inferior. That person has as much dignity, as much individuality, as any of the customers whom the person serves. A nation such as this, preaching fairness as well as social mobility, relies on the principle of equality. Equality is both a value and a slogan in the United States. Your job doesn't define who you are. You are who you are in spite of your surroundings. Today you might work at Dunkin' Donuts. Tomorrow you might be the owner.

It has been said that social mobility in the United States isn't what it used to be. That compared to countries in Europe and perhaps even in Asia, it is much harder today to move out of the working class and into the upper echelons of society. The reasons are manifold. The recession plays an important role. It is harder to be risky nowadays, to explore new ventures. Yet the value of American individualism is deeply ingrained in the country's psyche and, I would argue, remains intact. The citizens in this country want to be seen as individuals. Not only as individuals but as exceptional individuals.

In Mexico and Central America, individualism and exceptionalism aren't features of the collective self. It isn't that the region isn't made of individuals or that each of these individuals isn't unique. But individualism as a value and exceptionalism as an individual and collective premise are not seen as traits. What the culture emphasizes is collectivism: the good of the many. As such, the highest form of good is sacrifice, not for oneself but for the members of our group. Sacrifice plays a major role in the United States as well. But its metabolism is different. Sacrifice and its sibling, voluntarism, underscore the collective good but only as an enhancer of the individual good. Americans like to be seen as devoted to helping others, but only insofar as that help ultimately benefits them. Otherwise, as an endeavor it is hard to justify.

It follows from what I'm saying that civility is culturally defined. This brings me to the core of my argument. I mentioned before that Latinos in the United States constitute the second largest concentration of Hispanics in the world. I also said that soon one out of every four Americans will have Latino descent. Let me add just one more bit of information: roughly one out of every four or five Mexicans lives in the United States now, the other two or three being in Mexico. Unlike other immigrant groups in the United States, who came at a specific time in history and then their immigration wave ceased, Mexican immigration across the Rio Grande has been a constant for more than a century. The Mexican Revolution, World War II, the Bracero Program, and the economic strife from the sixties onward have given continuity to the current. Add to this the element of geographic closeness. Mexico is just on the other side of the border. This closeness results in a constant back and forth that delays the process of assimilation. If and when someone is able to return to the place once called home with relative ease, the delay prolongs itself even more.

These factors also define other members of the Latino minority: Puerto Ricans, Colombians, Guatemalans, Salvadorans . . . This means that unlike other immigrant groups, assimilation for Latinos has its own quirks. The questions are frequently asked: Are Latinos assimilating to the United States? Are they perhaps too many, which means they have found mechanisms through which not to assimilate but to live in tribelike enclaves? And then there's the difference between melting pot and salad bowl. Today Latinos are asked to assimilate by learning to speak, write, and read English without giving up our Spanish, that is, our roots.

Whatever opinion you have about that process of assimilation, one thing is evident: a dramatic transformation has been taking place. Expressions like "Sí, patrón," "Mande usted," and "Para servirle" are heard among the newly arrived, but they aren't used by the next generation, the one born in the United States. Or, if we stick to the immigrants themselves, even those who crossed the border give up these types of enunciations after a handful of years in the United States. To me this is what assimilation is about. Yes, one learns to be an altogether different person. The acquisition of a different mindset is part of that learning.

I'm not a social scientist. Social scientists do longitudinal studies that help them turn a hypothesis into a thesis. I'm a cultural commentator. My commentary explores the way people act and the forces behind those actions. Language is to me a key. Spanglish, the mestizo tongue, is a manifestation of what Latinos are about. Spanglish juxtaposes Spanish and English. That is, the speaker switches codes. Depending on where the speaker is located, there might be more used from one of these languages than from the other. This is only one strategy.

The three strategies employed by a Spanglish speaker are: code switching, simultaneous and often automatic translation, and the invention of neologisms. To the ears of a nonspeaker, Spanglish sounds chaotic. It is, but one needs to remember that chaos is another form of order. Conjugations, for instance, might be performed haphazardly. Spanglish speakers who are also somewhat fluent Spanish speakers often give up the conditional tense. *Yo hablaría, tú hablarías, él/ella hablarían*: in English, "I would speak, you would speak, he/she would speak." In this reformulation of language patterns, the conditional in particular is required in order for the speaker to be courteous, to use polite talk. That is, a Spanish speaker seeking to be civil employs the conditional as a display of good manners. Its disappearance is thus suggestive of changing behavioral modes.

It might sound simplistic, but politeness isn't intrinsic to Spanglish. On the contrary, Spanglish displays rawness. And harshness, too. That's because as a hybrid language Spanglish has a history. It didn't suddenly just come out of the blue. There was Spanglish in the late nineteenth century, at the time of the Bracero Movement, during the Vietnam War years. None of these stages displayed more civility. So are Latinos civilized? Yes. Do we display civility? We certainly do, although our approach to cortesía is rapidly changing in the United States. Is our civility in danger? Neither more nor less than it is for the rest of the United States.

At a time when politeness and good behavior appear to be endangered species, Latinos are following the same pattern as everyone else. We are also bombarded with insolent, vicious, cruel media images. And we live in overpopulated cities ruled by the law of the jungle. In us these behavioral patterns involve the renunciation of some atavistic ways of speaking that did express a different type of civility in the past—decoro, afabilidad—but that, apparently, no longer have a role to play in the present.

In closing, let me reiterate my thesis that Hispanic culture is actually more civil than American culture, as evidenced by the formal forms of speech in our language and by the priority of the community over the individual. It might appear that as Latinos become assimilated to the United

States this minority become less civil. In truth, what happens is that we are adopting a different view of what civility is. My thesis is also that civility is culturally defined and that in Hispanic culture civility means deference to authority and respect for the family and the community. But is there a difference between the way Latinos perceive civility in public discourse, or the lack thereof, and the way the majority culture perceives it? And is the lack of civility an issue in Latino public culture in the way that it seems to be in the mainstream media, say?

By way of an answer, I want to go back to my original digression on the general feeling of nostalgia people in the United States feel for a time in the past in which good behavior really mattered. A recent poll suggests that two out of three Americans are unhappy with the country's lack of civility and see this decline in good manners as a major national problem. Seventy-two percent of those polled believe that the government, with the constant bickering between Republicans and Democrats, is a prime example of the lack of civility. And the assumption is that such lack of civility has an impact on the overall political process. The same poll suggests that 49 percent of Americans are tuning out of the political process and that 63 percent of those who tune out do it because they are fed up with political bickering.

Unfortunately, the poll doesn't break the data into cultural groups. What do Asian Americans think about the nation's declining standards of civility? African Americans? There's no data on what Latinos think either. So let me speculate. Personally, I doubt that the Latino minority is really concerned with the decrease of polite behavior in the public sphere. The reason is simple. While learning to become Americans, we don't dwell too much on what the country has lost by way of politeness; we simply focus on what we're learning to do to be like everyone else.

But once again, Latinos aren't a unity but a multiplicity. My feeling is that those Latinos who have been in this country for generations regret the current decline in manners, whereas those who are recent arrivals don't know much or don't care about that decline. As for the *dysfunctional* political climate (notice I've brought back this adjective), this is an altogether different issue that deserves our full consideration. Latinos comes from a region of the world where politicians cannot be trusted as a matter of fact. They are egotistical, corrupt, and abusive. This is because the entire political structure in the Hispanic world is built on shaky foundations. Only recently—that is, within the last twenty years—have we witnessed the arrival of democracy as a system of government vested in the people.

For someone to understand what a vote might do, it is crucial to experience it firsthand. Hence, trusting politicians isn't something Latinos know how to do well. We're certainly learning . . . By assimilating to the United States, we learn precisely that: our individual vote counts. If a child grows up in a family where the parents are always fighting, that person is likely to think that all parents do the same. To see politicians here squabbling about every little thing doesn't look strange to some of us who have never seen politicians behave nicely.

So there you have it: civility is culturally defined, and culture is never static.

[2012]

JOSÉ GUADALUPE POSADA

A Profile

$\mathcal{S}$ INCE THE TURN OF THE CENTURY, POLITICAL CARTOONS
and murals in Mexico have been considered forms of street art. Still a highly
cultivated medium, political cartoons were published from the 1850s on in
prints and chapbooks that captured the imagination of the masses—rarely
of the sophisticated, highly literate elite. Like journalistic accounts, they
offered quick insight into contemporary affairs, and then they perished. In
the decades before the Socialist revolution of 1910, millions were enlightened and entertained by José Guadalupe Posada's lurid, eye-catching, marvelous engravings, which were often accompanied by jocular lyrics. Murals,
on the other hand, were less ephemeral, more detailed and colorful. In the
thirties, the busy passerby might see aspects of Mexico's history painted
from a Marxist point of view in murals by Diego Rivera, David Alfaro
Siqueiros, and José Clemente Orozco. While Posada was incapable of seeing the pedagogic possibilities of muralism as a form of political activism,
preferring to rely on the graphic arts to educate the populace, Rivera and
his circle later acknowledged their debt to Posada's hyperbolic illustrations,
both in their art and in their writings, and by doing so created a bridge
between the two forms of street art.

But Posada, it seems to me, was more than just a populist artist. He
invented the most fascinating freaks and grotesque monstrosities, and in
that regard he is comparable to Goya, Rudolph von Ripper, Alfred Kubin,
Sibylle Ruppert, and the creators of the fabulous beasts and demons of the
medieval and Renaissance worlds.

Posada was born on February 2, 1852, at number 47 Calle de Los Angeles
(later Calle de Posada) in the city of Aguascalientes in central Mexico. (Some
encyclopedias give his year of birth as 1851.) The fourth of six—some sources

say eight—children, of which only three survived, he was baptized in the Parroquia de la Asunción. Both of his parents were of Indian descent and illiterate. Germán Posada, his father, was a baker who owned a small shop; Petra Aguilar, his mother, was a housewife. Their oldest son, José María de la Concepción, died when still a child. The second, José Cirilo, born in 1839, became a schoolteacher. He taught José Guadalupe to read and write, until the latter and his younger brother Ciriaco were sent to a municipal school in the San Marcos neighborhood. Apparently, Posada enjoyed drawing even as a child, for he made humorous portraits of José Cirilo and his young pupils. Unfortunately, none of these early artistic experiments can be found.

As an adolescent, Posada studied with Antonio Varela at the Municipal Academy of Drawing in Aguascalientes. By 1867 he began practicing the "trade of the painter," and the following year he apprenticed in the lithography workshop of Trinidad Pedroza. Politically active, Pedroza supported the creation of a local government and spoke out against the ineffectiveness of city politicians—particularly the influential Colonel Jesús Gómez Portugal—and the economic and military intervention of France and the United States in Mexican affairs. In addition to lithography, Posada learned the basic printmaking techniques of engraving wood and metal. He also began producing lampoons and illustrations for magazines and books, selling some to Pedroza's own independent newspaper, *El Jicote*. Many of them featured Colonel Portugal as their main target.

Biographical information is scarce, so it is impossible to say precisely when or how Posada's political conscience was awakened. Some, like Octavio Paz, Mexico's foremost contemporary essayist and poet, claim that Posada's ideology has actually been misunderstood. According to Paz, Posada's work was not the prototype of *el arte de protesta* but simply a recording of what he saw. Since the artist was surrounded by the poor and uneducated, his subject matter just happened to look "progressive." Paz, however, wrongly oversimplifies Posada's artistic spirit. While it is true that political manifestos do not exist in his oeuvre—the tracts of Pierre-Joseph Proudhon and scientific socialism not having reached him from Europe—he had a "socialist" weltanschauung and always expressed a strong social conscience. Even without a specific message, in image after image Posada clearly condemns injustice. And while he may not have subscribed to a particular philosophical or governmental remedy for the ills of his epoch, his lampoons nevertheless are testimony to the inequities and instabilities of his fragile country.

At times his stand regarding certain public figures is ambiguous. He could support the president and condemn his enemies, only to ridicule the ruler later.

Figure 10: José Guadalupe Posada, *¡Caso raro! ¡Una mujer que dio a luz tres niños y cuatro animales!* Zinc etching, Library of Congress, Prints and Photographs Division, Swann Collection.

And, as mentioned, politics or political figures were by no means the focus of his lampooning. Folklore and "magical" happenings, subjects popular with everyone, provided ample grist for his cartoons. Regardless of his choice of subject, though, Posada was unmistakenly allied with the dispossessed.

༄

The subversive element in Posada's work is humor—an ingredient that makes his images as compelling today as they were in his time. Through humor, Posada denounced delinquency, assassinations, and corruption. Through humor, he sympathetically described the struggles of popular heroes. According to Paz, Posada's comic equivalent is the French playwright Alfred Jarry, himself a creator of popular prints, who drew inspiration for the absurd world of his King Ubu from Posada's imagery. Although both are rooted in the nineteenth century, they are also our contemporaries, Paz claims, and will be contemporaries of our children through the timeless appeal of their humor.

Even in his earliest works, Posada is a satirist. While maintaining loyalty to his visual perceptions, he never forgets to inject a comic element. There is a hint of the Rabelaisian—or, better, Quevedesque—touch he would later perfect. Usually his early images synthesized an accompanying text or interpreted it with stereotypes and symbols. At this point in his career, he had not yet developed the distinct style of his later works. Perceiving his craft as a means of graphically, but not always sensuously, explaining the daily news, he printed portraits of diplomats, demons, virgins, lawyers, and bankers and depicted comets, natural disasters, and national events.

While Benito Juárez, a pure-blooded Indian lawyer, was Mexico's president, *El Jicote*, with its constant criticism of politicians and the establishment, angered the local authorities and was forced to close. Nineteen-year-old Posada was considered a political agitator. He and Pedroza realized that they had to leave Aguascalientes as soon as possible, so together they went to the city of León de los Aldamas in the state of Guanajuato, where they opened a commercial lithographic business in 1872. It was a prosperous and very religious city, and Posada made a living mainly from producing Christian stamps, as well as cards, invitations, stickers, and labels for cigar packages and liquor bottles. For the time being, politics were left behind.

In 1873 Pedroza returned to Aguascalientes, and Posada was left in charge of the shop. Although he knew that he was not a good businessman, Posada enjoyed being his own boss. In 1875 he married María de Jesús Varela. (He had a son, but not by his wife. The boy died in his teens.) All in all, the future looked bright. A terrible flood, however, devastated León in 1887, and Posada lost everything. In 1888 he moved with his family to Mexico City, where he opened a workshop downtown, on Calle de Santa Teresa and subsequently on Calle Santa Inés (later Emiliano Zapata).

While the history of muralism in Mexico has been well researched, lithography has been relatively neglected. Early on, the technique was used primarily to illustrate scientific treatises, but largely owing to the influence of the French artist Honoré Daumier, it quickly became a popular artistic medium. Mexico's first lithographic workshop was established in 1826 by Claudio Linati and was used to produce the newspaper *El Iris*. Posada was familiar with the prints of early Mexican lithographers such as J. M. Villasana, Hipólito Salazar, and Santiago Hernández. Close scrutiny of his images, though, reveals that he also was acquainted with the work of a handful of European avant-garde artists, specifically Edgar Degas, Édouard Manet, and Henri de Toulouse-Lautrec.

In Mexico City, Posada made contact with the artist and engraver

Figure 11: José Guadalupe Posada, *¡Esta es de Don Quijote la primera, la sin par, la gigante calavera!* Type metal engraving, Library of Congress, Prints and Photographs Division, Swann Collection.

Manuel Manilla, who introduced him to Antonio Vanegas Arroyo, an editor and publisher of street gazettes and a true pioneer of modern journalism. Arroyo recognized not only Posada's artistic talent but also his prodigious drive; he offered to hire him, with a promise of complete artistic freedom. Posada sold his own shop and began a prolific career with Arroyo, producing hundreds of thousands of cartoons, love letters, schoolbooks, card games, penny dreadfuls, and commercial advertisements like posters for circus performances or bullfights.

On occasion, Posada would illustrate satirical verses or simple news reports written by Arroyo or Constancio Suárez, a poet from the state of Oaxaca. The trio of editor, illustrator, and poet became and remained a very famous and extremely productive and powerful voice until 1895, when Suárez died. Posada and Arroyo continued their partnership, and with the benefit of Arroyo's entrepreneurial spirit, Posada reached millions with his images, becoming a spokesman for Mexico's collective soul.

It is commonly thought that during his association with Arroyo, Posada created the calavera—a humorous, vivid drawing of dressed-up skulls or skeletons engaged in activities such as dancing, cycling, guitar playing, drinking, or masquerading. In fact, it was Manuel Manilla who first drew these fanciful characters, publishing calaveras in newspapers and street gazettes as early as 1883. Posada, however, was the one who popularized them, and thus he is often mistakenly credited with their invention. In a European context, calaveras derive from the medieval imagery of the *danse macabre*, or Dance of Death. Peter Wollen dates the tradition to fresco paintings of the fifteenth century and then to a series of woodcuts by Hans Holbein in 1538. Posada so personalized the imagery, though, that the calaveras have become metaphors for his homeland: they are to Mexico what Uncle Sam is to the United States. Originally, Posada simply intended to commemorate Mexico's Day of the Dead on November 2, when the poor and illiterate picnic and sleep in cemeteries to be close to their beloved dead. But the calaveras were immensely popular. They captivated audiences by poking fun at the adventures of Cervantes's *Don Quixote* or José Zorrilla's play *Don Juan Tenorio*. Now, sculptural sugar calaveras are consumed every year to celebrate the holiday. Later generations of artists were also influenced by the macabre characters, including Orozco, who, like Posada, started his career as a cartoonist, and Rivera. Rivera's mural *Dream of a Sunday Afternoon in Alameda Park*, in Mexico City's now-destroyed Hotel del Prado, depicts a female calavera *catrina*, a society belle, wearing a scarf and hat. To the skeleton's left, arm in arm with her, stands Posada; to her right is Frida Kahlo, Rivera's tormented wife, and a childish self-portrait of the muralist himself.

Many of Posada's calaveras bear no signature, and over the years the works of countless imitators and forgers have been falsely attributed to him. Even images like *Calavera huertista* and *Calavera Zapatista*, both possibly the creation of Manilla, have sometimes been mistakenly ascribed to Posada.

Posada became a master of the chiaroscuro. Overcoming the limitations of engraving and lithography, he injected his images with force and passion. Antonio Rodriguez explains Posada's primary printmaking techniques in his book *Posada: The Man Who Portrayed an Epoch:*

> Before settling in Mexico [City] Posada had used the technique of the lithograph. When he went to work for Arroyo . . . , he needed to find a more suitable method for clear, spectacular illustrations that were sharp in line and could be rapidly reproduced. With this in mind he adapted a method already in use in the workshop which consisted of engraving drawings on a plates of lead or an alloy of lead and zinc, almost as in wood engraving. Among the tools he used . . . were various types of burins, among them the "velo," or multiple-line tool rather like the teeth of a saw, the various points and grooves of which produced parallel tracks on the surface of the plate. Later, under the pressure to compete with newspapers that were using modern photo-engraving procedures, Posada . . . [replaced] the burin with a combination of varnishes and acids. With the old technique, the engraver opened grooves in the plate (of wood and metal), knowing that only what was not engraved . . . would be printed on the paper. With the new technique, the artist drew or painted his sketches with a pen or brush dipped in protective varnish, and when the other parts of the sheet were eaten away on dipping the sheet in acid, the sketch remained intact for printing. . . . [This method] is rapid and allows great freedom.

Political cartoons and idiosyncratic comic strips are immensely popular throughout Mexico, and Posada is considered the founding father of the genre. Every significant historic event of his epoch appears in his cartoons. He ridiculed the dictatorship of Porfirio Díaz, a mixed-blooded general from Oaxaca who fought the French invasion in the 1860s, whereby Napoleon III installed the Austrian Archduke Maximilan of Hapsburg as emperor of Mexico. At first appearing to be a progressive liberal, Díaz led an abortive coup against the charismatic president Benito Juárez in 1871. He organized another revolt and eventually became president, ruling Mexico tyrannically from 1876 to 1911, except for one four-year term. Posada also made fun of Mexico's huge foreign debt and of the colonization of Cuba by the United States. He lampooned his country's bourgeoisie for their arrogance and used sensational canards to stir up additional excitement.

When the revolution began, Posada was fifty-eight years old and had produced fifteen thousand engravings. He was a supporter of Francisco Madero, a wealthy lawyer who militarily opposed Díaz and became president in 1911—only to be murdered two years later by one of his men, Victoriano Huerta. He also sympathized with Emiliano Zapata, a guerrilla from the state of Morelos who fought for the peasants and agrarian reform. During these years, Posada's engravings depict national heroes and symbols, such as women soldiers. Jean Charlot, one of the artist's dedicated admirers, wrote, "The Revolution was a Posada 'still' come to life, its tableaux charted by his able brown hand before it had even begun." Unfortunately, he did not live to see the end of the conflict.

In 1910, around the time that his wife died, Posada created another famous character, don Chepito Marihuano, a middle-class bachelor who counterbalanced Posada's satiric, at times cruel, voice with a moralistic one. Because of his strong influence with his audiences, Posada may have had apprehensions about providing criticisms without solutions. Departing from his customary pessimism, the artist took a positive approach, using don Chepito to persuade the ignorant to adopt civic manners. Don Chepito made fun of social foibles but afterward offered a pedagogic message. His every appearance was educational, demonstrating rules regarding behavior, ethics, and honor.

For more than twenty years, Posada lived in a poor neighborhood near the Tepito market, at number 6 Avenida de la Paz (later Jesús Carranza). It was there he died, penniless, on January 20, 1913, of gastroenteritis. He was buried in a pauper's grave in the Dolores cemetery. Seven years later, after no one had claimed his mortal remains, his bones were exhumed and tossed in a communal grave. While not uncommon, the mass burial can be seen as a metaphor for Posada's anonymity.

Posada embodied Mexico's renaissance in his perception of the country as independent of Europe and in his desire to establish a national art with indigenous motifs and symbols dating to the Conquest. National and international events parade through his imagery: the awaited earthquake of 1899, which was considered an omen of the Apocalypse; the burning of a library in Chicago; the famous criminal trial of María Antonia Rodríguez, who was accused of killing her compadre. His political heroes were bandits and Robin Hoods; and his political cartoons express concepts and themes later expounded in Mexican murals. Within his simple and sometimes static images, he displays a considerable amount of inventiveness and fantasy, as in the cartoon of a woman who gives birth to three children and four animals or the one of a girl with a face on her buttocks. One could argue that Posada foreshadows elements of the so-called magic realism style of literature—with its dramatic juxtapositions of reality and fantasy—as embodied in the writings of Gabriel García Márquez and Juan Rulfo.

Posada's imagery was so varied, his burin so prolific that it is difficult to know how best to approach his body of work. Roberto Bardecio and Stanley Appelbaum have established a thematic hierarchy: calaveras, disasters, national events, religion and miracles, don Chepito Marihuano, chapbook covers, chapbook illustrations, everyday life, and miscellaneous prints. One could also approach his oeuvre chronologically and biographically, examining the art as it developed in the context of his life. Or one can simply ignore any logical sequence and approach the work chaotically—which is my preference. The artist is best appreciated when external frameworks are not imposed on him. His spirit erupts in each autonomous engraving or lithograph, and the encounter between image and viewer is pure pleasure.

Posada's life after death was yet another act of creation. He did not find an immediate following. For the next decade, the Academia de Bellas Artes de San Carlos, a national institute founded in 1778 to preserve traditions and techniques in the visual arts, ignored emerging indigenous trends in favor of imported styles and ideas. To counterattack this, the Taller de Gráfica Popular was formed in 1937 under the Socialist regime of Lázaro Cárdenas. The group supported new artistic movements and tried collectively to create a revolutionary street art. At the same time, artists of the so-called Mexican school—in particular Rivera and Orozco—frequently produced lithographs strongly influenced by Posada. Together with Emilio Amero, Jean Charlot, Miguel Covarrubias, Carlos Mérida, Pablo O'Higgins, and Rufino Tamayo, the two muralists created a lithographic tradition of great impact following the teachings of Posada.

Two sources might be credited with restoring Posada to prominence. In 1920, the early modernist painter Dr. Atl (Gerardo V. Murillo) "rediscovered" Posada. It was Jean Charlot, however, a French immigrant to Mexico and a friend of the muralists, who showed around Posada's prints and wrote about him during the twenties in the context of cubism. He brought the engraver to the attention of Rivera, Orozco, and Siquieros, who were so enchanted with his artistic spirit that they embraced him as their master.

Rivera once stated that Posada "was so closely associated with the spirit of the Mexican people that he may end up just as an abstraction"—in other words, his legacy would become a collective one, which has indeed happened. Orozco saw Posada as one of the greatest artists, "one able to teach an admirable lesson in simplicity, humility, equilibrium, and dignity."

In *Posada: Messenger of Mortality*, Peter Wollen analyzes Posada in Borgesian fashion: through the eyes of his successors. He examines, for example, similarities between him and the early European avant-gardist Gustave Courbet—a painter of earthy, and sometimes crude, realism—and he discusses the affection some of the cubists, such as Piet Mondrian, had for the Mexican cartoonist because of their reevaluation of noncanonical and "primitive" forms of art. Wollen also refers to Posada's influence on Russian *lubki*—posters and small books containing ballads, tales, and tracts—made by Mikhail Larionov and other Golden Fleece and Donkey's Tail artists. Larionov knew of Posada through his friend Rivera, whom he frequently visited in Paris.

Other cultural links can be found, such as Posada's appeal to the Russian director Sergei Mikhailovich Eisenstein and to Surrealists such as Alfred Jarry and André Breton, who cherished the calavera for its cruel, yet humorous, morbidity. In an enthusiastic article, Breton wrote that

the rise of humor in art to a clear, pure form seems to have taken place in a period very close to our own. Its foremost practitioner is the Mexican artist Posada who, in his wonderful popular engravings, brings home to us all the conflicts of the 1910 Revolution. They tell us something about the passage of comedy from speculation to action and remind us that Mexico, with its superb funereal playthings, is the chosen land of black humor.

According to Wollen, Eisenstein first saw Posada's work in Berlin in 1929, at the house of playwright Ernst Toller. The Russian filmmaker, himself an aspiring artist, shared the Mexican printmaker's interest in crowds, revolution, and tumultuous events, as seen in his movies such as the 1925 *Battleship Potemkin, October*, which was made in 1927, and the unfinished *¡Que viva Mexico!* In his autobiography *Immortal Memories*, Eisenstein explains how, when he was learning to draw, his drawing went through a stage of purification in his striving for a mathematically abstract and pure line, and how he was influenced at the time by Rivera, Mexican primitivism, and the "cheap prints" of Posada.

In what may be the ultimate praise, Rivera compared Posada to Francisco de Goya. In drawing his analogy, Rivera had the artists' populism in mind. But, as I argued before, the links between the enlightened eighteenth-century Spaniard and the premodernist Mexican are even more obvious, at least at one level: both created an enduring zoology of imaginary beings. Rivera wrote of Posada:

> Entirely original, Posada's work speaks with a pure Mexican accent. . . . If we accept Auguste Renoir's dictum that the true work of art is "indefinable and inimitable," we can safely say that Posada's engravings are works of art of the highest order. Posada can never be imitated; he can never be defined. In terms of technique, his work is pure plasticity; in terms of content, it is life itself: two things that cannot be imprisoned in the straitjacket of a definition.

Rivera loved the Posada of the urban poor, the lumpen street people. But equally enjoyable, and most attractive to me, is the Posada who transports us to a universe of gothic, at times grotesque, magical, and bizarre incidents, or Posada the anarchist, dwelling on catastrophe, satire, and death. Death, in fact, is his primary preoccupation, as far as I am concerned—not an existential, painful death, but one that is irrevocable, social, and egalitarian. The gothic facet of Posada has, unfortunately, gone unattended. His universe is full of bats, griffins, skeletons, animal hybrids, snakes, explosions, pistols, demons, ghosts, and deformities. He draws attention to fear, despair, and criminality. His monsters are not pure abstraction; they are symbols, allegorical images, metaphors. They have a life of their own yet are tied to the human reality. They deserve a place next to the sphinx, the multiple-headed dragon, and the behemoth, as well as Pieter Brueghel's vision of hell. Posada was able to portray the sadism, torture, madness, superstition, and paranoia of his time through these incredibly complex, outstandingly imaginative characters without ever losing touch with the Mexican soul, perhaps because they inhabit it.

Why is this master of street art relevant today? Because he was a genius without artifice or pomposity. Because he truly spoke to the masses. Because he was attracted to the calamitous and absurd, as mankind will always be. Because rarely does an artist manage to bridge the gap between popular and sophisticated tastes as he did through his lampoons and cartoons. To put it simply, because Posada *is* Mexico.

[1990]

CONVERSATIONS

LANGUAGE
AND EMPIRE

(with Verónica Albin)

VERÓNICA ALBIN: Are words neutral?

ILAN STAVANS: Language obviously isn't an empty bank of conventionally accepted sounds and graphs. It is infused with history. Each of the words at our disposal has undergone a series of permutations. A word's etymology only points to its roots. The permutations enable us to peel away the layers of meaning accumulated through time. Take *Bible*, for instance: a designation we use for the sacred Jewish and Christian scriptures consisting of the Old and New Testaments. It comes from the Greek βίβλος, that is, "the books." Upon being exposed to it, an extraterrestrial wouldn't appreciate the accrued meanings. How *did* a classical term—not Aramaic, not Hebrew, not even Latin—become the most influential term in the world?

VA: Most people use language mechanically, though. They have no interest in linguistics.

IS: How is a bone marrow transplant performed? What does a microchip do? Language is never static. Scientific and technological advance, for instance, modify the way we approach words. But even without these developments, as people we're also restless, subverting etymologies, reinventing meaning.

VA: You've been quite a controversial figure in the study of language. Are you a linguist by training?

IS: I'm a happy amateur, just like Antonio de Nebrija or Andrés Bello. Being a layperson with a passion allows for enormous freedom. It is

149

an antidote against conformism. It precludes you from having to be a slave to institutional protocols.

VA: In what sense?
 IS: One doesn't need to pay homage to the rigid parameters of an established discipline.

VA: Have your studies in the history of language turned you into a linguist, though?
 IS: I prefer the word *philologist*. Like the word *humanist*, it has unfortunately gone out of use, in American English, at least. But it is closer in spirit to the approach I believe one needs to take to understand language.

VA: How would you describe that approach?
 IS: An all-encompassing one. If language is history, one needs to use whatever tools are available to appreciate it: sociology, philosophy, science, anthropology, religion, lexicography, politics, literature . . .

VA: What does a philologist do?
 IS: Philology is the study of language in all its possibilities. In other words, the study of culture.

VA: You've been accused of mixing yourself in your field of study.
 IS: Could it be otherwise? Language is *us*.

VA: But should a philologist studying an emerging way of communication also translate a work of literature into it, as you did in rendering the first chapter of *Don Quixote of La Mancha* into Spanglish?
 IS: It is a mistake to hide behind the coldness of the scientific method. The scientist tackles a phenomenon from the outside, uncommittedly. How could that succeed when language is everything—our speech, our dreams, our ideology, the food we eat, the fashions we embrace, et cetera? A philologist cannot look at language from a distance. He needs to get his hands dirty. His explorations are forms of advocacy.

VA: Does it bother you to be the target of animosity? The reaction to your reflections on Spanglish has generated a worldwide debate.
 IS: Not in the least.

VA: Your books are engaging, learned, and enormously readable. They are released by major publishing houses and targeted to a large audience.

IS: Academics love to build self-enclosed turfs through obscure, obstructing jargon. It's nonsense. Ludwig Wittgenstein said it best in 1922, in his *Tractatus Logico-Philosophicus*: "What can be said at all can be said clearly; and whereof one cannot speak thereof one must be silent." By the way, I believe silence should also be an area of study for linguists. It is an essential aspect of communication.

VA: You have explored silence in many of your works.

IS: It is a topic that intrigues me. Isaac Babel rebelled against the Man of Steel by ceasing to write. In 1934 he told the Congress of Soviet Writers: "I have invented a new genre—the genre of silence." Furthermore, in a story I just finished set in Belgium, I argue that that country engaged in a silence that turned it into an accomplice of National Socialism and that that silence proved devastating to Belgian Jewry. Shakespeare, by the way, was also intrigued by it. In *Henry VI, Part 2*, act 3, scene 2, Suffolk says:

> Would curses kill, as doth the mandrake's groan.
> I would invent as bitter-searching terms,
> As curst, as harsh, and horrible to hear,
> Deliver'd strongly through my fixed teeth,
> With full as many signs of deadly hate,
> As lean-faced envy in her loathsome cave:
> My tongue should stumble in mine earnest words.

And Edward Gibbon worried about it as well. So what does the *OED* have to say about silence? "The fact of abstaining or forbearing from speech or utterance (sometimes with reference to a particular matter)" and "the state or condition resulting from this." And then it states: "muteness, reticence, taciturnity." It also suggests that silence is repressed speech, that it is the cause of a compulsion to cease speaking on a particular occasion, and, finally, that silence is proof that an argument has been overcome.

As I mentioned in my essay "The Impossible," included in *Dictionary Days*, it still isn't clear to me, existentially, what silence is. Is it stillness? Is it absence? Stillness is an attribute of being. Absence, on the other hand, is the disappearance of being. Like most people, in my youth I loved sound—all kinds of sounds: speech, music, the noises heard in a sports arena . . . I love silence now: silence from my children's sighs and shrieks, my students debating a certain topic, a symphony by Brahms. As adulthood has settled in, I've become more attracted to silence. Silence is quietness. But at different stages in life it acquires distinctive connotations.

Every word at our disposal has its own double: a nonword. Every dictionary that has ever produced a catalog of words available to a particular group of people also creates its counterpart, a lexicon of unavailable words, words that are not possible, cannot be uttered, words that cannot exist or come into being.

VA: Is this lexicon of impossible words a dictionary of silence?

IS: Wouldn't it be fitting to seek the definition of silence and, yes, come across a vacuum, an empty page? But I'm not the first to consider this. In my essay "Pride and Prejudice," I gave that credit to Aleš Debeljak, who compiled a Slovenian dictionary of silence.

VA: You've also perfected the genre of the interview . . . *Dominical*, the Sunday supplement of *El Mundo* in Spain, called you "un comunicador nato" (a natural communicator). Do you have any idea how many media Q&As you've done in radio, TV, and newspapers?

IS: Several dozen, perhaps over a hundred.

VA: I gather you've been thinking about language since childhood. When did you begin studying it in a more systematic way?

IS: The moment I immigrated to the United States in 1985, I became fascinated with the topic of translation. About a decade later, I embarked on an exploration of the twists and turns of Spanglish. This led me to do sustained readings in linguistics, religion, and politics. I became interested in the development of Spanish, English, French, Portuguese, and German as self-sufficient tongues and in their vicissitudes through time. How to explain their life cycles? To what extent did conquest and colonization change these languages? Lexicons became an obsession. What role do dictionaries play in their maturity? In regards to the transition from *castellano* to *español* to the Spanish spoken in the Americas, the work of Amado and Dámaso Alonso, Arturo Capdevila, Ramón Menéndez Pidal, Raimundo Lida, Angel Rosenblatt, Fernando Ortiz, Fernando Lázaro Carreter, Rafael

Lapesa, and Antonio Alatorre was invaluable. In retrospect, I see what I've done as simply connecting the dots.

VA: Is Spanglish a language in formation?

IS: It has been moving from the purely oral to the written realm. There are novels, poems, stories, essays available in it already. These include Ana Lydia Vega's "Pollito Chicken," Giannina Braschi's *Yo-Yo Boing!*, María Eugenia Morales's "T'was the Night," Felipe Alfau's *Chromos*, Cecilio García-Camarillo's "Talking to the Rio Grande," and Susana Chávez-Silverman's *Killer Crónicas*, as well as the music of Juan Luis Guerra, Café Tacuba, and Cypress Hill. People are looking into a standard orthographic spelling, even for a systematic syntax. But Spanglish is also something else: a state of mind. It allows us an opportunity to appreciate the creation of a new minority culture in the United States. As the discovery of new galaxies allowed astronomers to better understand the secrets of our universe.

VA: Yet Spanglish has often been seen as a bastardization of the language of Castile, an inferior mode of communication, a "restricted" code of the impoverished classes. You have brought this construct under attack, remarking on its richness.

IS: Why shouldn't the zest and improvisational drive of Spanglish speakers be applauded? Who establishes the parameters of richness and poverty in language? When I come across a fluent Spanglish speaker, I'm in awe at the versatility of the language. It seems not to know any barriers.

VA: In your introductory essay in *Spanglish: The Making of a New American Language*, which includes your explorations on the hybrid tongue (you refer to it as "la jerga loca"), a lexicon of approximately six thousand terms, and your translation of *Don Quixote*, you mention that academicians are allergic to it. They itch and scratch and dismiss it as a nuisance.

IS: Academics are eager to defend against all odds the security of their tenured positions. They also pride themselves as educated. For them to get involved with the lower strata is a waste of time, a nuisance. More than once I've come across a linguist whose research involved exposure to a Spanglish speaker. What does he do? He registers in a comfortable hotel. Once a day he spends a couple of hours in La Loisaida, as the Lower East Side is known among Spanglish speakers, then dines at an elegant restaurant. He shapes his paper in the isolation of his office in an ivory tower institution.

VA: Octavio Paz claimed: "Spanglish is neither good nor bad. It's abominable."

IS: Paz was utterly blind to the reality of Latino culture in the United States. The first chapter of *The Labyrinth of Solitude* is nothing short of embarrassing. It is ironic that so enlightened an intellectual should be so blind to a crucial aspect of la mexicanidad. Paz isn't the only antagonist, though. The list of Latin American intellectuals who have gone on record against it is long. In fact, during the III Congreso Internacional de la Lengua Española, celebrated in Rosario, Argentina, in 2004, whose theme was linguistic identity and globalization, José Saramago, Nobel Laureate from Portugal—a non-Spanish-speaking country—stated that he hated Spanglish because it threatened to dilute the language of Cervantes into a broth that is 50 percent English and 50 percent Spanish. Saramago's equation is wrong, of course: Spanglish is never a 50–50 brew. In any case, I'm not surprised.

VA: Why?

IS: There is a sense in Latin America, and it obviously reaches as far as Portugal, that nothing good or worthwhile will come out of Hispanic culture in the United States.

VA: Is this due to the construct of rascuachismo?

IS: Rascuachismo is an aesthetic of the dispossessed; it suits Spanglish to the dot. If Saramago and others who embrace a Marxist ideology paid closer attention to its social origins, they would embrace it wholeheartedly.

VA: Have you discussed this with Saramago?

IS: When we met in Boston, we talked politics of another sort. He had just spent time in Ramallah, and he compared the Israeli army to the Nazis.

VA: Is there an agenda on your part in endorsing Spanglish?

IS: What kind of agenda?

VA: By subverting the academicians' opinion of Spanglish being nothing more than a *jerga rascuache*, by transforming it from an unacceptable mode of speech to one that is hip, and interesting, and valuable, and worth studying, you're also pushing for a reconsideration of Latino identity in general, right?

IS: Sure. There is nothing wrong with Spanglish. It is a legitimate form of speech. English is the only ticket to success in the United States. Every Latino needs to be fluent in it. But not at the expense of Spanglish. Why can't the two—or, better, the three, for Spanish forms the triptych—coexist?

VA: Doesn't this benefit you?

IS: How so? To be honest, there are days when I tire of talking about Spanglish—not *in* Spanglish but *about* it. But then I recognize my role as agitator, with which I'm comfortable. Don Francisco, the host of the Univisión variety show *Sábado Gigante*, once introduced me as "the destroyer of the Spanish language." He, needless to say, meant it as a joke, for he and his audience are fluent in it. Imagine what would happen if a single individual had, at the tip of his fingers, the power to unravel an entire language!

VA: Some have also described you in the *New York Times* as an assimilationist, even branded you as an Uncle Tom.

IS: El Tío Tom . . . I'm not making myself clear to them. Actually, I embrace the opposite principle: resistance through language. I often think of Jean Anouilh's version of Sophocles's *Antigone*, staged in Paris in 1944. His mission wasn't to stage a Greek tragedy as much as it was to incite his countrymen to rebel against the Nazi usurpers.

VA: Should Latinos actively rebel against Americans, then?

IS: Rebellion is most successful when it is subtle.

VA: What does your friend Richard Rodriguez, author of *Hunger of Memory*, think of Spanglish?

IS: I don't think it sparks his mind. He's mostly interested in miscegenation.

VA: *Tu wat extent can an Espanish orthografy bi uʒd tu reprizent Inglish?*

IS: This movement is sheer folly. Although it was born in England in the 1950s when Mont Follick, a professor of comparative philology at the University of Manchester, in his capacity as a Labour MP promoted a Spanish-based spelling system he had devised in the 1930s, it is currently kept alive by a bunch of gringos who argue that since the English language has an almost inscrutable orthography, and who posit that since a number of states in the union will soon follow the route of California and Texas—i.e., they will have a white minority and a multiethnic majority—[they] propose teaching English to all—Latinos and Anglos—using the phonetic spelling of Spanglish. This emphatically leads to the threat of the browning of America, which makes conservatives go wild.

VA: Was your translation of *Don Quixote* into Spanglish a one-time shot? Have you continued the endeavor?

IS: Part 1 of Cervantes's novel is almost finished.

VA: When do you expect to publish it?

IS: Not until the entire manuscript is done.

VA: If Spanglish is still in formation, without its own syntax, what are your morphological parameters?

IS: I tackle the issue in a nota bene in *Spanglish*. In seeking to reflect the polyphonic and polymorphic nature of the tongue, I used elements from Nuyorican, Dominicanish, Cubonics, Chicano Spanglish, and other varieties. Mine is a middle ground.

VA: The effort is . . . well, quixotic. Are you also hoping to update the lexicon?

IS: Since the book appeared in 2003, I've been accumulating more entries. I have close to two thousand already. My intention is to one day create an Internet lexicon.

VA: Ah, that PalmPilot vade mecum you've talked about, where one might envision rapid access to the latest meaning of a word. The Internet is certainly a much more flexible medium than the printed word.

IS: It is also more democratic. I'd like to invite Spanglish speakers to offer fresh terms.

VA: It could be maddening . . .

IS: Every entry in *Spanglish* was rigorously checked. At least three occurrences needed to be recorded. And the spelling, when possible, was standardized by means of discussion with colleagues. The same approach would need to be taken in the Internet version.

VA: Do you ever get down to analyzing morphologically a single sentence?
IS: In the classroom, I frequently zoom in and out of grammatical patterns, scrutinizing morphological and syntactical structures.

VA: You've been primarily concerned with Spanish in the United States. In the article "Giving Spanish Its Due," published in the *Chronicle of Higher Education*, about the responsibility of Spanish departments to teach undergraduates using an interdisciplinary approach, you wonder: "Is Spanish a foreign language in the United States?"
IS: It is the most often taught language on American campuses after English, often superseding in the amount of students the combined enrollment totals for French, Russian, German, Italian, Greek, Latin, and Hebrew. This isn't a quantitative issue but a historical one. Spanish has been a fixture in the southwestern territories of what is the United States today since the colonial period. It might have been eclipsed in certain periods, but it never lost its gravitas. And the demographic explosion of Latinos makes it the nation's "official second language."

VA: You've also referred to "el español en América," not as a unity, but as a plurality.
IS: I saw an ad not long ago that read: "Se habla español en varios idiomas." Spanish is spoken here in various languages. The astonishing complexity of the Latino minority can't be ignored. Before the Treaty of Guadalupe Hidalgo, signed in 1848 at the end of the Mexican-American War, the Spanish spoken by Iberian explorers, missionaries, and *adelantados* metamorphosed into the type used in northern Mexico. But there were self-sufficient exceptions: *el español novomexicano*, for instance; the idiosyncratic form used by Californios, some Chilean, others Mexican; and so on. At the close of the nineteenth century and the early decades of the twentieth, that type was dramatically enriched by exiled communities such as Cubans in Key West and Puerto Rican *tabaqueros* in New York. Over time, Dominican, Colombian, Ecuadorian, and Salvadorian vernaculars, to name just some, were added to the stew. Within each of these national subgroups, there are also lexical variants. The result is a delightfully aromatic posole. What kind of Spanish is used by Don Francisco? Is it the same heard on

Spanish-language national radio? Yes, nowhere on the globe (and perhaps at no other time in human history) has the language of Antonio de Nebrija been at a more decisive crossroads.

VA: Reporters in particular see this crossroads as perilous. Is Spanish in danger in the United States?

IS: News of its demise goes back at least to the Spanish-American War of 1898. For instance, Rubén Darío, the Nicaraguan *modernista*, believed *el inglés* would ultimately take over. Here is his "Los cisnes" of 1905:

> ¿Seremos entregados a los bárbaros fieros?
> ¿Tantos millones de hombres hablaremos inglés?
> ¿Ya no hay nobles hidalgos ni bravos caballeros?
> ¿Callaremos ahora para llorar después?

I quote from Greg Simon's and Steven F. White's version:

> Are we to be overrun by the cruel barbarian?
> Is it our fate that millions of us will speak in English?
> Are there no fierce shining knights, no valiant noblemen?
> Shall we keep our silence now, to weep later in anguish?

VA: So should we worry?

IS: Like any living organism, languages go through a life cycle: they are born out of necessity, spread as a result of invasion and colonial enterprise, undergo a series of mutations, and die when their speakers no longer have use for them. Spanish in the United States will last as long as it needs to—not a second more. Other immigrant languages have faced a similar destiny.

VA: Is Spanish an immigrant language?

IS: Yes and no. Insofar as it was brought by newcomers from the Caribbean Basin, Latin America, and Spain, it certainly is. Ironically, to some extent it is also an aboriginal language in that prior to the Declaration of Independence in 1776, it was already in use in what is today the United States, from the Southwest to the Commonwealth of Puerto Rico.

VA: In the forward to *Growing Up Latino: Memoirs and Stories*, you talk about the difference between *ser* and *estar*.

IS: I echo Borges: "El español es facilísimo." But I might add that it suffers from severe limitations, for instance, its reluctance to compound words.

The nuances of "to be" in Spanish, on the other hand, are exquisite. Other languages are poorer on this front: Italian makes the same distinction in that it has *essere* and *stare*, but doesn't exploit the nuances quite as richly as Spanish does; French is limited to *être* (etymologically related to *estar*), which, interestingly, is conjugated in some grammatical persons like *ser* ("Je suis un bouffon," "Nous sommes tant aimés," "Ils sont enfin libres"); Hebrew disregards the complication; as for Russian, it is even drier, for it has no auxiliary verbs whatsoever: no *ser* and no *estar*. Russians say, "I professor" or "I doctor," but Russian does have an infinitive meaning ("to be a professor") that makes use of the instrumental case for declensions: *profesorom, doktorom*.

VA: Do all languages have the same blueprint?

IS: Think of the nineteenth-century Romantic concoction introduced by Polish oculist and linguist Ludwik Lejzer Zamenhof: Esperanto. Although it was taught throughout the world, Esperanto never quite achieved the international recognition its inventor hoped for it. This is because artificial languages have their own metabolism; they aren't connected to the principal engine behind the communication effort. Let us not forget that language is the pull of a common memory based on tradition, literature, and national pride. Language is love of country. Languages are born out of necessity; they emerge when a group needs to distinguish itself, at the verbal level, from its surroundings. The need isn't enough, actually. The historical circumstances must be ripe. How did Old English evolve? What kind of break did a work like Geoffrey Chaucer's *Canterbury Tales* create? Think of the development of Hittite, Phoenician, Babylonian, and Persian.

VA: Why did some perish and others survive?

IS: Languages are "exposed to the elements," so to speak. They are at the mercy of historical forces.

VA: How about the death of a language?

IS: When there is no longer a necessity for it, a language disappears. That is the pattern of Hittite, Babylonian, and Phoenician. They also fossilize, like Aramaic and Latin. And at times they also die abrupt deaths. Yiddish, for instance, almost vanished by 1945 in Auschwitz and other concentration camps under Adolf Hitler's war machine. Another example of a language that faced death by edict is Spañolit, aka Ladino, when in 1492 the Jews who spoke it were expelled from Spain by Isabella. Yiddish has managed to stay alive (albeit barely) thanks to the diligent work of people like Aaron Lansky, founder of the National Yiddish Book Center in Amherst, and Spañolit is hanging on fragile spiderwebs thanks to Dr. Emese bain-Medgyesi, director of the Europees Bureau voor Taalminderheden (European Bureau for Lesser Used Languages) in Brussels, to Haim Vidal Sephiha, founder of the Vidas Largas Association in Paris, and Aaron Koen, director of La Autoridad Nasionala del Ladino in Israel. But when language death is concerned, we must not forget the attempts of the Generalísimo Francisco Franco to eradicate Gallego, Aragonés, Euskara, Catalan, Valenciano, Mallorquín . . . Tyranny, famine, expulsion, and massacres have a terrible effect on language. When reading about the bloodbath in Rwanda and Burundi, for instance, I cannot help but wonder if the Hutu and Tutsi tongues, with their common base in the Bantu branch of the Niger-Congo family, are likely to survive.

VA: And Spanish?

IS: The fall of the last Moorish stronghold, Boabdil's Granada, and the consolidation of the Spanish Empire at the hands of the Catholic monarchs Ferdinand and Isabella, brought forth a unified national spirit. It coalesced under a single banner: one state, one religion, one language. It also recognized Spanish as the de facto official language. From his *cátedra* at the University of Salamanca, Antonio de Nebrija, who once was Bishop of Avila, is the spokesperson for the cause. "Language," he said in his prologue to the *Gramatica castellana*, published in the annus mirabilis of Spanish history, "has always been the perfect instrument of empire." He added: "After Your Highness takes under her yoke many barbarian towns and nations with strange tongues, and with the conquering of them, they will need to receive the laws that the conqueror puts on the conquered and with those, our language." At the time Sebastián de Covarrubias's *Tesoro de la lengua castellana o española* is released, under the aegis of the Holy Office of the Inquisition, in 1611—in between parts 1 and 2 of *Don Quixote*—he is ambivalent, even in the title, between the terms I mentioned before: *castellano* and *español*. Which one to use? The ambivalence remains palpable today.

VA: You've mentioned Nebrija and Bello. *ABC* in Madrid once described you as "our modern Nebrija."

IS: As a Renaissance man, Antonio Martínez de Cala y Jarava, born in Lebrija (Seville) and known to the world as Antonio de Nebrija, was a true humanist. He believed in language as a springboard (the *Scienza nuova* is the denotation given by Giambattista Vico) for the birth of a new man and a way to understand the universe as a whole. I would have loved to meet him. He was versed in Greek and Latin, the languages of erudition of his day and age. In addition to grammar, he was also committed to the study of theology, rhetoric, jurisprudence, history, medicine, and cosmogony. He believed Spanish to be "obra de la providencia."

VA: How about Andrés Bello?

IS: The Venezuelan Bello was a polymath of the first order. His mind moved in several directions at once: linguistics, poetry, jurisprudence, history . . . He founded the Universidad de Chile and was its chancellor from 1843 to 1865. His reflections on Spanish are incisive. He published lucid studies in lexicography and proposed a series of emendations to Spanish American orthography, most of which were rejected. His overall quest was to preserve the language as "media providencial de comunicación" of the people in the Americas so that "la confusión de idiomas, dialéctos, y jerigonzas, el caos babilónico de la Edad Media," could be avoided. To achieve his objective, he wrote the *Gramática de la lengua castellana destinada al uso de los americanos*. Pedro Henríquez Ureña thought highly of it. Almost four hundred years after Nebrija, he still understood Spanish to come from above, a gift from the Almighty.

VA: In a much-quoted essay, "Translation and Identity," you discuss the indigenous languages in the Americas. What kind of verbal landscape was there prior to 1492?

IS: Spain was in the midst of its misnomered Golden Age, *El Siglo de Oro*, when Christopher Columbus arrived in San Salvador. The admiral sent a couple of his captains, Rodrigo de Escobedo and Rodrigo Sánchez de Segovia, with instructions to keep an eye out as they and others took possession of the island. About the indigenous peoples, the Genoese admiral wrote in his diary: "They must be good servants, and intelligent, for I can see that they quickly repeat everything said to them. I believe they would readily become Christians; it appeared to me that they have no religion." Indeed, the Spanish language arrived *con fuerza* with the conquistadores. The type of unsophisticated adventurer-cum-knight interested in making the voyage was from Extremadura. The exception, for there is always one, was Hernán Cortés, who, although an Extremeño, had studied law, and his *Cartas de relación* show a clear and sophisticated mind. But let me answer your question from the subaltern's perspective. In the Americas, around two hundred distinguishable codes of communication were in use, from Aymara to Zapotec. In Mexico alone the linguistic variety was simply breathtaking. A list of aboriginal tongues includes Yumano, Chinanteco from Quiotepec, Chinanteco from Palantla, Chinanteco from Latani, Matlazinca, Zapoteco from Ixtlan, Mixteco, Amuzgo, Popoloca, Tepehua, Chol, Chontal from Tabasco, Tzeltal, Tzotzil, Tojolabal, Jacalteco, Kanjobal, Pima, Pápago, Yaqui, Cora, Huichol, Nahuatl, Purépecha, and Kikapú, to mention a few. The Iberian newcomers weren't interested in linguistic lushness, though. Their mission was to conquer and colonize. To accomplish their task, they brandished the sword and the cross. At first sight, the former might appear more powerful; in the long run, the latter probably had a longer-lasting impact.

VA: Through *catequismo?*

IS: *Catequismo* is a euphemism for spiritual and intellectual subjugation. It is the rationale behind the enterprise of mestizaje, i.e., the transculturation that resulted from the superimposition of Catholicism over the idolatrous religions of the pre-Columbian world. In retrospect, it can be argued that syncretism as a strategy is at the heart of the Hispanic American experience. It is also what characterizes the vicissitudes of Spanish in the United States. The capacity to absorb from the environment, to recycle that absorption while mixing it with our ancestral views, is a signature of our culture. Some describe this as the sign of colonialism. But colonialism isn't altogether negative; it offers resources to cope with hybrid times like ours.

VA: On the other hand, endorsing the native (though not always the nativist) viewpoint has been fashionable in Latin America.

IS: Think of Augusto Roa Bastos, José María Arguedas, Humberto Ak'abal, María Sabina, Rigoberta Menchú . . . And prior to them, Sor Juana Inés de la Cruz, *la Décima Musa*, who spoke of the magic and wisdom of the native peoples of Mexico.

¿Que mágicas infusiones
de los indios herbolarios
de mi patria, entre mis tetras
el hechizo derramaron?

In Margaret Sayers Peden's translation:

What are those magical infusions
of the herbalist Indians
of my land, that spread their spell
through all the letters from my pen?

In Sor Juana's century, just as in ours, the Indian population has tradi-
tionally remained *ninguneada*. The English equivalent is "ignored,"
but *ningunear*, an enchanting *mexicanismo*, is more idiosyncratic.
Among the scholars of Indian literature is one I admire profusely
and whose reputation in the United States is null: Fray Ángel María
Garibay. A priest and a rara avis in Mexican scholarship, Garibay is
unjustly unknown in the United States, especially among Latinos.
Dead in 1967 at the age of seventy-five, his erudition was of the highest
order. Although he was a Hebraist and a translator of Greek and Latin
classics, his major contribution is to be found in his interest in pre-
Columbian languages and literatures. He specialized in Nahuatl and
focused on the oeuvre of Fray Bernardino de Sahagún, the primary
source of information about Aztec civilization. The contemporary
thinker that most resembles him is his student, the remarkable Miguel
León-Portilla, author of the popular *The Vision of the Vanquished*.
Garibay was brave, a quality frequently missing in intellectuals.

VA: Why is "Spanish Golden Age" a misnomer?

IS: Have you ever read José Vasconcelos's *Breve historia de México?* It is
built on a triptych of fallacies: it isn't brief, nor is it a history; and it's
not about Mexico, really. The same ought to be said about el Siglo
de Oro español: it lasted longer than a century; gold was an excuse
for merciless abuses of power; and it wasn't only about Spain and its
citizens, but about a vast continent across the Atlantic sacked by the
voraciousness of the Iberian enterprise. A golden age for whom? Not
for the dwellers in the colonies; not for women, children, the ill, and
the unschooled; and certainly not for the Jews and Muslims on Spanish
soil. The year 1492 brought an end to *La Reconquista*. It also invited
Spain to use language as an instrument of colonization. It isn't unlike

the use by the United States today of the media to accomplish the task. Rock, blues, jazz, Hollywood movies, fashion, fast food are all badges of empire. Likewise, Spanish was the conduit that allowed the Iberian Peninsula to force itself on the native population.

VA: In the essay "Translation and Identity" you discuss translation as a modus vivendi in Spain and the Americas in the fifteenth century.

IS: Prior to the Expulsion Edict of 1492, urban centers like Toledo were emblems of cohabitation, *La Convivencia*. In the twelfth century, Toledo was home to the Escuela de Traductores (established by King Alfonso X, known as "the Wise"), to which Juda ben Moses ha-Kohen, a doctor in charge of revising the *Tablas Alfonsinas* as well as translating *El libro conplido en los iudizios de las estrellas*, was affiliated. The escuela also counted among its affiliates Ali Aben Rabel, also known as don Abraham, a personal physician to King Alfonso X, who translated Ibn Haitham; Isaac ibn Sid, who compiled *Los libros del saber de astronomía del Rey Alonso* in Spanish; and Juda Mosca, who translated *Lapidario* by Aegidius de Thebaldis. In Granada today a statue in honor of Yehuda ibn Tibón, perhaps the most distinguished translator of the escuela, stands proud. Spain has always been a cradle of languages and dialects. In addition, by the sixteenth century the educated crust of society was also fluent in Greek and Latin, and some had access to Aramaic and Hebrew. Overall, the period is known for its baroque inclinations. Borges described its style as verging on caricature. It certainly is one that emphasizes *las apariencias*, i.e., not reality, but the expression of reality. The Spanish saying "Las apariencias engañan" dates back to those times. Think of Nebrija's *Gramática* along with the *Comentarios reales* by the Inca Garcilaso, the comedias by Lope de Vega, and *Las soledades* by Luis de Góngora. And, of course, Baltasar Gracián's *Criticón*. Language was perceived as a veil. Translations, on the other hand, were tributes to the masters: Francisco de Quevedo pays homage to Torquato Tasso by rewriting him. And Cervantes imagined his novel *Don Quixote* to be a loose translation from an Arabic manuscript by one Cide Hamete Benengeli.

VA: Earlier in the conversation you mentioned the Bible. You've analyzed its various Spanish translations used in the New World, from colonial times to the present.

IS: The topic is perfect to·understand the intricate relationship between translation and empire. An edict from the Holy Office of the Inquisition issued in Toledo in 1551 forbade the translation of the Bible into Spanish and other vernaculars. But demography sooner or later sets the pattern of culture. The first translation was actually commissioned by Alfonso X in 1260; it is known as the *Biblia Alfonsina* or *española*. It is a paraphrase of the *Vulgata*. There are also the *Biblia de Alba*, preserved in the Biblioteca del Duque de Alba. And the Biblia of Alfonso V, translated from the Hebrew and Latin. The famous Biblia of Ferrara, Italy, appeared in 1553 translated from the Hebrew by two Portuguese Jews: Duarte Pinel (aka Abraham Usque) and Geronimo de Vargas (Yom Tov Levi Atias). In the latter, the syntax is strange; still, it is the principal source of dissemination of the Christian faith in the New World. There is also the so-called *Biblia del Oso* of 1569 and the rendition by Cipriano de Valera (1602). In other words, in spite of the edict, Spanish versions were made available. Furthermore, the history of those versions is an exercise in selective misreading: sexual scenes disappear, pagan references are attenuated, and the Jewishness of the text is made to justify the advent of Jesus Christ. Take the example of the *Biblia de Alba*. Don Luis de Guzmán, grand master of the Order of Calatrava, commissioned it. He sought "vna biblia en rromance, glosada e ystoriada," a Bible to be translated into *romance*. Its purpose, Guzman claimed, would be to make available the Holy Scripture in the language of the uncultured masses. The edition was to have explanations, annotations, commentary, and illustrations. Whom did de Guzmán commission it to? A rabbi by the name of Moses Arragel. In a long and tortured letter the rabbi adamantly refused the commission, raising all sorts of objections. It was precisely the letter, fifteen chapters' worth of explanation, which convinced de Guzmán that Arragel was the right man for the job. Skeptics argue that the rabbi's complaint was in fact an astute demonstration of his competence. In any case, Arragel refused the offer once, then agreed to the task. His translation was done in 1433 from the original Hebrew and Aramaic. It was funded by Pope John II. In his introduction (drafted after he completed the job), Arragel claims he is not about to criticize Christian beliefs nor praise Jewish ones. Yet he makes a record of the egregious incisions done to the text in the past. For instance, he writes: "Since I have done no more than relate or record [*memorar*], everyone is left free to believe, dispute [*disputar*], and defend their law as much as they can." But the rabbi did not shy away from pointing out "mistakes" in his commentaries, such as the one proffered after the translation of Exodus 1:5: *"Seventy souls.* In Hebrew there are no more [than this]; but in the translation of Saint Jerome there are 'seventy-five'; and it is the same in the *Actus Apostolorum,* chapter seven; and Nicolau de Lira says that the law mentions the number twice, once saying seventy, and the next seventy-five; but in the Hebrew there are only seventy in both instances." The reprints of the *Biblia de Alba* often left out Arragel's commentary. His own identity as a Jew was eclipsed. This sequence of abuses is proof that translation and manipulation have gone hand in hand.

VA: Let's explore more the crossroads of language and colonialism.

IS: As empires sally forth, their languages undergo contamination. To be exposed to other cultures is to lend and borrow. Imperial languages become mechanisms of control. But they are also transformed from the inside. Again, let's focus on Spanish. Its adventures on this side of the Atlantic Ocean might be seen as an attempt to breach the national borders, to explore other landscapes. But those explorations result in a weakening of the central linguistic core. To put it in other words, they expose the language to different influences. And those influences eventually shape its course. The Spanish of the Americas has indeed acquired its own characters, each modeled after a different natural and human climate. The variety of the River Plate is unique, as is the one from Lima. Then there are the vernaculars Lunfardo and Cocoliche from Argentina (mainly from Buenos Aires) that incorporate Italian words; and there are creoles like Opita, Valluno, and Rolo from Colombia. These are comparable to Cockney, Joual, Gaunersprache, Gíria, Bargoens, Germanía, Hiant-Chang, and Gergo, among others.

VA: Is Lunfardo like Spanglish?

IS: To some extent. Borges was quite interested in Lunfardo. In fact, everything about the Argentine language fascinated him. Along with José Edmundo Clemente, he published a slim volume in 1968, *El lenguaje de Buenos Aires,* which includes his essays "El idioma de los argentinos," "Las alarmas del doctor América Castro," and a curious meditation, "Las inscripciones en los carros," on the aphorisms found painted on Argentine vehicles. About Lunfardo Borges said: "Es jerigonza ocultadiza de los ladrones. El lunfardo es un vocabulario

gremial como tantos otros; es la tecnología de la furca y de la gánzua"
(It is the enigmatic slang of thieves. Lunfardo is an occupationally specific language, just like any other: it is the technology of muggers and
picklocks). In other words, the language of crime and prostitution.
The author of "The Aleph" argued that authentic Argentine poetry
was to be found in the lyrics of tangos and milongas. But Lunfardo is
the language of cant born in Argentina in the second half of the nineteenth century. It is defined by class. Spanglish is more multitudinous.
It goes beyond a particular social group. It isn't a mere vocabulary of
displeasure and aggression.

VA: You've accused the Real Academia Española (RAE) of maintaining a tight fist on the speakers of Spanish. You've also criticized
the *Diccionario de la lengua española* (DRAE) as an instrument of
repression.

IS: The RAE is stuck in the past. Gabriel García Márquez, also one of its
critics, once lost count of the time it takes for a word coined in Quito,
Ecuador, to make it to the DRAE. Its members believe their eighteenth-
century institution is responsible for safeguarding the Spanish language. Safeguarding it from what? Their motto is "Limpia, fija, y da
esplendor," which—and I'm not the first to suggest it—sounds like a
detergent commercial. There are approximately 40 million people in
Spain. The total number of Spanish-language speakers in the world is
estimated at 400 million. In Mexico alone there are over 100 million.
And the number of Latinos in the United States is over 40 million.
Why should Spain remain the central command? Shouldn't a less cen-
tralized, more democratic approach to the language of Cervantes and
Nebrija, with that of Sor Juana, Darío, and Borges, be devised? The
affiliates of the RAE never act as independent units. They are extremi-
ties of the one in Madrid.

VA: An empire always refuses to look at its colonies as equals.

IS: Instead, it sees its own efforts at educating the colonials—*los bár-
baros*—as philanthropic. Lately I've been reading about the pater-
nalistic attitude of the British toward India. For instance, in 1835,
Thomas Babington Macaulay—later known as Lord Macaulay—
addressed the question of what type of culture should the population
of India be exposed to under British rule. Should the natives learn science in English? Today his response sounds like an endorsement of

conservativism. It reminds me of Saul Bellow's statement, in an op-ed piece published in the *New York Times* in 1988, at the height of the culture wars, in which he asked: "Who is the Tolstoy of the Zulus? The Proust of the Papuans?" Similarly, Lord Macaulay argued: "All parties seem to be agreed on one point, that the dialects commonly spoken among the natives of this part of India, contain neither literary nor scientific information, and are, moreover, so poor and rude that, until they are enriched from some other quarter, it will not be easy to translate any valuable work into them. It seems to be admitted on all sides, that the intellectual improvement of those classes of the people who have the means of pursuing higher studies can at present be effected only by means of some language not vernacular amongst them. What then shall that language be? One-half of the Committee maintains that it should be the English. The other half strongly recommends the Arabic and Sanskrit. The whole question seems to me to be, which language is the best worth knowing?"

VA: I assume Lord Macaulay chose English.

IS: He was an honest man. "I have no knowledge of either Sanskrit or Arabic," he said. Lord Macaulay then goes on to justify the superiority of European civilization. "I have done what I could to form a correct estimate of their value," he added. "I have read translations of the most celebrated Arabic and Sanskrit works. I have conversed both here and at home with men distinguished by their proficiency in the Eastern tongues. I am quite ready to take the Oriental learning at the valuation of the Orientalists themselves. I have never found one among them who could deny that a single shelf of a good European library was worth the whole native literature of India and Arabia. The intrinsic superiority of the Western literature is, indeed, fully admitted by those members of the Committee who support the Oriental plan of education." Finally, Lord Macaulay stated: "It will hardly be disputed, I suppose, that the department of literature in which the Eastern writers stand highest is poetry. And I certainly never met with any Orientalist who ventured to maintain that the Arabic and Sanskrit poetry could be compared to that of the great European nations. But when we pass from works of imagination to works in which facts are recorded, and general principles investigated, the superiority of the Europeans becomes absolutely immeasurable. It is, I believe, no exaggeration to say, that all the historical information which has been collected from all the books written in the Sanskrit language is less valuable than what may be found in the most paltry abridgements used at preparatory schools in England. In every branch of physical or moral philosophy, the relative position of the two nations is nearly the same."

VA: I like his use of the word *relative*.

IS: Lord Macaulay could be described as a relativist, even though his ideas are absolutist.

VA: In sum, you don't see empire as evil, do you?

IS: Empire is a synonym of progress. To be against it is to fall into an idealistic trap. There have always been, and will always be, colonizers and colonized. In linguistic terms, they push language to change. English is often described as the lingua franca of today. Yet as it reaches beyond its boundaries, it is undergoing dramatic transformations, giving room to spin-offs like Spanglish. It isn't improbable that one day these spin-offs will become imperial themselves. It is part of the same cycle.

[2007]

AGAINST BIOGRAPHY

(with Donald Yates)

DONALD YATES: Do you think it is difficult to write about a living author?

ILAN STAVANS: My approach, and perhaps the approach of all biographers, is to see the biographee as dead, not because one prefers him to be in the grave, but because the past, in spite of its instability, isn't a moving target, at least not as much as the present, and certainly far less than the future.

DY: What do you mean by "unstable"?

IS: The past is always open to reinterpretation. But the facts are set.

DY: Would you agree that García Márquez is probably the most prominent Latin American author writing today?

IS: His work is enormously influential. My biography uses him as a compass to explore how Latin American culture changes in the twentieth century, from being a backwater landscape to becoming the stage for magical realism. García Márquez, as you know, is the leading exponent of that aesthetic trend, which remains incredibly amorphous, not to say controversial. In particular, I'm fascinated by the fact that in the age of the Internet, García Márquez's exoticism remains hypnotizing to such wide audiences, maybe because the more wired we get, the stronger is our longing for a simpler, more primitive way of being.

DY: Unlike the case with Borges, the Internet is alien to García Márquez's world.

IS: Intrinsically, yes, but in the Internet age García Márquez's fame has spread at the speed of light. Google his name and you get more than 35 million hits—not bad for a *mamador de gallos*, a teaser, according to the popular Colombian expression, one who made his way from the misbegotten coastal town of Aracataca to the international stage in 1967 with a novel that, when published in Buenos Aires, altogether changed the way people perceive the Americas.

DY: In what way?

IS: Before 1967, when *One Hundred Years of Solitude* appeared, the former Spanish colonies on this side of the Atlantic were perceived as backward, undeveloped, and unworthy of high-caliber literature. After the novel's publication, the same views acquired an altogether different tone. Latin America was still primitive, but it held itself closely to its ancestral mythology, a fact García Márquez vindicated with his portrait of Macondo. The region's premodern status had an explanation.

DY: Would you say he romanticized the region's past?

IS: García Márquez's fiction is romantic in that it describes a habitat where modernity hasn't been fully digested. In *One Hundred Years of Solitude*, one of my all-time favorite books, technology—a mnemonic machine, for instance—has miraculous qualities. There are also trains, planes, automobiles, and other devices, of course, yet Macondo, even at the end, feels pristine. In contrast, Borges, who was García Márquez's elder by almost three decades, in stories like "The Aleph," "The Library of Babel," and "The Garden of Forking Paths," foretold the advent of the World Wide Web. Interest in Borges remains undiminished since he became an international sensation in the early sixties because he forces the reader to be active but also, and to a large extent, because of his prophetic talents. Isn't it ironic that a blind, self-taught man from Buenos Aires without any advanced degree was able to see further than most of his contemporaries?

DY: Borges dealt with what we could call unmeasurables—infinity, eternity, identity, metaphysical questions that can have no prescribed containment. Therefore, no matter how technology expands, Borges's chosen themes will place him outside of and untouched by the finite concerns of others. I suppose you could say he was always seeking to attain inconceivable limits.

IS: Indeed, there's a tendency—obnoxious, in my eyes—to paint him as outwardly superhuman. To me his concerns, philosophical and literary, were quite earthly. Don't we all dream of God as a puppeteer?

DY: No doubt some persons do. But despite the helplessly deterministic image that concept entails—obviously, it is a way of suggesting the nature of our existence—Borges couldn't have embraced it.

IS: I disagree. Although he espouses free will, Borges is a fervent supporter of determinism.

DY: For Borges there would constantly be someone behind the puppeteer manipulating him, and then behind that presence someone else who was . . . The mirror is something that invariably troubled him, a recurring object in his writings. Place the puppeteer between two facing mirrors, and then attempt to identify which of the resulting images is the last of them. I find Borges permanently seeking what could be considered the first cause but repeatedly coming up short. *Seeking* is a key word in understanding his writings. His stories and essays so often take the form of inquiries that in the end fail to come up with a final answer. Even, as you note, in "Death and the Compass." He gave what I think was a revealing title to his first book of essays, published in 1925: *Inquisitions*.

IS: I have a different opinion. He doesn't resign himself to failure. Instead, he finds the first cause an amusing if childish idea. This is because Borges is interested, not in the end of a search, but in the act—and art—of searching. Proof of it is his pseudo review "The Approach to Al-Mu'tasim" and the story "Averroës's Search." He employs the word *inquisition*, with stringent, morally unavoidable connotations in Spanish, playfully.

DY: So we have differing views of what the search meant for Borges. You believe that the search, writing about the search, was its own justification. My belief is that he truly wanted to find the consolation of some sort of final revelation, and I do perceive in his writings a sense of melancholy despair—in no way an underlying attitude of playfulness—over his not having been able to achieve that. But let me move on. Have you met García Márquez?

IS: Yes, briefly. And I have books signed by him to me. But I have no interest in official biographies.

DY: Do you mean biographies that have the blessing of the subject or of his estate? Are you saying that there is really no intrinsic merit in this seal of approval?

IS: I'm against biography. I'm appalled by the way it has become an apology, an exoneration of the causes of human frailty. In their work biographers build a rationale that allows them to tolerate the intolerable behavior in their subjects. I'm not interested in that. I'm only attracted to biography as an excuse. I believe the genre of biography—looking at the curve of a person's life from birth to death— offers a valuable strategy to understand the way talent is shaped, the strategies used to respond to the stimulation from the environment, what maturity is, et cetera. I not only approach García Márquez's life, but I use him as a compass to understand the intellectual transformation taking place in Latin America in the second half of the twentieth century. After all, he's been at the center of crucial historical moments: he was a child when the massacre of workers took place in La Ciénaga; he witnessed El Bogotazo, when the left-wing political leader Eliécer Gaitán was assassinated, while he was a college student; he worked for Prensa Latina, Cuba's news agency, soon after Fidel Castro consolidated his power in Havana; he was a public face in the fight against right-wing dictatorships like Augusto Pinochet's in Chile; he was involved in the Heberto Padilla affair; he was close to the Sandinista Revolution in Nicaragua; he befriended not only Castro but President Bill Clinton, among other master politicians; he served as a mediator with Subcomandante Marcos and the Zapatistas in Chiapas; and so on.

DY: Why do the García Márquez biography in two volumes?

IS: My original intention was to approach the endeavor in a single volume. But the information was enormous and the space to reflect on it insufficient. I wanted to process the material as a cultural critic, not as a standard biographer. Plus my editor was eager to bring the work out while García Márquez is still alive. So I suggested dividing the project in two. The first volume deals with his life from his birth in 1927 to the moment the English-language translation of *One Hundred Years of Solitude*, by Gregory Rabassa, was released in 1970.

DY: Is there a rationale for the cutoff date?

IS: I'm an American critic, even though I was born in Mexico. In my biography I look at García Márquez from that perspective. Obviously I pay enormous attention to the *Rezeptionsgeschichte* in the Spanish-language world, but my primary audience is in the United States.

DY: The first volume is being published in early 2010, is that right?

IS: Yes, it's called *Gabriel García Márquez: The Early Years*.

DY: And the second?

IS: I will wait until after García Márquez's death. I need to digest what that death will mean . . . Needless to say, there have been other biographers: Mario Vargas Llosa, Dasso Saldívar, and the "anointed" Gerald Martin.

DY: I have seen the Vargas Llosa book. What was the title? I believe there was some controversy over it.

IS: It was his doctoral dissertation in Madrid: *García Márquez: Historia de un deicidio*. Years ago, my parents found a copy of the 1971 Monte Ávila edition and gave it to me as a present. It's a rather admirable exercise, even though it contains some errors. But after a fistfight between them, the Peruvian forbade any reprint of it.

DY: Do you believe the biographer, if he is the biographee's contemporary, should spend time with the author?

IS: I don't. Biography and fiction have a common goal: to make an invented person's life believable in the eyes of the reader. One uses facts and the other uses the imagination, but the difference is inconsequential. Your case is different, since not only did you meet Borges but you became his friend. Does friendship tarnish any appearance of objectivity in your task as biographer?

DY: When New Criticism came into vogue, it held the extreme position that details associated with an author's day-to-day life had no bearing on the evaluation of his writings. In other words, the text is all there is to work with. More recently, we have seen a trend develop that moves away from the view that information related to the author's existence is inconsequential. If you believe that this is a reasonable position to adopt, wouldn't you agree that there could be some validity in taking one step further and acknowledging that a personal relationship with the author could provide additional insight into the interpretation of his work?

IS: I'm not sure. Are you writing a biography or a memoir?

DY: My book on Borges will have a dimension that sets it apart from those biographies written by persons who had no significant relationship with him. In the final analysis, a biographer works with what he has.

IS: Why not just write a memoir? Maybe I can anticipate your answer: you don't want to produce a narrative about how you met Borges, what the two of you did together, but to use your privileged insider's view to explicate why he looked at the world the way he did.

DY: A book that would deal only with a friendship—what we said and did over the years of our relationship—would, as you intimate, be very deficient, not only in its capacity to explain his view of the world, but in meeting the expectations of the reader of a biography: to offer an explanation of what that author wrote and why he wrote what he did.

IS: Didn't Emir Rodríguez Monegal and María Esther Vázquez do exactly that? The two of them knew Borges well, maybe better than you, and still produced biographies, the first in 1978, the second in 1996. In my mind, Rodríguez Monegal, who taught at Yale, ended up producing a strikingly unappealing psychoanalytic case study. On the other hand, Vázquez's effort is more enjoyable.

DY: Rodríguez Monegal called his book a "literary biography," by which he meant that he intended to focus on the texts that Borges wrote himself or with the participation of friends or interviewers and move all "the usual biographical data" to a subordinate role. This pleased Borges, who admired reticence in biographies. He adopted as his framing device Borges's "Autobiographical Essay," written with his friend and translator, Norman Thomas di Giovanni, and published in the *New Yorker* in 1970. Rodríguez Monegal reproduced much of Borges's original text and interjected his own information into the interstices. Admittedly, downplaying "the usual biographical data" and stressing only written texts is a difficult position for a biographer to maintain, and, in fact, Rodríguez Monegal was tempted to indulge in a certain amount of psychological theorizing that some critics thought was the principal flaw in an otherwise admirable evocation of the Buenos Aires literary milieu from which Borges emerged.

María Esther Vázquez, who in 1977 and 1984 had published collections of interviews with Borges together with much biographical information, expanded this material into a full-length study called *Borges esplendor y derrota* (Borges, Splendor and Defeat), which she published as a biography. Vázquez was an important figure in Borges's life for some twenty-five years, a fact that she doesn't downplay in these pages. I consider her book to be a blend—as mine will be—of memoir and biography.

IS: Just like you, Rodríguez Monegal actually wrote his biography in English, as did James Woodall and Edwin Williamson. In your view, what's there at stake in writing the biography of a subject in a language that wasn't his?

DY: I don't see anything crucial at play here. The merit of the study should reasonably attach to the qualities of the biographer, in whatever language he writes. You'll recall that Borges wrote his "Autobiographical Essay" with di Giovanni in English. It and Rodríguez Monegal's book both eventually found their way into Spanish. I see nothing inherently inappropriate in that process.

IS: You're missing something important. By choosing to write the "Autobiographical Essay" in English, Borges was catering to an American audience. He inserted himself into the autobiographical tradition of the New England transcendentalists, Oscar Wilde, and William and Henry James. Had the piece been written originally in Spanish, it would have been dramatically different. In fact, throughout his life Borges refused to allow the piece to be made available in Spanish, as if he wanted to keep an intimate part of his life away from Spanish-language readers. A pirated version circulated for some time, yet the official translation by Aníbal González, with María Kodama's seal of approval, appeared in 1999 under the imprimatur of Galaxia Gutenberg/Círculo de Lectores/Emecé, thirteen years after Borges's death, to coincide with the centennial of his birth. As is the case of memoir, writing biography in a specific language means targeting a particular audience. It also means inserting oneself into a specific literary tradition. Let me expand this thesis a bit. As literary genres, both memoir and biography have developed differently in English and Spanish. This is because the cultures that fostered these parallel traditions understood personal revelation—and indiscretion—in dramatically different ways. An artifact like Domingo Faustino Sarmiento's *Facundo; or, Civilization and Barbarism* shared little with *The Education of Henry Adams*. I'm using two random yet significant examples to make my case. Others by people like Sor Juana Inés de la Cruz, Frederick Douglass, Richard Rodriguez, and Rigoberta Menchú could likewise be cited. Sarmiento's book is a hybrid—part diatribe about the gauchos in Argentine, part political argument against the Rosas tyranny. *Henry Adams*, instead, is an experiment in the limits of democracy. By opting to write in English (even though, as you pointed out, translation spreads the gospel across borders) the memorialist and biographer use a set of tools that respond to the needs of a singular civilization. In doing so, there's stuff that needs to be digested that might seem obvious to the audience in another language.

DY: I have a different view of Borges's attitude toward his "Autobiographical Essay." We really owe its composition to di Giovanni, who had heard Borges speak often and at length about his life and career and believed that much valuable information could be brought together in a single coherent account of his experiences. He urged Borges to work with him in setting all this down in an essay that could be included in the collection of his translations of a number of Borges's stories that he had committed to preparing for E. P. Dutton in New York. That book was published in 1970, with the title *The Aleph and Other Stories (1933–1969)*. Di Giovanni had negotiated a contract that entailed book publication by Dutton and a "first refusal" clause that gave the *New Yorker* magazine first look at anything that di Giovanni and Borges produced together. So from the outset, Borges understood that his audience would be primarily North American. Accordingly, he offered explanations and elaborations of subjects that would be perfectly familiar to an Argentine reading audience. When di Giovanni pushed for the essay's translation and publication in Buenos Aires, Borges balked, pointing out that those unnecessary clarifications of Argentine topics would make him seem ridiculous. This apparently created some friction between them. I honestly don't think Borges was concerned, as you say, about keeping an intimate part of his life away from Spanish-language readers. There cannot have been much of a confessional nature revealed in that essay that Borges had not already put forth in the scores of interviews he had given over the years to Argentine journalists.

IS: I've heard the story about how the "Autobiographical Essay" was crafted and the way the relationship between Borges and di Giovanni deteriorated to the point that di Giovanni was all but excluded from the three volumes prepared by Viking under the tutelage of María Kodama, and with the supervision of the Andrew Wiley literary agency, for the centennial celebrations. Indeed, much has been said about the actual breakup with di Giovanni and the extent to which he was not a translator but a bully. I spoke with him a number of times in London in the late nineties. He viewed himself as having been wronged by Borges's small circle of friends. In any case, Borges's naïveté is never what it pretends to be. But let's go back to biography. In total, there are at least a dozen biographies of Borges. In fact, I venture to think that no other Latin American writer has been biographed with such insistence.

DY: I think that Borges's writings have a certain quality about them that seems to invite comment, provoke reaction, and to discourage the reader from adopting a passive attitude toward what he is reading. In some persons, the biography is a way of responding to this feature of his writing. In others, it calls for some sort of examination or probing or interpretation. You are well aware of how many hundreds and hundreds of articles and books have been written about Borges. The number is astonishing and shows no sign of tapering off. It is as if Borges were holding a mirror up to his readers and drawing out of them a deeply personal response.

IS: Is there a need for another biography?

DY: Of the existing biographies that you indicate, two of the recent ones have been written by persons who didn't know him. My contact with Borges and his work goes back well over half a century and extends over those years when I had access to him—and to his family and friends—and during which he gave me a lot of information in response to questions I asked about him and his work that I dutifully wrote down. I will stake out my own perspective and have my own things to say. The book will be a hybrid of sorts, an overview of his literary career together with an accounting of my personal relationship with him.

IS: Borges himself loved to write microbiographies. Examples of these are everywhere in his oeuvre, starting with *A Universal History of Infamy*. He was also an avid reader of standard biographies. But he could never write one himself.

DY: You are right about the microbiographies. He believed that the essence of a person's life could be captured in just a few scenes. It is true, too, that he was skeptical of the standard biographical model. He once archly suggested that there is a degree of implausibility inherent in a book in which a person undertakes to communicate to someone else the thoughts and experiences that belonged exclusively to a third person. But you'll recall that he did experiment with the biographical genre in 1930 when he put together his impressionistic account of the life and works of the young Argentine poet of the Buenos Aires outskirts, Evaristo Carriego. It is anything but a traditional biography. It was perhaps to acknowledge or justify his bringing together descriptions of aspects only loosely related to Carriego's life that he prefaced the book with an epigram from De Quincey. It read: "A mode of truth; not of truth coherent and central, but of truth angular and splintered."

IS: *Evaristo Carriego* is closer to what I think a biography should do: not only deliver facts but interpret them. Information isn't knowledge. But I'm still unclear as to what the function of the biographical genre is for you.

DY: In general, I believe its purpose is to satisfy the curiosity of its reader. This depends on the subject of the book. In the case of a biography of an author, the reader is most likely to be a person familiar with that author's work. I would say that he reads the biography in search of clues to the experiences in the author's life that led him to write what and how he did. Do you agree?

IS: For me biography is less about an individual than about a culture. Of course, one cannot write a study of the entire Hispanic civilization but . . .

DY: Although you did exactly that in 1996 with *The Hispanic Condition*, a sociohistorical investigation into Latino life in the United States.

IS: But that book isn't a biography. What attracts me to biography is that it can seek to understand not only an important cultural player but the culture that shapes him too.

DY: Your view of biography is more encompassing. Have you written one before?

IS: Only a small meditation called *Bandido: The Death and Resurrection of Oscar "Zeta" Acosta*, about a Chicano lawyer and activist during the civil rights era who disappeared mysteriously in 1973 in Mazatlán, Mexico. Zeta wrote a couple of cult books: *The Revolt of the Cockroach People* and *The Autobiography of a Brown Buffalo*. Other books of mine, including *Resurrecting Hebrew*, about Eliezer Ben-Yehuda, an early Zionist who was instrumental in adapting biblical Hebrew to modern times, rotate around a probing figure who, as I see it, is at the vortex of multiple forces: political, religious, ethnic, and cultural.

DY: How different would your García Márquez biography be if you wrote it in Spanish?

IS: An altogether different book. Being an immigrant, I cherish my role as an interloper. I look at American civilization from the outside in. And I'm no longer an insider in Mexico either. My volumes of García Márquez are written from the edge—*desde la orilla*. I'm sure you'll understand the concept, since la orilla is an archetypical ingredient in Borges's oeuvre. Not only did he write also from the edge, but he had a fascination with *los orilleros*.

DY: Yes, Borges himself was an orillero by nature, a man from the fringe, in no way "downtown" or mainstream. That was an integral aspect of his character and contributed greatly to the particular voice in which he wrote. Borges may have had his differences with his brother-in-law, the Spanish critic Guillermo de Torre, but the latter identified as well as anyone the source of Borges's outsider's perspective. He said that Borges had "an attitude of innate distrust of anything affirmative and a perverse preference for doubts and perplexities of a philosophical as well as aesthetic nature." That says a lot.

IS: Staying on the topic of language, I want to talk more about translation. You translated portions of *Labyrinths*, with James Irby, in 1962. How did the project originate?

DY: In a graduate class I took at the University of Michigan in 1954 taught by Enrique Anderson-Imbert, one of the required reading texts was a collection of Borges's short stories titled *La muerte y la brújula*. I had long been a devotee of detective fiction and had begun writing crime stories myself. I was so impressed with the brilliance and originality of the title story, which was Borges's version of a traditional detective-versus-criminal narrative, that I immediately wanted to try to bring it into English. Through an Argentine friend, I was able to secure Borges's authorization to undertake the translation.

After "Death and the Compass," Borges encouraged me to take on more translations from that collection, as well as from a volume of detective short stories that he had written with his friend Adolfo Bioy-Casares, called *Six Problems for Don Isidro Parodi*. Or, in fact, anything else of his that I thought might have some promise.

I translated three more stories from *La muerte y la brújula* as well as the first of the Don Isidro Parodi cases and began to consider the possibility of assembling a book-length collection of his work in English. In time, after several rejections, I was offered a contract by James Laughlin at New Directions. When I learned that my former classmate at Michigan, James Irby, who was writing his dissertation with Anderson-Imbert on the subject of the structure of Borges's stories, had also been translating a number of his prose pieces—essays and fiction—just to get the feel of his style, I asked if he would let me read them. Seeing that they were very good, I asked him if he would like to join me in the New Directions project, and he agreed. That was the start. We found a number of other existing translations that we liked and got permission to include them, too. *Labyrinths: Selected Writings of Jorge Luis Borges*, with a preface by André Maurois, appeared in the spring of 1962.

IS: Arguably, this was the volume that introduced Borges to the English-speaking world. It has gone through a zillion reprints. Was he pleased with it?

DY: As you know, Borges's long-time friend and collaborator Adolfo Bioy-Casares kept a diary of their countless conversations, carried out usually after dinner at Bioy's home, where Borges for years commonly spent his evenings. A sixteen-hundred-page volume published in 2006 miraculously—and even mysteriously—reproduces hundreds of hours of their conversations. In an entry for July of 1962, I find that Borges's initial reaction to the New Directions publication of *Labyrinths* was not very favorable. He said he didn't like its physical appearance, which he claimed was an important feature of a book. Oddly, however, his description of it didn't match the book's appearance. More serious was his dissatisfaction with the translations. He appeared to think that it had been translated by a single person. But there were seven translators in all. He said that the book's "translator" commonly looked for the easiest similar English term for a Spanish word. He gave the example of *habitación* being translated as "habitation" instead of "room." I have no idea where that occurred. Nonetheless, he was very cordial and open with me when I came to Buenos Aires a month later. You're right, the book has been very successful. Especially in England, where the Penguin edition of *Labyrinths* is regarded as a kind of classic.

IS: I understand that Borges came to Michigan State University on four occasions: 1969, 1972, 1975, and 1976. The last of these was as visiting professor for four months. Talk to me about this experience.

DY: Late in 1969, Borges and di Giovanni came to the States for a symposium to be held at the University of Oklahoma. They arrived early so that they could visit other schools where they had been invited. On his first trip to East Lansing, Borges spoke about his work and answered questions posed by di Giovanni before a large and appreciative audience. In 1972, he returned to Michigan to receive an honorary doctorate, after which he and I set out on a cross-country lecture tour. In 1975, the MSU Department of English dedicated its annual literary conference to Borges and his work. My assignment was to go to Buenos Aires and bring him back for a week in October. He so enjoyed the experience and the glorious autumn weather (which he had to sense, since he had lost his sight in 1955) that he asked if there were some way for him to return for a longer stay. I said it might be possible during the next academic term in the winter of 1976. He came in January, accompanied by María Kodama, and stayed until April. He taught two classes in the Department of Romance Languages and gave a series of public lectures in English, and we traveled to many places. That was a very important period in my life.

IS: The angle of detective fiction is at the center of Borges' enterprise, starting with "Death and the Compass." You've been attracted to it since early on and have never ceased to trace its contributions to his narrative structures and techniques.

DY: That is true. In fact, I think we could go all the way back to Borges's first attempt at writing his own prose fiction to find his employment of a crime narrative technique. That was the story that has come to be known as "Man on Pink Corner," which was included in *A Universal History of Infamy*, published in 1935. "Death and the Compass" came some seven years later, but it is certainly his major contribution to detective fiction literature. The more I examine his writings the more I am convinced that this genre has informed a considerable part of his work. It entails, after all, a traditional structure that an author fills out in his own individual, and oftentimes inimitable, way. That was certainly the case with "Death and the Compass." You know the story well, Ilan. No one had ever written a detective tale like that before. Not even Chesterton, whom Borges admired greatly. In fact, that story is like a Father Brown tale in reverse. Borges wasn't interested in writing genre stories of a sort that other authors had written before. That is one of the important features of his narrative genius: a profound disregard for the commonplace.

IS: Although little known, detective fiction in Latin America is an important genre.

DY: More so now than ever before. The manifestations in Latin America of what is called "popular culture" have emerged today as respectable subjects for academic study. You, Ilan, have written a book on that topic—your *Antihéroes*, published in 1993, and later in English translation in 1997. The subtitle is *Mexico and Its Detective Novel*. Popular culture, it seems, is at the core of how you see the world.

IS: Even though Borges and García Márquez are considered highbrow—more so the Argentine than the Colombian—the fact is that both are committed to what you describe as popular culture. Borges wasn't only interested in detective fiction (the armchair version), but in science fiction, too. "The Aleph" is a tribute to, among others, H. G. Wells; and "Tlön, Uqbar, Orbis Tertius" is a futuristic story, just like "A Weary Man's Utopia" and maybe "August 25, 1983." Plus he wrote for women's magazines like *El Hogar*. García Márquez also infuses his fiction with pop artifacts: the anonymous placards in *In Evil Hour*, for instance; or the references to *cumbias*, airplanes, and the Wandering Jew in *One Hundred Years of Solitude*.

DY: Let me get back for a moment to the obligations of the biographer. To what extent should travel be one of the biographer's basic tools?

IS: To a large extent. That travel shouldn't only be geographical, it should also be cultural.

DY: In what sense?

IS: Biography is the art of looking at one culture intimately by using a chosen subject as a road map. I traveled to Colombia, Spain, and Mexico to research García Márquez's life. But my travels were also through conversations, food, dance, TV, and movies. How about you?

DY: Between 1962 and 2008, I made seventeen visits to Buenos Aires, several for the space of a year (sabbaticals, Fulbrights, et cetera). Traveling to Buenos Aires has been like returning to a second home. This has allowed me to become familiar with the *porteño* way of life and most importantly to accompany Borges for long periods on his daily rounds. You mentioned conversation as a key factor in absorbing a sense of the place where you are. This was especially true of time spent with Borges because conversation was a vital necessity for him, as it is for you. He was absolutely tireless, both physically and mentally, and seemed uncomfortable with letting a dialogue lapse into silence.

IS: Although I believe travel is crucial for translation, I recently had a conversation with Richard Wilbur, who told me the opposite: translation doesn't derive from direct geographical experience. I don't know if you're aware of it, but Wilbur translated some of Borges's poems without knowing any Spanish. What do you think?

DY: Poetry involves many subtle and mysterious factors, but what you say Wilbur accomplished is one that I honestly have never considered. I should think that he would have had to replace the use of a good English-Spanish/Spanish-English dictionary with some other source of enlightenment regarding the words he was bringing into English.

IS: Wilbur believes a good translator is first and foremost a good poet. And a good poet, to do a fine translation, can go a long way by seeking help from someone in that original culture—a cultural mediator—who is able to convey the meaning, tone, and intention of the poem. He translated Anna Akhmatova in the same way.

DY: Now that you explain it, this process seems reasonable. And, as you say, beginning with a good poet is a prime consideration.

IS: Still, translation has been a passion of mine.

DY: And one of mine, too. Aside from my role in putting together *Labyrinths*, I have translated novels and short stories by many River Plate authors. Recently, I've been translating the stories of a virtually unknown Argentine writer named Edgar Brau. I think he is enormously talented, and he has a recognizable debt to Borges. In 2006, Michigan State University Press published his *Casablanca and Other Stories*. And I've just finished the translation of Brau's *Argentine Suite*, a collection of four narratives that deal with the torture and "disappearance" of suspected subversives in Argentina during what has come to be called the Dirty War. So the passion continues unabated.

IS: What appeals to you in the art of translation?

DY: Well, I never had to answer that question before. I began by translating the detective stories of Argentine author and translator (English to Spanish) Rodolfo Jorge Walsh. He, in turn, translated my fiction. It seemed like a comfortable way to cement a relationship between two persons from two different parts of the world who were both writers and translators. When it came to Borges, I was so dazzled by his brilliance that I considered it an honor to bring to a new audience—in what he called his "preferred language"—the manifestations of a literary talent that I had not encountered before. With time, the act of translation became for me a gesture of friendship extended to Argentine and Uruguayan authors whom I had met. I have translated very little that was not written by people that I have known personally. Now that I'm giving it some thought, what appeals to me is that translations are in a way like a scotch and soda and a cigar shared with a friend in a magical space.

IS: A gesture of friendship. I'm moved by your thought. Translation is also, at times, the opposite: an invitation to obfuscation. As translators, we paint ourselves as agents of dialogue. But egotism plays a far larger role than is often acknowledged. Recently I've been reviewing the twenty-something full-fledged English translations of *Don Quixote*. The bunch of translators involved in the task indulged not only in plagiarism but in backstabbing.

DY: Well, that's unfortunate. Since a translator is essentially a sort of selfless volunteer, whose role in authorship is automatically reduced to a secondary level, it's disturbing that so much larceny and ego should come into play. In your case, Ilan, I note that translation is something unusual. You write in both English and Spanish and have translated back and forth from these languages. And you have also translated from the French, Hebrew, and Yiddish.

IS: I believe the translator's authorship is no longer secondary. It might have been that way for centuries, but translators are more activists now than they used to be. They are simultaneously friends and confidants, literary critics, book agents, and in-house editors. All these activities are performed for miserable pay but not a meager reputation. In any case, probably the most decisive moment in my life took place in 1985, when I picked up my things and, as an immigrant, moved to the United States. I knew the effort would be decisive, but I couldn't have envisioned its infinite consequences.

DY: Such as?

IS: The moment is a marker: it delineates my life into a "before" and an "after." Everything I've done is connected with it. I not only acquired a new language but I adopted a new self: a new personality. Being a bilingual writer means having two homes. Or, better, it suggests living in a permanent state of transit. For me translation isn't a profession but a way of life. On a daily basis I navigate different realms by employing different tongues.

DY: And you've also studied the mixing of some of those tongues, like Spanglish.

IS: Yes, I'm fascinated by the *zona liminar*, the border region, the in-betweeness that connects people from different realities.

DY: Is biography also a zona liminar for you?

IS: Unquestionably.

DY: In the end, Ilan, I think we are expressing, with different words, a similar sense of satisfaction in our translating and are in agreement that biography is a genre that needs to be tested. Thank you for having passed on to me your insights.

[2009]

REDRAWING
THE *HISTORIETA*

(with Neal Sokol)

NEAL SOKOL: You have acknowledged to be a huge fan of the tradition of Mexican comic strips—known as *historietas*—as well as of José Guadalupe Posada's "lampoons for the masses." And you've written a seminal essay on Latin American poster art, called "The Art of the Ephemeral." You are also an admirer of the graphic novel and underground comics pioneers Will Eisner and Art Spiegelman. Let me start by asking you: strictly speaking, is *Mr. Spic Goes to Washington*, the third installment (after *Latino USA* [2000] and *¡Lotería!* [2001]) in your series of artistic collaborations that attempt to marry "highbrow and pop culture," a *historieta?*

ILAN STAVANS: *Historieta* is the Spanish word for a comic strip. It refers to a graphic narrative designed to entertain and, on occasion, to educate. In Mexico, I spent my teens reading historietas made in the country or in other parts of Latin America for internal consumption: *Condorito, La familia Burrón, Mafalda, Memín Pinguín, Kalimán,* et cetera. I also consumed Rius's buffoonish histories of just about everything: Sigmund Freud, the history of Communism, the making of the Volkswagen sedan. In *Mr. Spic Goes to Washington*, I pay homage to those rich, multifaceted cultural artifacts I grew up with and through which I discovered the value of pop art.

NS: As a mass-market phenomenon, the historieta sells millions in Mexico. According to an industry overview in the *American Business Review*, "at the industry's height, nearly 90 percent of the literate Mexican population regularly read historietas." And yet, unlike the Japanese *manga* crossover explosion among American comic books fans, the historietas have hardly registered here despite their pulpy leaning. Their limited export potential seems baffling. A *Village Voice* profile praising the art form described historietas as "*As the World Turns* in a *barrio*" directed by soft-porn filmmaker Russ Meyer or "*Superfly* meets *Charlie's Angels*." It seems like a bankable formula, but it hasn't panned out so far in the United States. Why has the historieta floundered for the most part on this side of the Rio Grande?

IS: American mainstream culture is just warming up to Mexican kitsch.

NS: *Mr. Spic Goes to Washington* is clearly influenced by historieta tradition. Are you worried that your readers might misinterpret your graphic novel? I recall the case in 2005, when, in the pages of the *Washington Post*, a Mexican historian, Enrique Krauze, rushed to the defense of historieta icon *Memín Pinguín* (described in the American media as a cross between *Dennis the Menace* and *Spanky and Our Gang*). Reportedly, Jesse Jackson, Al Sharpton, and President Bush were set off by a *Memín Pinguín* commemorative postage stamp. According to Krauze, for "Americans, the figure, with his exaggerated 'African' features, appears to be a copy of racist American cartoons. To Mexicans, he is a thoroughly likable character, rich in sparkling wisecracks, and is felt to represent not any sense of racial discrimination but rather the egalitarian possibility that all groups can live together in peace. During the 1970s and '80s, his *historietas* sold over a million and a half copies because they touched an authentic chord of sympathy and tenderness among poorer people, who identified with *Memín Pinguín*."

IS: Just as in other parts of the world, Mexican kitsch is racy and outrageous. It needs to be understood within its own context. The attempt with my historieta is to transpose—to translate—that outrageousness to our environment.

NS: I suppose some might brand the historieta as a manifestation of *rascauchismo*, a term you discuss in various corners of your work, particularly in your essay "The Riddle of Cantinflas" as well as in *Bandido*, your biographical meditation on the Chicano lawyer and outlaw Oscar "Zeta" Acosta. But to my understanding, the historieta has real roots in the Mexican publishing world dating back to 1896.

IS: The first historietas were based on European literary classics. Today the idea is used frequently everywhere. I have with me a cartoon version of the first volume of Proust's *Á la recherche du temps perdu*.

NS: I heard, at one point, that the former mayor of Mexico City, Andrés Manuel López Obrador, published his very own historieta to trumpet his achievements. Some saw this as self-serving propaganda. For many years, the Mexican government subsidized the historieta industry. In the conversations you had with Verónica Albin collected in the book *Knowledge and Censorship* (2008), you discuss restrictions on free speech in the Hispanic world. How did such sponsorship impact free speech in Mexican comic books? Does the law prevent comic book artists from explicitly lampooning political figures?

IS: The liaison is complicated. For years most publications were government sponsored. Think of Octavio Paz's magazines *Plural* and *Vuelta*, torches and paragons of freedom. Depending on the time, each of them depended on federal money for the acquisition of paper as well as for ads. The historieta industry isn't any different. Does that infringe on free speech? It surely does. But remember: censorship is the mother of metaphor.

NS: *¡Lotería!* and *Latino USA* are different. The first is a coffee-table book with art pieces by Teresa Villegas, about the Hispanic game that is similar to bingo. The second is illustrated by Lalo Alcaraz, a Chicano artist, is a humorous cartoon history spanning five hundred years, from Columbus to Selena. You developed *Mr. Spic Goes to Washington* with the Venezuelan-based painter Roberto Weil. How did the project come about?

IS: After finishing *Latino USA*, I suggested to Alcaraz that we collaborate again. But he went through a difficult personal period and was unable. I thought I would wait, but the plot of *Mr. Spic Goes to Washington*, a parody of Frank Capra's 1939 movie with Jimmy Stewart, in the same fashion of *Don Quixote* turning the tradition of chivalry novels on its head, kept popping up into my consciousness. Then, in 2007 I started writing a syndicated Spanish-language newspaper column. In a conversation with Javier Marín, the editor-in-chief of one of the publications where the column is featured, I told him about the graphic novel. He automatically contacted Roberto Weil, a talented Venezuelan illustrator. Weil and I became virtual friends (we've never met in person). The historieta was produced over a period of twelve months.

NS: The book is being published as the groundbreaking 2008 presidential campaign is under way, in which, for the first time, a woman and an African American candidate for the Democratic Party have commanded worldwide attention.

IS: *Mr. Spic Goes to Washington* is intended as a survey of Latinos in the political landscape.

NS: At one point, someone in the historieta says that "a visionary Latino is a dead Latino."

IS: Bill Richardson, governor of New Mexico, was also in the contest for the nomination of the Democratic Party. Although it would be far-fetched to call him a visionary, he's the first Mexican American to seek the nomination for president of the United States in a major party.

NS: Yet the historieta is also a denunciation of internal Latino politics. After all, Senator Spic is assassinated by another Latino.

IS: Yes. The will to fly among Latinos, to acquire political clout in the national stage, is often curtailed by debacles at the heart of the community, which, in its present state, is nothing if not Balkanized.

NS: I have noticed that you have often revisited this topic concerning the tensions within the Latino community in interviews. You discussed it with Neil Conan on NPR's *Talk of the Nation*. You had a similar conversation on PBS's *The NewsHour with Jim Lehrer*, back in 2001. You told Ray Suarez: "Puerto Ricans and Cubans have not always lived in peace. Mexican Americans and Central Americans have also had their tensions. We're white, we're black, we're upper class, we're middle class, we're lower class." How would the story of *Mr. Spic Goes to Washington* play out if had you changed the protagonist's background—if Senator Spic, was, for example, of Cuban, Dominican, or Puerto Rican ancestry?

IS: It would need to be redrawn from A to Z. Senator Spic is a former L.A. gang member. His background, detailed in a flashback, connects him with immigrants crossing the border illegally. He's from the south, not from the east—neither a *balsero* nor *bachatero*, but a *pocho*. And although he likes graffiti, he isn't into hip-hop.

NS: You are a keen follower of the "intellectual debate on the value of comic strips or serious stories that take the form of comic strips." The "hard content" of *Latino USA* was hailed in the press and in the classroom. Now that alternative comics have gone mainstream, is the debate closed?

IS: Curiously, as a tradition the graphic novel, even though it has a strong foundation in the Spanish-speaking world, is still not grounded among Latino readers. There are first-rate practitioners (Carlos Saldaña [*Burrito: Jack of All Trades*], Rafael Navarro [*Sonámbulo*], Laura Molina [*Cihualyaomiquiz*], Lalo Alcaraz [*La Cucaracha*], Richard Dominguez [*El Gato Negro*], and Javier Hernandez [*El Muerto: The Aztec Zombie*], as well as Wilfred Santiago, Marco Corona, José Muñoz, and Carlos Sampayo), but the readership within the community is small.

NS: Why?

IS: There isn't a homegrown shelf yet that has awakened the interest of readers. Also, there's a valuable tradition in Mexico of *fotonovelas*, photographic novels. (My father appeared in several of them.) To my knowledge, the format has never been used north of the Rio Grande, maybe because it's expensive.

NS: Fittingly, the *Los Angeles Times*, in a quote in the back of the book, says: "Ilan Stavans, scholar, historian, polyglot, theoretician of two diasporas, is one of those rare intellectuals who seems willing to try his hand at anything." Is there a risk in overextending yourself?

IS: I'm sure there is. But should that stop me?

NS: Who do you envision as the readership for *Mr. Spic*—students, comic book devotees . . . ?

IS: A wide audience: adolescents, people interested in graphic novels, identity politics, Latino culture.

NS: Your book *Spanglish: The Making of a New American Language* (2003) was published by Rayo, a division of HarperCollins. The imprint is devoted to publishing books by and about Latinos. Will Soft Skull, a division of Counterpoint, follow the same route and heavily market your historieta among Hispanics?

IS: Nothing is for Latinos alone. This is the United States . . .

NS: You have said in the past that the comic book format can be used to "digest complex" historical and political themes. Humor also plays a big part in making that process work. In *Latino USA* and *Mr. Spic Goes to Washington* you playfully indulge in "types, archetypes, and stereotypes." Your touch in *Latino USA* can be at times whimsically lighthearted, but in the historieta the humor on show is darker in nature. Why the shift in tone?

IS: Perhaps because I'm older. Also, the age of Latino pride is over. Ours, in fact, is the age of outrage.

NS: How so?

IS: Being Mexican *en los Estados Unidos* today is like being a virus. We're being deported. And the Bush administration has built a wall to keep us out. The fear is uncontainable: Mexicans are ruining this beautiful country!

NS: In 2002, you claimed on NPR that Latinos are "living in terrific times." You seemed optimistic that Latinos could be "witnesses and also participants to this new possibility of being an American." In the historieta, the "American Dream" turns into the "American Nightmare." Has the "Hispanization of the United States" that you forecasted been halted in its tracks? Or does *Mr. Spic Goes to Washington* document what you have called another "necessary growing pain of an emerging minority"?

IS: The *hispanización* is taking place before our eyes. The question now is about responsibility: what do we Latinos do with the power bestowed on us? Can we handle it?

NS: In your 1993 essay in the *American Prospect*, "Hispanic USA: The Search for Identity," you noted that "yesterday's victim" could become "tomorrow's conquerors." But in the historieta the protagonist, Senator Spic, finds his voice in the political pilgrimage from the periphery of culture to center stage, only to be tragically silenced by the corporate world and their Washington cronies. You have compared Latinos to a sleeping giant that will soon awake. Is the Latino place in the American political system still dormant, in your estimation?

IS: Yes, and the historieta dreams about that sudden awakening. President Bill Clinton shows up at the end, eulogizing the protagonist as the leader who paved the way for a more comfortable political role for Latinos.

NS: That explains the epigraph: "Sacrifice is the measure of leadership." Is the protagonist of *Mr. Spic Goes to Washington* "seduced by the American political system"? Is your book a cautionary tale about the perils of political integration? You have noted in the past that some Latinos are less likely to identify "with the collective symbols of American culture."

IS: Integration is, first and foremost, about loss. Only after that loss is acknowledged are the fruits of a life in a democratic, multicultural environment able to be harvested.

NS: When a Latino politician rises in the ranks and becomes a Washington insider, is he or she considered an outsider to the community? In your words: "He's left so he's a traitor; he's successful so he no longer speaks for us."

IS: Yes, that conflicting emotion is at the core of Hispanic civilization, where success is paid dearly.

NS: Is there a real-life political model that you based the historieta on?

IS: I wished he was based on someone, but I created him to fill the vacuum that exists today. We have no Latino leaders to be proud of, no one to inspire us.

NS: You sound pessimistic.

IS: Actually, I'm hopeful. I want *Mr. Spic Goes to Washington* to make people think, not about what they have, but about what they don't have . . .

NS: At one point, the protagonist is attacked for being an impostor. It's the same attack that has been labeled against you.

IS: Aren't we all impostors? If there's an urtext for Senator Spic, is Woody Allen's *Zelig*.

NS: Can you talk about the impact and influence of the art of Will Eisner and Art Spiegelman on you?

IS: Eisner made the graphic novel a tool to explore theological questions. I have his *A Contract with God* trilogy in my bed table. I also admire his historical disquisition on *The Protocols of the Elders of Zion* and, in general, his exploration of Jewish life as folly, fragility, and fragmentation. Spiegelman's *Maus I* and *II* moved the discourse about memory and the Holocaust into an altogether new realm. Comedies like *Life Is Beautiful* are impossible without it. Another decisive artist is Joe Sacco, whose super book *Palestine*, about the plight of the Palestinians in the Occupied Territories, was frequently in my mind when doing *Mr. Spic Goes to Washington*.

NS: What's next in your love for historietas?

IS: I would like to produce a bestiary, e.g., a compendium of grotesque imaginary creatures, related to the Hispanic world. I also want to write one about a female border superhero whose power comes from specially grown tortillas.

[2008]

SOURCES

"¡Viva el Kitsch!," *Michigan Quarterly Review*; "Immigration and Authenticity," *Michigan Quarterly Review*; "Mother of Exiles" was delivered as the Martin and Rona Schneider Lecture at the Brooklyn Public Library; "A Dream Act Deferred," *Chronicle of Higher Education*; "Arrival: Notes from an Interloper," *Transition*; "Unmasking Marcos," *Transition*; "¡Lotería! or, The Ritual of Chance," *AGNI* and *¡Lotería!* (with art by Teresa Villegas, University of Arizona Press, 2004); "Santa Selena," *New Republic*; "The Novelist and the Dictator," *Chronicle of Higher Education*; "The Riddle of Cantinflas," *Transition*; "Mario Vargas Llosa: Civilization versus Barbarism," *Chronicle of Higher Education*; "The Art of the Ephemeral," *Latin American Posters*, edited by Russ Davidson (Museum of New Mexico Press, 2006); "Sandra Cisneros: Form over Content," *Academic Questions*; "Civility and Latinos" was delivered in February 2012 as part of the conference "Civility and American Democracy: A National Forum," sponsored by the National Endowment for the Humanities, at the University of Massachusetts Boston; "José Guadalupe Posada: A Profile," *Journal of Decorative and Propaganda Arts*; "Language and Empire" (with Verónica Albin), *Spanish and Empire*, edited by Nelsy Echávez-Solano and Kenya C. Dworkin y Méndez (Vanderbilt University Press, 2007); "Against Biography" (with Donald Yates), *Michigan Quarterly Review*; and "Redrawing the *Historieta*" (with Neal Sokol), *Literary Review*.

INDEX

Page numbers in italic text indicate illustrations.